Wallace's Dialects

DAVID FOSTER WALLACE STUDIES

Vol. 3

Series Editor

Stephen J. Burn, University of Glasgow, UK

Advisory Board

Kasia Boddy, University of Cambridge, UK
Marshal Boswell, Rhodes College, USA
Paul Giles, University of Sydney, Australia
Luc Herman, University of Antwerp, Belgium
Mary K. Holland, The State University of New York at New Paltz, USA
Steven Moore, Independent Scholar, USA

Volumes in the Series

Vol. 1. *Global Wallace*
Lucas Thompson
Vol. 2. *The Wallace Effect*
Marshall Boswell
Vol. 3. *Wallace's Dialects*
Mary Shapiro

Wallace's Dialects

Mary Shapiro

BLOOMSBURY ACADEMIC
NEW YORK • LONDON • OXFORD • NEW DELHI • SYDNEY

BLOOMSBURY ACADEMIC
Bloomsbury Publishing Inc
1385 Broadway, New York, NY 10018, USA
50 Bedford Square, London, WC1B 3DP, UK
29 Earlsfort Terrace, Dublin 2, Ireland

BLOOMSBURY, BLOOMSBURY ACADEMIC and the Diana logo are trademarks of
Bloomsbury Publishing Plc

First published in the United States of America 2020
This paperback edition published in 2021

Copyright © Mary Shapiro, 2020

Series Editor's Introduction © Stephen J. Burn, 2020

For legal purposes the Acknowledgments on p. 201 constitute an extension
of this copyright page.

Cover design: Daniel Benneworth-Gray
Cover image © Creative Commons

All rights reserved. No part of this publication may be reproduced or transmitted in any form or by any means, electronic or mechanical, including photocopying, recording, or any information storage or retrieval system, without prior permission in writing from the publishers.

Bloomsbury Publishing Inc does not have any control over, or responsibility for, any third-party websites referred to or in this book. All internet addresses given in this book were correct at the time of going to press. The author and publisher regret any inconvenience caused if addresses have changed or sites have ceased to exist, but can accept no responsibility for any such changes.

Library of Congress Cataloging-in-Publication Data
Names: Shapiro, Mary, (Professor of linguistics) author.
Title: Wallace's dialects / Mary Shapiro.
Description: New York: Bloomsbury Academic, 2020. | Series: David Foster Wallace studies; vol. 3 | Includes bibliographical references and index. | Summary: "A linguistic analysis of the portrayal of dialect (regional and ethnic) and idiolect in David Foster Wallace's works" – Provided by publisher.
Identifiers: LCCN 2019047437 | ISBN 9781501348471 (hardback) | ISBN 9781501348495 (pdf) | ISBN 9781501348488 (epub)
Subjects: LCSH: Wallace, David Foster–Language. | Wallace, David Foster—Knowledge–Language and languages. | Dialect literature, American–History and criticism. | Oral communication in literature. | Speech in literature.
Classification: LCC PS3573.A425635 Z868 2020 | DDC 813/.54–dc23
LC record available at https://lccn.loc.gov/2019047437

ISBN: HB: 978-1-5013-4847-1
PB: 978-1-5013-7113-4
ePDF: 978-1-5013-4849-5
eBook: 978-1-5013-4848-8

Series: David Foster Wallace Studies

Typeset by Deanta Global Publishing Services, Chennai, India

To find out more about our authors and books visit www.bloomsbury.com and
sign up for our newsletters.

Contents

List of Abbreviations vi
Series Editor's Introduction vii

1 Language, Linguistics, and Literary Dialectology 1
2 Foreigners and Foreignness 27
3 Ethnicity and Segregation 47
4 Ethnicity and Assimilation 81
5 Regionality and the White Working Class 101
6 Texan Pride and Southern Shame 117
7 Midwestern and Rural 135
8 Boston and Urban 159
9 "Dave Wallace" and His Readers 171
10 Language and Humanity 195

Acknowledgments 201
Bibliography 202
Index 217

Abbreviations

ASFTINDA	*A Supposedly Fun Thing I'll Never Do Again.* New York: Little, Brown, & Co., 1997.
BFAN	*Both Flesh and Not.* New York: Little, Brown and Company, 2012.
BIHM	*Brief Interviews with Hideous Men.* Boston: Little, Brown, & Co., 1999.
Broom	*The Broom of the System.* New York: Avon Books, 1987.
CTL	*Consider the Lobster.* New York: Little, Brown, & Co., 2005.
GWCH	*Girl with Curious Hair.* New York: W.W. Norton & Co., 1989.
HRC Wallace Papers	The Harry Ransom Center David Foster Wallace Papers (1971-2008), Austin, TX.
Jest	*Infinite Jest.* Boston: Little, Brown, and Company, 1996.
Oblivion	*Oblivion.* New York: Little, Brown and Company, 2004.
The Harry Ransom Center	The Harry Ransom Center Bonnie Nadell Collection of David Foster Wallace (1980–2008), Austin TX.
TPK	*The Pale King.* Little, Brown and Company, 2011.
"Shipping out"	"Shipping out." *Harper's Magazine* 292, no. 1748 (1996): 33–56.
"/Solomon Silverfish/"	"/Solomon Silverfish/." Reprinted in *Sonora Review* 55 (2009): 67–96.
Water	*This Is Water.* New York: Little, Brown, & Co., 2009.

Series Editor's Introduction

In Mark McGurl's reading of Wallace as "a student—and later teacher" (30–31), the late novelist is presented as a figure intellectually and personally locked into a university career by virtue of a kind of failure of vocational imagination. "It apparently never occurred to him," McGurl writes, "to find a way to pay the bills other than to become a teacher" (32), and so Wallace's acute sense of the limitations of Program culture is framed as a paradoxical, even hypocritical, inclination to worry "out loud and at length about the many implications of the rise of creative writing programs but without letting those worries impede his headlong entry into the career of creative writing teacher" (31). Yet the closer we look at that career, the less complacent and certainly the less passive Wallace's decision to become a teacher appears. The fullest account that we have of Wallace as a teacher—Charles B. Harris's edited collection, *Proofread or Die!* (2016)—suggests, in fact, that a different paradox underlies Wallace's relationship to the university. That is, that while much academic attention (McGurl's included) emphasizes Wallace's role as "a student of the likes of Pynchon" (McGurl 30)—tracing the often vital ways Wallace incorporated the lessons learned from his ancestors in his recombinant fictions—Wallace's own attention as an academic tended to be on language, rather than literature. Harris opens his collection by noting that Wallace "preferred other assignments" to creative workshops or even advanced literary classes, instead "volunteering to teach composition courses" (xxviii). Doug Hesse, similarly recalls that Wallace "had asked to teach English 244: Applied Grammar and Usage for Writers . . . He was a stickler for language to put it mildly, and he really thought that right teaching could fix things for students" (162n1). When he did teach workshops, students such as Suzanne Scanlon recall that his baseline requirement was that writing "be grammatically correct" (115). From this perspective, it is perhaps unsurprising that one of the earliest references to Wallace's work in secondary literature appears not in a literary journal, but in his mother's grammar primer, *Practically Painless English* (1990), where she offers the following example of how to properly present a book title: "My very favorite novel is *The Broom of the System*" (51).

What difference does it make to our understanding of Wallace's fiction that its author was not simply a masterful manipulator of narrative devices who was deeply read in multiple literary traditions, but was also, on a deeper level, a dedicated student of language: its mechanics, its structures, and its usage? Few scholars (myself included) have the training and knowledge to tell us, because answering this question requires not just detailed knowledge of a complex and expansive oeuvre but also specialist training in philology, dialectology, and linguistics. Mary Shapiro's achievement in *Wallace's Dialects*, then, stems in part from her rare ability to draw these two distinct strands together. While the previous two books in this series work (like much Wallace scholarship), by using intensive close readings to leverage Wallace's tangled intertextual relationships, reveal either how he was a student of a far greater swathe of writers than "the likes of Pynchon" or how he manifests himself as a uniquely ambivalent tutelary presence in the work of his contemporaries and younger writers, *Wallace's Dialects* directs its intensive readings on the particularities of characters' speech, to provide the first really detailed and specialist account of what Tom LeClair called (almost twenty-five years ago) Wallace's "stylistic tours de force in several dialects" (35).

What we have at the end of this book is a richer and more precise understanding of the relative depth of Wallace's engagement with those "several dialects." But, crucially, this understanding is not simply abstract information. Shapiro's rigorous attention to both Wallace's voluminous output and earlier Wallace scholarship helps reveal *why* Wallace deployed particular dialects, and strategic deviations from standard usage, in particular situations. This is pioneering work that clarifies and sometimes corrects our sense of how well Wallace knew certain speech patterns, and of how his choice to deploy a particular dialect intersects with increasingly central questions about his construction of race, gender, and class in a given work.

Stephen J. Burn
University of Glasgow

1

Language, Linguistics, and Literary Dialectology

If words are all we have as world and god, we must treat them with care and rigor; we must worship.
—David Foster Wallace, letter to Jonathan Franzen (Quoted in Max[1])

You can't escape language: language is everything and everywhere.
—David Foster Wallace, "Authority and American Usage" (*CTL* 70)

In the two decades since David Foster Wallace's *Infinite Jest* catapulted him to literary rock star status, his inventive and poetic uses of language have been frequently praised, but little studied from a linguistic point of view. Wallace's numerous, if fleeting, dialect portraits (always at least implicitly contrasted with the distinct dominant voice of Wallace himself, embodied by various alter ego narrators) illustrate fissures in American society, force readers to acknowledge and face their own prejudices, and challenge readers to empathize with others across these divides. Some of his dialect portrayals have been particularly vilified, even as the voice of the author himself triggered intense reactions (both positive and negative) from readers. Looking at these performances of dialect not just locally (how they function as part of the particular essay, story, or novel) but also as part of a larger project, a semiotic web of voices that occur across Wallace's work, allows a better understanding of why Wallace might have made particular linguistic choices.

Wallace is held less in awe today than just a few years ago when McGurl[2] referred to him ironically as "a leading candidate for contemporary canonization" (in both the religious and the literary senses). Increased awareness of his admitted obsessive stalking and abuse of poet Mary Karr has triggered some deserved revulsion, and Wallace is sometimes dismissed

---

[1] D. T. Max, *Every Love Story Is a Ghost Story: A Life of David Foster Wallace* (New York: Viking, 2012), 166.
[2] Mark McGurl, "The Institution of Nothing: David Foster Wallace in the Program," *boundary* 2 41, no. 3 (2014): 27–54, esp. 33. DOI 10.1215/01903659-2812061.

as "a symbol of lit-bro culture."[3] A recent satirical *New Yorker* piece on "How to Read *Infinite Jest*"[4] mostly mocks readers' pride in (falsely) claiming to read the challenging tome, and an online magazine article deemed those who love it "insufferable."[5] In an *L.A. Review of Books* interview,[6] Wallace scholar Clare Hayes-Brady characterizes much of the criticism of Wallace during his lifetime and shortly after his death as "hagiographic," and calls the "inevitable critical backlash" healthy; nonetheless, she argues that he was an author of immense talent and complexity and that there is room for much more critical examination of his work. This is especially true with respect to Wallace's distinctive and even radical uses of language, which have occasionally been misunderstood, and may have caused some of the "backlash" to go further than it should. Although largely apolitical, this monograph considers how Wallace's use of dialects relates to some of the more political readings of his work, such as Joffe,[7] who argues that Wallace "worked hard to present himself as the compassionate, egalitarian, and progressive writer, all while reinstating the centrality of his white masculinity" (25). It is possible, I hope, to question Wallace's politics while still admiring his brilliance with language and the scope of his literary ambitions.

An in-depth look at Wallace's dialect representations contributes to an understanding of Wallace's worldview—not just who is allowed to speak for themselves but also whose speech is represented as nonstandard, and whose is presented without noticeable dialect features (sometimes despite descriptions of the speech by the narrator or by other characters that indicate otherwise). For those characters whose nonstandard dialect is directly encoded, a look at which specific features Wallace incorporated into those representations allows fresh consideration of how he differentiated the speech of individual characters, showing not just personality differences but a more realistic presentation of how language functions in daily life, expressing multiple aspects of speakers' identities and also their perceptions of the situations in

---

[3] Steve Paulson, "Wallace in the #MeToo Era: A Conversation with Clare Hayes-Brady," *Los Angeles Review of Books* (September 10, 2018). https://lareviewofbooks.org/article/david-foster-wallace-in-the-metoo-era-a-conversation-with-clare-hayes-brady/.

[4] Clare Friedman, "How to Read *Infinite Jest*," *The New Yorker Magazine*. Print edition November 5, 2018. Online October 29, 2018. https://www.newyorker.com/magazine/2018/11/05/how-to-read-infinite-jest

[5] Jason Rhode, "Why Insufferable People Love *Infinite Jest*," *Paste Magazine.com* (June 29, 2018). https://www.pastemagazine.com/articles/2018/06/why-insufferable-people-love-infinite-jest.html

[6] Paulson, "Wallace in the #MeToo Era."

[7] Daniela Franca Joffe, *"In the Shadows": David Foster Wallace and Multicultural America*. Ph.D. Dissertation, University of Cape Town, 2017. http://open.uct.ac.za/handle/11427/26899.

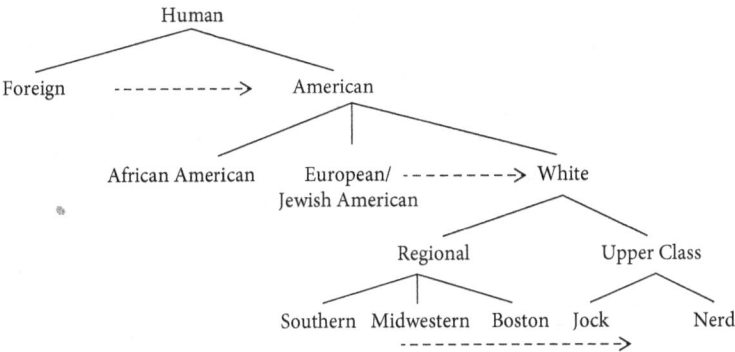

Figure 1 Taxonomy of Dialects in Wallace's Work.

which the speech is produced. Wallace's work, both nonfiction and fiction, provides an interesting "folk dialectology," reflecting and often subverting Americans' beliefs about different language varieties and the speakers who use them.

A catalog of Wallace's dialect depictions reveals a splintering, recursive fractal image of different varieties of the English language with large gaps at each level, like the Sierpinski gasket which Wallace said inspired the structure of *Jest*.[8] Following this introduction, which explores Wallace's knowledge of linguistics as well as how dialect representations have generally been used in literature, the monograph will follow the structure of Figure 1, showing the pressure felt at every level of social categorization to move from the left side of the diagram toward the rewards enjoyed by the people on the right side.

Chapter 2 considers foreign characters in Wallace's work. The choice to include only a few foreign characters may be motivated by his frequently expressed intent to explore what it means to be American: Showing some examples of what is "not-American" helps to home in on what is, but it is not necessary to show every possible alternative. Although his work is often referred to as "encyclopedic," Wallace's strategy for illustrating social categories is reductive, focusing readers' attention and providing an implicit social critique. Chapter 3 examines Wallace's controversial depictions of African American dialects, showing the continued segregation of people who cannot assimilate into a "melting pot" of default whiteness. Again, there are noticeable gaps in Wallace's work, with very few Latinx characters,

---

[8] David Hering, "Infinite Jest: Triangles, Cycles, Choices, & Chases," in *Consider David Foster Wallace*, ed. David Hering (Los Angeles and Austin: Sideshow Media Group Press, 2010), 89–100, esp. 89.

very few Asians, and no hybrid, blended identities. Chapter 4 investigates the pressure on European immigrants to assimilate, focusing in particular on the Irish American Pemulis family in *Jest* and the Jewish Americans in "Solomon Silverfish" and "Say Never." Although the predominate whiteness of Wallace's work is construed as a default absence of ethnicity, working-class characters often have regional dialects, as explored in general in Chapter 5. As with national and ethnic identities, Wallace is reductive, manipulating only a few possible regional identities. His Southern characters, Midwestern characters, and Eastern (Bostonian) characters are discussed in Chapters 6 through 8, respectively. Chapter 8 also demonstrates that although regionality is a function of the working class in Wallace's worldview, there is a chance for upward mobility for those who can excel as jocks or nerds. At each level (nationality, ethnicity, regionality), Wallace distinguishes "not-me" from "me," instantiating the distinctions in language used by different characters. All the "not-me" voices are implicitly contrasted with the voice of the "Dave Wallace" narrative persona that emerges across Wallace's works (often fictionalized in sound-alike focalizing characters); Chapter 9 outlines how that voice facilitates an ongoing relationship with readers, focusing particularly on positive politeness and conversational strategies. Despite all the social divisions Wallace encoded, the final chapter argues that he viewed language as something fundamentally human that could bring everyone together.

Wallace continually drew readers' attention to language, not merely as an illustration of what Hayes-Brady[9] identifies as his central concern, "human connection and the establishment of the self among selves," but as a fundamental component of that concern: it is through language that we establish identity and connect with others. Derdeyn[10] notes that Wallace used "experimental elimination" to "reveal the self among selves," focusing on peeling away different "relational identities." Dialect differences are an important way that he illustrated this.

Wallace's work is widely acknowledged to be preoccupied with the act of communication, as reflected in the number of characters who lose their voice, who speak words others have crafted for them, who think about and speak about and judge each other's ways of speaking, who speak but are not heard, and so on. He frequently drew attention to the inherent

[9] Clare Hayes-Brady, *The Unspeakable Failures of David Foster Wallace: Language, Identity, and Resistance* (New York: Bloomsbury Academic, 2017), 93.
[10] LeeAnn Derdeyn, "Love the Jackalope: Historicity, Relational Identity, and Naming in David Foster Wallace's 'Lyndon,'" *College Literature* 45, no. 4 (Fall 2018): 747–72, esp. 769.

difficulty of communication as well as its value, the human need to be heard and understood, the importance of sincere communication in establishing meaningful connections with other human beings. Critics such as Olsen,[11] Boswell,[12] and Hayes-Brady[13] have amply examined Wallace's investigation of Wittgenstein's ideas throughout his work, and Wallace himself discussed Wittgenstein at some length both in his review of Markson's *Wittgenstein's Mistress* and in "Authority and American Usage" (A&AU). Critics have also productively applied Bakhtin's ideas of monologism and dialogism in Wallace's work (e.g., Nichols[14] and Kelly[15]), but have seldom considered the actual linguistic variables manipulated.

At stake in a sociolinguistic reading of Wallace's work is not just questions of authenticity (whether he adequately captured different dialects, and whether he had any right to try to), not just additional fodder in disciplinary debates about the value of linguistic criticism or stylistics, but an opportunity to understand an important dimension of Wallace's work that has been heretofore little considered. As Mair[16] remarks, "In a discipline where the greater part of effort and ingenuity have gone into developing ways of speaking about writers' personal stylistic idiosyncrasies, it is difficult to account for effects which are achieved by imitating the speech of others."

Wallace's dialect representations are more symbolic and playful than mimetic, perhaps partly because he was aware of his own limitations and lack of access to various dialects, but also undoubtedly because he was more interested in making statements *about* language—and the social realities it reflects—than he was in linguistic analysis of dialects per se. It's perhaps ironic, therefore, that this monograph insists on conducting such analysis—but given how many contradictory statements have been made about his dialect representations, it seemed like a useful exercise to sort these out.

Much has been written about Wallace's observation that his first novel, *The Broom of the System*, was "a coded autobio that's also a funny little poststructural gag" about his "fear that he was nothing but a linguistic

---

[11] Lance Olsen, "Termite Art, or Wallace's Wittgenstein," *The Review of Contemporary Fiction* 13, no. 2 (1993): 199.
[12] Marshall Boswell, *Understanding David Foster Wallace* (Columbia: University of South Carolina Press, 2003).
[13] Hayes-Brady, *The Unspeakable Failures of David Foster Wallace*.
[14] Catherine Nichols, "Dialogizing Postmodern Carnival: David Foster Wallace's *Infinite Jest*," *Critique: Studies in Contemporary Fiction* 43, no. 1 (2001): 3–16.
[15] Adam Kelly, "Development Through Dialogue: David Foster Wallace and the Novel of Ideas," *Studies in the Novel* 44, no. 3 (2012): 267–83.
[16] Christian Mair, "Literary Sociolinguistics: A Methodological Framework for Research on the Use of Nonstandard Language in Fiction," *Arbeiten aus Anglistik und Amerikanistik* 17, no. 1 (1992): 103–23, esp. 107. https://www.jstor.org/stable/43023593.

construct,"[17] but perhaps the most important take-away from this is Wallace's awareness that whatever else we might be, we are most certainly *also* linguistic constructs—that identity is performative, and specifically created and re-enacted through language use. Wolfram and Schilling-Estes[18] begin their survey of US dialects by emphasizing that people "make judgments about regional background, social status, ethnicity, and a host of other social and personal traits based simply on the kind of language people are using." They deem these judgments "inevitable," and note that language differences may be "the single most reliable indicator of social position in our society."

Perhaps to nonlinguists the minutiae of linguistic description is, as *Pale King* narrator "Dave Wallace" says of tax policy and administration, "massively, spectacularly dull" (83). But the point the narrator makes in that book is that devoting close attention to such minutiae has an unexpected payoff—that one can push through the boredom to discover a whole world of hidden significance.[19] Language is not just a tool for communication to be taken for granted, it is the primary way people express identities and navigate social interactions, and therefore deserves close attention. As folk-linguistic terminology is often inadequate[20] for precise descriptions of language, and the technical terminology is unfamiliar and off-putting to those primarily interested in the study of literature, I have attempted to achieve a compromise that may please nobody, but should make this monograph accessible to all.

Although it is necessary to consider each work in its own context, and the reasons internal to that work why Wallace may have chosen to represent various dialects, it is also instructive to look across Wallace's work, to reveal the points he kept trying to make about language and society, how the latter is reflected in the former, with linguistic fault lines continuing to divide us. Wallace acknowledged, toyed with, and ultimately subverted the linguistic prejudices that many readers surely feel, while also encouraging

---

[17] Larry McCaffery, "An Expanded Interview with David Foster Wallace," in *Conversations with David Foster Wallace*, ed. Stephen J. Burn (Jackson: University Press of Mississippi, 2012), 21–52, esp. 41.

[18] Walt Wolfram and Natalie Schilling-Estes, *American English*, 2nd edn. (Malden, MA: Blackwell, 2006), 1.

[19] Ralph Clare, "The Politics of Boredom and the Boredom of Politics in David Foster Wallace's *The Pale King*," *Studies in the Novel* 44, no. 4 (2012): 428–46; Brian Douglas Jansen, "'On the Porousness of Certain Borders': Attending to Objects in David Foster Wallace's *Infinite Jest*," *ESC: English Studies in Canada* 40, no. 4 (2014): 55–77; and Arthur Cockfield, "David Foster Wallace on Tax Policy, How to Be an Adult, and Other Mysteries of the Universe," *Pittsburgh Tax Review* 12 (2015): 89–109.

[20] William Labov, *Sociolinguistic Patterns* (Philadelphia: University of Pennsylvania Press, 1972), 248.

a love of language in a larger sense as liberatory. Many different theoretical frameworks have been applied to Wallace's works: In addition to structural approaches and the applications of various philosophies, scholars have also productively incorporated a biomedical approach,[21] Marxist criticism,[22] disability studies,[23] and embodiment more generally[24]—this sociolinguistic approach is intended to supplement, not supplant, these.

In reading *across* Wallace's work, I am going against his view that "each piece of art's its own unique object, and its evaluation's always present-tense."[25] This monograph does not offer a full interpretation of any particular work of Wallace's; rather, I attempt to show that his work as a whole reflects certain attitudes about both language and society that can inform any reading of any individual piece. Hudson[26] has pointed out that many scholars have over-relied on Wallace's statements about his own work in a variety of personal interviews and essays, shaping the field of Wallace Studies in the way that he wanted. Although Wallace frequently discussed language and linguistics, he never commented explicitly (that I can find) on any of the dialect portrayals he created.

Wallace as Authority on Language

Wallace took pleasure in the nuts-and-bolts of language, not just thinking about language on a philosophical level but also paying close attention to the specifics of lexicon, morphology, syntax, phonetics, phonology, semantics, and pragmatics. I have described elsewhere[27] his ability to manipulate linguistic variables simultaneously on multiple levels of language within a single phrase in order to achieve a particular effect, and I offer a few more examples of this mastery in passing in this book. It is unclear to what extent he was playing with certain

---

[21] Elizabeth Freudenthal, "Anti-Interiority: Compulsiveness, Objectification, and Identity in *Infinite Jest*," *New Literary History* 41, no. 1 (Winter 2010): 191–211.
[22] Stephen Shapiro, "From Capitalist to Communist Abstraction: *The Pale King*'s Cultural Fix," *Textual Practice* 28, no. 7 (2014): 1249–71.
[23] Emily Russell, "Some Assembly Required: The Embodied Politics of *Infinite Jest*," *Arizona Quarterly: A Journal of American Literature, Culture, and Theory* 66, no. 3 (2010): 147–69.
[24] Peter Sloane, "The Divided Selves of David Foster Wallace," *Tropos* 1, no. 1 (2014): 67–73.
[25] McCaffery, "An Expanded Interview with David Foster Wallace," 28.
[26] Cory M. Hudson, "David Foster Wallace Is Not Your Friend: The Fraudulence of Empathy in David Foster Wallace Studies and 'Good Old Neon,'" *Critique: Studies in Contemporary Fiction* 59, no. 3 (2018): 295–306.
[27] Mary Shapiro, "The Poetic Language of David Foster Wallace," *Critique: Studies in Contemporary Fiction* 60, no. 1 (2019): 24–33. DOI: 10.1080/00111619.2018.1441121.

variables consciously and to what extent he just had a good ear, recognizing when a particular construction "worked." *Broom* Editor Gerald Howard[28] recognized Wallace's "virtuoso deployment of linguistic facility and narrative velocity," and Fadiman[29] said "Wallace doesn't bend grammar, but he bends English." In the foreword to the twentieth-anniversary edition of *Infinite Jest*, Bissell[30] calls it "a genuinely groundbreaking novel of language," rhapsodizing about its "exuberant" use of register, "fearless" neologizing, as well as its inventiveness with sentences. I am clearly not the only reader who persisted through seemingly endless paragraphs, knowing I would soon be rewarded with a striking and memorable phrase, something worth reading aloud and quoting to others.

"Obsessed with grammar"[31] and a "hard core syntax wienie,"[32] Wallace kept physical notebooks as well as a computer file of words he wanted to work into his writing, often making note of particular pronunciations. He deliberately crafted sentences that were (in his words) "a real bitch to read,"[33] punned relentlessly, and commented on his own uses of language in footnotes. However much delight he took in his linguistic virtuosity, it was never just a game or a joke to him, never just showing off, but rather an essential part of sincere communication, the only vehicle for minds to meaningfully connect with other minds. Individually, Wallace's characters provide interesting fodder for sociolinguistic analysis, sometimes illustrating and occasionally belying his famous "good ear," but together they form a chorus of voices that reveals not just how language functions in US society but also how the very society itself is constructed and maintained.

Wallace's extraordinary prowess with language—as well as his obvious delight in it—makes his views of language (embodied both in direct pronouncements and in the ways his characters use language) feel weightier and more authoritative. This is, after all, someone who served on *American Heritage Dictionary*'s panel of language authorities and who spent over sixty pages ostensibly reviewing Bryan Garner's *A Dictionary of Modern American Usage* (1998)[34] but actually summarizing and commenting extensively on prominent debates within the field of linguistics.

---

[28] Gerald Howard, "Afterword," in *The David Foster Wallace Reader*, ed. Bonnie Nadell et al. (New York: Back Bay Books/Little, Brown and Company, 2015), 63–4, esp. 63.
[29] Ann Fadiman, "Afterword," in *The David Foster Wallace Reader*, ed. Bonnie Nadell et al. (New York: Back Bay Books/Little, Brown and Company, 2015), 759–62, esp. 760.
[30] Tom Bissell, "Foreword" to 20th anniversary edition of *Infinite Jest* (Boston: Little, Brown, & Co., 2016), xi–xv, esp. xii.
[31] Max, *Every Love Story Is a Ghost Story*, 166.
[32] Max, *Every Love Story Is a Ghost Story*, 34.
[33] McCaffery, "An Expanded Interview with David Foster Wallace," 25.
[34] Bryan A. Garner, *A Dictionary of Modern American Usage* (New York: Oxford University Press, 1998).

As an undergraduate, Wallace wrote two honors theses: the first, for his English major, was published not long thereafter as *The Broom of the System*. The other, for his philosophy major, since published as *Fate, Time, and Language* (2011), is a sophisticated take on the semantics of physical modality. *Jest*'s Hal Incandenza includes a similar paper in his college application, along with "Neoclassical Assumptions in Contemporary Prescriptive Grammar" (7), and casually deploys linguistic terminology that is not readily available to most people, such as "glottal stop" (907). Hal's mother Avril, one of the "Militant Grammarians of Massachusetts" (987), has "Dowty, Wall and Peters's seminal *Introduction to Montague Semantics*" open on her desk in one scene (760). *The Union of Theoretical Grammarians in Cambridge*, a film by James O. Incandenza (*Jest* 987, endnote 24), features MIT language riots inspired by a debate between Avril and Steven Pinker over "the political implications of prescriptive grammar," although an early handwritten draft has the debate between Noam Chomsky and Barbara Partee, about "the reduceability of universal syntax to formal first-order logic" (HRC Wallace Papers, container 15.5). Wallace seems to have had particular animus toward Pinker, whose ideas about descriptivism he argues with in A&AU, although he did apparently ask his students to read Pinker's "Grammar Puss" (1994) (HRC Wallace Papers, Teaching Materials, container 32.7). Readers familiar with the real linguists, texts, terms, and philosophical debates in the discipline will be impressed by Wallace's awareness of these; readers to whom these are opaque will perhaps be even more so, although they may also identify with Joelle van Dyne, who (when Hal talks about "something called Haplology") has the desire "to slap the sleek little show-offy kid upside the head" (745).

Wallace was the son of a philosophy professor father and an English professor mother, whose grammar textbook, *Practically Painless English* (1980),[35] he frequently assigned to his own students. The Wallace family term "SNOOT" described "a really extreme usage fanatic" (*CTL* 69), "someone who knows what *dysphemism* means and doesn't mind letting you know it" (*CTL* 70), "just about the last remaining kind of truly elitist nerd" (*CTL* 70). The acronym, he claimed, stood either "'Sprachgefühl Necessitates Our Ongoing Tendance' or 'Syntax Nudniks of Our Time,'" depending on "whether or not you were one" (*CTL* 69). Wallace explored at length his own prescriptive and descriptive tendencies in this essay, finding fault with both approaches to language when taken to the extreme.

---

[35] Sally Foster Wallace, *Practically Painless English* (Englewood Cliffs, NJ: Prentice Hall, 1989 [1980]).

Wallace's Amherst College course on the history of the English language used the well-known textbook by Baugh and Cable (3rd edition, 1978);[36] Wallace still had this in his personal library at the time of his death, annotated and underlined, with the marginal note: "EXAM—know major dialect areas in U.S." His research notebook for A&AU (originally the 2001 *Harper's* article "Tense Present: Democracy, English, and the Wars over Usage")[37] shows that he consulted Baugh and Cable again as he was writing that essay (HRC Wallace Papers, container 30.2); it is not clear at which time he wrote a marginal note "snotty" beside Baugh and Cable's description of "*vulgar* or *illiterate speech*" as "the language of those who are ignorant of or indifferent to the ideals of correctness by which the educated are governed" (313). The phonetics chart in Baugh and Cable is marked up, and Wallace also owned and heavily underlined the first four chapters of Peter Ladefoged's *Elements of Acoustic Phonetics* (1962). Roache[38] problematizes the "tendency to take an author's marginalia as spontaneous disclosures of 'pure thought' or unambiguous truth," but it seems safe to assert both that he at one point learned the major dialect regions of the United States (though he might have quickly forgotten the details after the test) and that he had strong feelings about more judgmental characterizations of language.

One could probably write an entire monograph on Wallace's handwritten annotations of Garner's usage manual, as he appears to have used color-coding to distinguish (in red) Garner's judgments and proscriptions for "Standard Written English" (SWE) from information Wallace may have found relevant to his own writing and uses of language (in green). In A&AU Wallace acknowledges his own biases and pet peeves, but also his appreciation for local and individual quirks. Although he admits in this article to occasionally correcting others' speech, and was described by at least one acquaintance as "a smug prescriptivist douche-bag,"[39] Wallace would be more aptly characterized as taking a pragmatic (rather than dogmatic) approach to language, as Crystal[40] defines this: having "an ability to adapt knowledge to meet the needs of differing circumstances and a readiness to judge cases on their merits." Wallace insisted that "many of these non-

---

[36] Albert Croll Baugh, and Thomas Cable, *A History of the English Language*, 3rd edn. (Englewood Cliffs, NJ: Prentice Hall, 1978).
[37] "Tense Present: Democracy, English, and the Wars over Usage," *Harper's Magazine* 302, no. 1811 (2001): 39–58.
[38] Roache John, "'The Realer, More Enduring and Sentimental Part of Him': David Foster Wallace's Personal Library and Marginalia," *Orbit: A Journal of American Literature* 5, no. 1, (2017): 11. doi: 10.16995/orbit.142.
[39] Max, *Every Love Story Is a Ghost Story*, 165.
[40] David Crystal, *The Language of Stories* (Woodstock, NY: The Overlook Press, 2004), 524.

SWE-type dialects have their own highly developed and internally consistent grammars, and that some of these dialects' usage norms actually make more linguistic/aesthetic sense than do their Standard counterpart" (*CTL* 98). He did not say that this is the case for *all* dialects, and some usages in any dialect may seem illogical or aesthetically displeasing to any particular observer.

Wallace does not distinguish at this point in A&AU between native dialects and learned registers/styles, such as the stilted and pretentious "Academese," which he later describes as a "verbal cancer" (114), adding, "I regard Academic English not as a dialectal variation but as a grotesque debasement of SWE" (*CTL* 114). He judges "most US academic prose" as "appalling—pompous, abstruse, claustral, inflated, euphuistic, pleonastic, solecistic, sesquipedalian, Helioagabaline, occluded, obscure, jargon-ridden, empty: resplendently dead" (*CTL* 81). With Lipsky, Wallace discussed his aversion to "puffed up" language like *utilize* for *use* or *prior to* instead of *before* (which is also the first usage he singled out for criticism in "Twenty-Four Word Notes" (*Both Flesh and Not*)): "Why did they just take up one third of a second of my lifetime making me parse *at this time* rather than just say *now*?" (Lipsky audio, Walsh and Bonds, n.d.). Almost as soon as the words were out of his mouth, Wallace recognized the responsibility he had as a writer to pay attention to his own usage, to make every word count. Indeed, the amazing string of fifteen adjectives quoted earlier is not simply intended to overwhelm (showing the extent of Wallace's disdain as well as the underlying justification and therefore justness of it), nor simply to comedically mimic such usages (though the pleonastic use of *Heliogabaline* is certainly also both pompous and obscure). In fact, each adjective makes a slightly different accusation. An excellent discussion of how Wallace parodies "Academese" in various passages of *Infinite Jest* can be found in de Bourcier.[41]

Another good dissertation may yet be written on Wallace's vocabulary lists (HRC Wallace Papers, container 32.10), tracing where he encountered the terms, categorizing them (archaic vs. specialized vs. regional vs. borrowed, etc.), whether he used them subsequently in his writing, and if so, how. There are many such lists of varying length, both typed and handwritten, some dated, some not, one specifying "from books," another labeled "grammar vocab—random." Some words on typed lists are circled, or added by hand afterward, some are marked with asterisks, and quite a few have blanks or question marks instead of definitions (including *incrunt, sipe, marcid,*

---

[41] Simon de Bourcier, "'They All Sound Like David Foster Wallace': Syntax and Narrative in *Infinite Jest, Brief Interviews with Hideous Men, Oblivion* and *The Pale King*," *Orbit: A Journal of American Literature* 5, no. 1 (2017): 1–30, esp. 4–8. https://doi.org/10.16995/orbit.207.

addorse, cataphract, palliard, irrangible, aspectant, grumous, anthroparian, dracular, spalaean, cimmerian, cuspidine, morling, graymalkin, mascled, pauldron, nemoral, grimoire, androleptic, albified, spattled, cyclocephalic, faltress, banjax, grue, and *mononate).* Some definitions appear to be Wallace's own—for instance, the meaning of *piscean* is given as "fishish."

The posthumous collection *Both Flesh and Not* (2012) includes before each essay a two-page selection from the wordlist Wallace kept on his computer, organized alphabetically, without line breaks or punctuation between entries, cleverly displayed running across the width of both pages together (forcing readers to read these sections differently than they do the rest of the book). A publisher's note invokes Wallace's "insatiable love for words and their meanings," and asserts that his invitation to serve on the Usage Panel of *The American Heritage Dictionary* was "one of the great thrills of Wallace's life" (vii). The collection contains the unabashedly opinionated "Twenty-Four Word Notes" (2004), which starts as mentioned earlier and ends by stating that "no really serious writer should be without" an *Oxford English Dictionary* "close at hand" (280).

As student and reader, Wallace paid close attention to language use. His college essay on *Moby-Dick*, for instance, points out that "this is incredible language, and this fourth paragraph (which, if you look at it closely, is actually one very long sentence) draws me into its flow" (HRC Wallace Papers, container 31.6). As writer and teacher of writing, he encouraged his students to do the same. His syllabus for the "Creative Nonfiction" course he taught in spring 1997 told students that "rather than aspiring to language as a transparent window through which objectively to view the world, writers of creative nonfiction create rather a dirty lens. Works of creative nonfiction usually bear traces of their artificing. The writer wants us to see the language or to see him or herself as its maker." In the syllabus for his "Extremely Advanced Composition" course in spring 2004, he specified that the goal was not "expressive writing," but "*communicative* writing" (emphasis in the original), adding that "the reader does not automatically care about you, the writer, nor does she find you fascinating as a person, nor does she feel a deep natural interest in the same things that interest you. The reader, in fact, will feel about you, your subject, and your essay only what your written words themselves induce her to feel" (HRC Wallace Papers, container 32.6).

Wallace had confidence in his ability to mimic others, telling McCaffery,[42] "I think I have a good ear for speech and speech rhythms." He wrote to editor Gerald Howard, in a letter dated April 25, 1988, addressing references to

---

[42] McCaffery, "An Expanded Interview with David Foster Wallace," 39.

"real public persons, places, organizations, businesses" in *Girl with Curious Hair*, that "David Letterman has never to my knowledge said 'Some fun now, boy'—at various intervals or not. It is, though, weirdly, just the sort of thing he'd say" (HRC Nadell Collection, container 1.8). Note that in the story in question ("My Appearance"), when Edilyn quotes Letterman to her husband, he replies, "Of course he really said that. . . . It's just the sort of thing he'd say" (*GWCH* 198). So to assert for legal purposes that Letterman *didn't* really say what Wallace represented him as saying, Wallace quotes his own fictional character asserting that Letterman *did* really say it.

Wallace bragged to Lipsky,[43] "I can sound kind of like anybody." Indeed, Lipsky describes Wallace as a gifted mimic,[44] as does his biographer.[45] Several critics have made similar points to his biographers, including Kelly,[46] and Cohen,[47] who praises his "perfect ear." LeClair[48] refers *Jest*'s "stylistic tours de force in several dialects." When Moore[49] credits Wallace with capturing "the way modern America sounds in all its cacophony better than any of his contemporaries," he may have been referring specifically to the swirl of background noises that appear in Wallace's fiction, the TV jingles, the car horns and sirens, the pock-pock of tennis racquets hitting balls—but part of this cacophony is undoubtedly the many different voices that Wallace tries to capture. Wallace was a master of invented onomatopoeia—for instance, this list for the sound a tennis racket makes hitting a ball in the cold: "*cut, king, pons, pock, cop, thwa, thwat*" (*Jest* 674)—which may inspire further confidence in his other linguistic abilities, including his assumed mimicry of dialects.

Wallace's use of language was often playful and funny, especially in his naming practices, but many of his jokes pointed to deeper truths. LaVache is a funny name even if you're not aware that "la vache!" is used as a mild oath in French to indicate surprise—much as English speakers once said "holy cow!"—and anyone aware of the literal translation must certainly then evaluate to what degree *Broom*'s LaVache Beadsman is bovine. The full name

---

[43] David Lipsky, *Although of Course You End Up Becoming Yourself: A Road Trip with David Foster Wallace* (New York: Broadway Books, 2010), 258.
[44] Ibid., 176.
[45] Max, *Every Love Story Is a Ghost Story*, 41.
[46] Kelly, "Development Through Dialogue."
[47] Samuel Cohen, "To Wish to Try to Sing to the Next Generation: *Infinite Jest*'s History," in *The Legacy of David Foster Wallace*, ed. Samuel Cohen and Lee Konstantinou (Iowa City: The University of Iowa Press, 2012), 59–79, esp. 75.
[48] Tom LeClair, "The Prodigious Fiction of Richard Powers, William Vollman, and David Foster Wallace," *Critique* 38, no. 1 (Fall 1996): 12–37, esp. 35.
[49] Stephen Moore, "In Memoriam David Foster Wallace," *Modernism/Maturity* 16, no. 1 (2009): 1–24, esp. 2.

of the "Ennet House Drug and Alcohol Recovery House" is given more than half a dozen times in *Infinite Jest*, with a "[sic]" added to one instance (171) in case readers have missed the redundancy in the repeated "House," which may trigger reflection on redundancies built into the twelve-step recovery programs in which the residents are obliged to participate. The acronym O.N.A.N. for *Jest*'s global superpower, the Organization of North American Nations, is likewise both amusing and thought-provoking regarding masturbation, selfishness, and waste. Wallace's treatment of dialects was similar to his naming practices—showing little concern for linguistic accuracy (i.e., realism), but always motivated, working congruently with other elements of the text to convey and underline important ideas.

Dialects versus Dialogue/Dialogism/Dialectics

Many scholars have investigated Wallace's breathtaking intertextuality, and his embodiment of Bakhtin's notions of heteroglossia and dialogism. Thompson[50] considers Wallace "the literary equivalent of a hiphop sampler," and Nichols[51] refers to Wallace's "superdialogized textual landscape . . . a linguistic environment ever teetering on the brink of centrifugal disintegration." Hering[52] devotes a chapter of his monograph to illustrating how Wallace parroted and pastiched other authors. Even Wallace's habit of writing in the margins of books he was reading was dialogic: "Wallace was in conversation—sometimes with the book he was reading and sometimes with an earlier version of himself."[53]

Literary scholars have tended to jump immediately to a discussion of what Wallace's dialect representations are meant to index, rather than analyzing the representations themselves. Kelly[54] masterfully discusses the role of dialogue and dialectics in Wallace's fiction (interpreting his works in dialogue with each other, as I do), but not of dialects per se. It does not help scholarly discussion of these concepts that the terms are so often confused in

---

[50] Lucas Thompson, *Global Wallace: David Foster Wallace and World Literature* (New York: Bloomsbury Publishing, 2016), 234.
[51] Nichols, "Dialogizing Postmodern Carnival," 6.
[52] David Hering, *David Foster Wallace: Fiction and Form* (New York: Bloomsbury Publishing USA, 2017).
[53] Molly Schwartzburg, "Observations on the Archive at the Harry Ransom Center," in *The Legacy of David Foster Wallace*, ed. Sam Cohen and Lee Konstantinou (Iowa City: Iowa University Press, 2012), 241–59, esp. 256.
[54] Kelly, "Development Through Dialogue."

popular discourse, or that the precise definition of "dialect" even just within the field of linguistics is notoriously slippery. There are, of course, many individual idiosyncrasies in the way people speak, and many different styles or registers that any given speaker may deploy in different circumstances, but there are also "variations which are systematic in one group," which "are generally noticed by members of other groups,"[55] including ethnic dialects, regional dialects, sociolects, and genderlects, as well as discourse communities (or "communities of practice") that may cut across demographically defined identity categories. A well-defined shared way of speaking tends to be the result not of "objective" identity characteristics that would be tracked on the census, but of a strong (dense and multiplex) social network.[56] No matter how strong the dialect that emerges, however, there will be individual variations in any individual's speech or "idiolect." Wallace put nonstandard language into the mouths of characters not to evoke negative stereotypes of any particular group, but to confront readers with a particular view of how language functions in US society to reflect and reinforce social divisions, and to demonstrate how characters express their identities both in affiliation with and in resistance to other recognized identities.

Kelly's[57] study focuses on three conversations (all of which take place in literally elevated settings): one hilltop conversation between *Broom* siblings LaVache and Lenore Beadsman, a mountaintop dialogue between *Jest*'s Rémy Marathe and Hugh Steeply (which is spread out over hundreds of pages), and the "multi-character debate that takes place in an elevator in §19" of *The Pale King* (TPK). Kelly insightfully notes "the anticipatory anxiety his characters feel in addressing others";[58] he does not comment on dialect per se, but it is apparent that LaVache and Lenore sound alike, despite gender and personality differences, that the IRS characters all share a corporate sociolect, but that Marathe and Steeply present a stark linguistic contrast. LaVache and Lenore are siblings, sharing regional dialect, relative youth, and family, so might plausibly sound alike. The IRS agents come from different backgrounds but have effectively subsumed their identities to a larger group identity, erasing regional, racial, gender, and other projections of identity. (They also receive new social security numbers, all with the same starting number, symbolizing their assimilation.) Marathe and Steeply are embodiments of different

---

[55] Sumner Ives, "A Theory of Literary Dialect," *Tulane Studies in English* 2 (1950): 137–82, esp. 142.
[56] James Milroy and Lesley Milroy, "Linguistic Change, Social Network and Speaker Innovation," *Journal of Linguistics* 21, no. 2 (1985): 339–84.
[57] Kelly, "Development Through Dialogue."
[58] Ibid., 270–1.

groups which represent different histories and philosophies. Their linguistic differences are key to never letting the reader forget this.

Literary Dialectology

> One of the first things you have to beat out of grad students is the habit of <u>always</u> using correct usage + grammar, even in pieces whose characters are not sophisticated. They seem oblivious of the fact that the <u>way</u> someone communicates says more about them than almost anything else.
> (HRC Wallace Papers, Teaching Materials, container 30.2)

> Writing down something that somebody says out loud is not a matter of transcribing. Because written stuff said out loud on the page doesn't look said out loud. It just looks crazy.
> (Wallace, quoted in Lipsky[59])

Readers are so accustomed to the routine sanitization of dialogue on the page that a more realistic rendering—encoding not just dialect differences but all the disfluencies of normal conversation—would be painful to read and would make characters seem incoherent, unintelligent, perhaps even unintelligible. Even linguists and dialectologists who want to capture all the nuances of real, spontaneous speech for academic purposes argue about what degree of fidelity of transcription is required.[60] Readers are "inherently resistant to the representation of dialect on the page,"[61] partly because of linguistic prejudice against nonstandard dialects in general or the ones represented in particular but also because of the extra work involved in decoding these. Oster[62] argues that in literary representations of dialect, "a foreignness that calls attention to itself by means of language" may be "an inviting insider experience" when "the 'foreignness' is one in which we already feel at home, or at least recognize a familiar friend or guest," but notes also the danger that readers "can feel shut out of it, or put off by what is foreign, either *because* it is foreign or simply because it is difficult to understand." Cole[63]

---

[59] Lipsky, *Although of Course You End Up Becoming Yourself*, 164.
[60] Ronald K. S. Macauley, "'Coz It Izny Spelt When They Say It': Displaying Dialect in Writing," *American Speech* 66, no. 3 (1991): 280–91.
[61] Jane Hodson, *Dialect in Film and Literature* (New York: Palgrave Macmillan, 2014), 107.
[62] Judith Oster, *Crossing Cultures: Creating Identity in Chinese and Jewish American Literature* (Columbia: University of Missouri Press, 2003), 93.
[63] Roger W. Cole, "Literary Representation of Dialect: A Theoretical Approach to the Artistic Problem," *The USF Language Quarterly* 14, nos. 3–4 (1986): 3–8, esp. 6.

refers to respellings of speech as "code noise" and argues that authors would not include this without "an overriding purpose." Authors may initially use some "code noise" to identify a character and trigger desired associations, shifting to more standard representation once these have been established, to lessen the demands on the reader.[64] Wallace never employed such a shifting strategy for the reader's sake—he believed in making the reader "do her share of the linguistic work."[65] There are a couple of instances (particularly with African American characters) where Wallace characters code-shift for their own reasons, but those shifts are away from the supposed standard to a more marked variety.

Hodson's[66] survey establishes that authors less frequently represent "nonstandard grammar" (i.e., syntax and morphology) than incorporate lexical items and nonstandard pronunciations, including an increased use of what Preston[67] calls "allegro speech," the "running together" of casual (but otherwise standard) speech, as in "waddaya want? What can I getcha?" Wallace, however, did just the reverse, avoiding "easy" representations in favor of more interesting ones, carefully selecting particular combinations of features, as can be seen in a preemptive note he wrote warning the copyeditor of *Infinite Jest* about "non-standard syntax in sections concerning the characters Minty, Marathe, Antitoi, Krause, Pemulis, Steeply, Lenz, Orin Incandenza, Mario Incandenza, Fortier, Foltz, J. O. Incandenza Sr., Schtitt, Gompert" (HRC Wallace Papers, container 20.5). Interestingly, this list omits several of the more radical dialect representations in that work, perhaps because it would have been more obvious to the copyeditor that Wallace was intentionally introducing nonstandard features into these.

Early dialect representations in American literature were frequently included for comedic effect, to signal ignorance or immorality,[68] and only very occasionally as "a powerful tool to counterhegemonic subversion."[69] A "local color movement" after the Civil War saw the increasing use of dialects for realism rather than humor, including (among others) prominent use by

---

[64] Hodson, *Dialect in Film and Literature*, 172.
[65] McCaffery, "An Expanded Interview with David Foster Wallace," 34.
[66] Hodson, *Dialect in Film and Literature*.
[67] Dennis R. Preston, "The Li'l Abner Syndrome: Written Representations of Speech," *American Speech* 60, no. 4 (1985): 328–36, esp. 328.
[68] Lisa Cohen Minnick, *Dialect and Dichotomy: Literary Representations of African American Speech* (Tuscaloosa: University of Alabama Press, 2007), 3.
[69] Gavin Jones, *Strange Talk: The Politics of Dialect Literature in Gilded Age America* (Berkeley: University of California Press, 1999), 133.

Twain, Stowe, Cable, Chopin, and Crane.[70] Skaggs[71] suggests that "careful control of . . . condescension" is a hallmark of the use of "local color" dialect representations, that "although the plain folk are presented as culturally inferior to the recorders, the stories display the many virtues of such commoners," allowing the reader to feel "doubly smug: he can condescend to the plain folk speaking in dialect while he still respects them, thus avoiding the moral pitfall of snobbery."

Linguists have mostly been concerned with these representations as historical data, focusing on the accuracy of the linguistic variation shown (often parsing the respellings used by authors to illustrate actual pronunciations), whereas literary theorists have largely remained focused on the purposes of such encoding of dialect in a given work. Mair[72] points out that "there is an awareness that what is encountered in a work of fiction is not a faithful transcription but an artefact," agreeing with Ives,[73] who notes that "each author has made his own decision as to how many of the peculiarities in his character's speech he can profitably represent." More interesting are "questions about linguistic distance between authors, characters, and readers,"[74] and how dialect representations may serve as "a critique of existing attitudes towards language."[75] Esau, Bagnall, and Ware[76] argue that variation in characters' speech "reflects the social stratification of the speech community, is used as a tool to establish social dominance, camouflages complicated patterns of overt and covert prestige, and indicates that opposing value systems may be linked to social class membership." And of course, authors may be motivated to represent dialects "by sheer playfulness."[77] Wallace biographer Max[78] recounts that on a road trip to Tucson with his friend Gale Walden, Wallace expressed the desire "to write a variation on William Gass's novel *Omensetter's Luck*.[79] The laconic hillbilly voice of the story appealed to him. As a 'weird kind of forger,' imitating it would be a fun challenge." The dialect Wallace eventually fashioned for "John

---

[70] Minnick, *Dialect and Dichotomy*, 8.
[71] Merrill Maguire Skaggs, *The Folk of Southern Fiction* (Athens: University of Georgia Press, 1972), 211–2.
[72] Mair, "Literary Sociolinguistics," 104.
[73] Sumner Ives, "A Theory of Literary Dialect," *Tulane Studies in English* 2 (1950): 137–82, esp. 138.
[74] Minnick, *Dialect and Dichotomy*, 11.
[75] Mair, "Literary Sociolinguistics," 122.
[76] Helmut Esau, Norma Bagnall, and Cheryl Ware, "Faulkner, Literary Criticism, and Linguistics," *Language and Literature* 7, nos. 1–3 (1982): 7–62, esp. 12–13.
[77] Mair, "Literary Sociolinguistics," 118.
[78] Max, *Every Love Story Is a Ghost Story*, 74.
[79] William Gass, *Omensetter's Luck* (New York: Penguin, 1966).

Billy" actually bears little resemblance to the one used in Gass's book, as I argue in Chapter 6, but Wallace certainly seemed to enjoy playing with it. When authors depict dialects other than their own, they risk misrepresenting them. Mair[80] argues that "an incomplete, distorted or otherwise incompetent transcription of nonstandard features in a literary work need not be an artistic flaw necessarily." Misrepresentation may result from relying on incorrect but widespread ideas about dialects, the general lack of education about these in schools (other than the imposition of the supposed "standard"), and the inaccessibility of much linguistic research. To complicate this further, a single linguistic variable may simultaneously index a variety of identities. The so-called r-lessness (the deletion of /r/ after vowels) can be found in dialects of African American English (AAE) (which despite popular stereotype do vary from region to region), Southern dialects, and various East Coast dialects. Likewise, multiple negation within a single clause is quite common in working-class regional dialects throughout the United States, regardless of ethnic identity. For obvious historical reasons, AAE in any region shares many features with white Southern dialects. The lack of isomorphism between language and subculture means that use of any dialect feature without overt description of the character (or commentary from other characters or narrators) may lead to confusion or misunderstanding of who the character is supposed to be. As Preston[81] summarized decades of matched-guise sociolinguistic perception experiments, "The path from stimulus to group identification to the triggering of attitudes towards the group so identified was not a trouble-free one," even with all the phonological cues of spoken language. Both *ain't* and multiple negation have been shown to trigger negative attitudes even when judges aren't sure of a speaker's regional or ethnic identity. Most readers are no more consciously aware than authors of how linguistic variables pattern along social lines. Niedzielski and Preston's extensive study of folk linguistics found that most Americans reduce questions of language use to *You ain't from around here, are you?* and *He don't talk so good, does he?*[82]

To force recognition of the intended identity, an unskilled author may paint with too broad a brush, resulting in caricature—which, if recognized as such, would be found offensive. Ives[83] shows that "the literary dialect is

---

[80] Mair, "Literary Sociolinguistics," 106.
[81] Dennis R. Preston, "Language with an Attitude," in *The Handbook of Language Variation and Change*, ed. J. K. Chambers, Peter Trudgill, and Natalie Schilling-Estes (Malden, MA: Blackwell, 2004), 40–66, esp. 52.
[82] Nancy A. Niedzielski, and Dennis R. Preston, *Folk Linguistics* (Berlin: De Gruyter Mouton, 2000), 306.
[83] Ives, "A Theory of Literary Dialect," 146.

likely to be more regular in its variants"; for instance, having a character "use initial [d] in every word in which an educated character would use initial [ð]" ("th" as in "they"), although "it is by no means certain that the man in real life would do so." Folk perception of dialects is usually categorical: people believe that "speakers of certain 'types' either use or do not use certain stereotypical variants,"[84] although the difference is usually a relatively small but statistically significant quantitative difference. Linguistic stereotypes are subject to confirmation bias:[85] listeners will notice only the usages that confirm their stereotype. Wallace may have consciously avoided the trap of being overly consistent in his dialect representations—but he may have just been occasionally sloppy with them.

Authors who have the linguistic skill to realistically depict a dialect other than their own may nonetheless be accused of cultural appropriation, although this was less of a concern in Wallace's lifetime. *The Corpus of Contemporary American English*[86] shows a spike in usage of this term in 2015; Google Scholar returns almost ten thousand "hits" for that phrase since then (likely many more by the time this monograph is printed), but only about a thousand total prior to 1996 (when *Jest* was published). Wallace was nonetheless possibly familiar with what Bourdieu[87] discussed as "strategies of condescension," when someone with prestige and authority appropriates a subordinated language in order to make a point. Nor is it necessarily a safer choice for authors who are native speakers of a nonstandard variety to write in their own vernacular, as it may then be perceived that their intended audience is restricted to those whose dialect is represented, producing what Graham Shorrocks[88] calls "dialect literature" rather than "literary dialect."

Wallace was surely aware that he was taking risks, yet his attempts to directly capture dialects (rather than just commenting on them) span his

---

[84] Nancy A. Niedzielski, and Dennis R. Preston, *Folk Linguistics* (Berlin: De Gruyter Mouton, 2000), 148.
[85] Joshua Klayman, "Varieties of Confirmation Bias," in *Decision Making from a Cognitive Perspective: The Psychology of Learning and Motivation*, Vol. 32, ed. Jerome Busemeyer, Reid Hartie and Douglas L. Medin (New York: Academic Press, 1995), 385–418; Manuel Padilla Cruz, "Interlocutor-Related and Hearer-Specific Causes of Misunderstanding: Processing Strategy, Confirmation Bias and Weak Vigilance," *Research in Language* 15, no. 1 (2017): 11–36.
[86] Mark Davies, *The Corpus of Contemporary American English (COCA): 560 million Words, 1990-Present*. (2008–), https://corpus.byu.edu/coca/.
[87] Pierre Bourdieu, *Language and Symbolic Power*, translated by Gino Raymond and Matthew Adamson (Cambridge: Harvard University Press, 1991), 68–71.
[88] Graham Shorrocks, "Non-Standard Dialect Literature and Popular Culture," in *Speech Past and Present: Studies in English Dialectology in Memory of Ossi Ihalainen*, ed. Juhani Klemola, Merja Kytö, and Matti Rissanen (Frankfurt: Peter Lang, 1996), 385–411, esp. 386.

career. Wallace once said that "maybe half of fiction's job is to dramatize what it is that makes it tough [to be a real human being]. The other half is to dramatize the fact that we still *are* human beings, now. Or can be."[89] All real human beings have idiolects, made up of differential access to different registers, dialect features associated with all their different identities, and idiosyncratic verbal habits and routines. Part of what makes it tough to be human is that people use language not just to create community within group lines but also to enforce group boundaries.[90] Linguistic prejudice is still a mostly socially acceptable proxy in US society for racism, classism, and other evils.[91]

Hodson[92] notes that in fiction, narrative commentary on dialects "allows writers to draw the reader's attention to dialect variation in ways that are much more difficult for film to achieve" (15) but that often, "audiences end up with the impression that they know what a dialect sounds like and what characteristics a speaker of that dialect is likely to have, even though they have no real life experience of interacting with speakers of that variety" (11). Most readers (who are not members of the dialect communities represented) do not know "whether the style is a representation of a genuine local dialect or whether it is an authorial stylistic manipulation to achieve a particular effect."[93] Wallace both availed himself of many opportunities to comment directly on language and on particular dialects and used direct representation of dialects without much concern for authenticity or equal airtime. Wallace's world is largely seen through the eyes of his white male protagonists, who prefer to indirectly report the speech of others, to the extent that anyone who is not white, male, youngish, cisgender, and heterosexual has trouble getting a word in edgewise. Most critics have treated this as a blind spot for Wallace, but given his hyper-self-awareness, his obsession with language, his sophisticated understanding of both the philosophy of language and the history of linguistics, it makes more sense to view this as a deliberate strategy. The marginalization of others is an implicit critique of Wallace's protagonists'

---

[89] McCaffery "An Expanded Interview with David Foster Wallace," 26, emphasis in the original.
[90] Katherine A. Collins and Richard Clément, "Language and Prejudice: Direct and Moderated Effects," *Journal of Language and Social Psychology* 31, no. 4 (2012): 376–96, esp. 389.
[91] Rosina Lippi-Green, *English with an Accent* (London and New York: Routledge, 1997); John Baugh, "Linguistic Profiling and Discrimination," in *The Oxford Handbook of Language and Society*, ed. Ofelia García, Nelson Flores, and Massimiliano Spotti (Oxford: Oxford University Press, 2017), 349–68; among others.
[92] Hodson, *Dialect in Film and Literature*, 2014.
[93] Crystal, *The Language of Stories*, 503.

insularity; their blind spots reflect more on them than on the "background" characters with whom they are unable to effectively connect. As Wallace observed, "Which dialect you choose to use depends, of course, on whom you're addressing. More to the point, I submit that the dialect you use depends mostly on what sort of Group your listener is part of and whether you wish to present yourself as a fellow member of that Group" (*CTL* 101). Not surprisingly, therefore, in his fiction, Wallace often uses dialect to comment on social fissures.

> People really do "judge" one another according to their use of language. Constantly. . . . But it's clear that at least one component of all this interpersonal semantic judging involves acceptance, meaning not some touchy-feely emotional affirmation but actual acceptance or rejection of somebody's bid to be regarded as a peer, a member of somebody else's collective or community or Group. (*CTL* 97)

In these quotes, Wallace presents a choice between distinct varieties, not a quantitative adjustment, scaling a bit up or down in the use of dialect features, converging or diverging with interlocutors, as social psychologists describe speech accommodation.[94] In Wallace's fiction, characters frequently assimilate (losing ethnic or regional dialects) to fit in with a new target community. Dialects depicted are almost never *named*—perhaps because he recognized that dialect labels come with prejudgment, but also perhaps because he did not represent any dialect as a monolithic, static, well-defined "object." There are very few black Wallace characters, but they do not all sound alike, for example. The dialects named in A&AU are "Black English, Latino English, Rural Southern, Urban Southern, Standard Upper-Midwest, Maine Yankee, East-Texas Bayou, Boston Blue-Collar" (*CTL* 98). Earlier in the article, in considering whether usage shapes popular views of correctness, Wallace asks *whose* usage matters: "Urban Latinos? Boston Brahmins? Rural Midwesterners? Appalachian Neogaelics?" (*CTL* 84). I'm not sure whether this last part of the question was intended to be taken seriously. Although there were certainly Scots-Irish immigrants who settled in Appalachia, there is no scholarly use of the term "Appalachian Neogaelic," and the Celtic influence on Appalachian English is greatly exaggerated in the popular imagination. Clearly, neither list is intended to be comprehensive,

---

[94] Howard Giles, ed. *Communication Accommodation Theory: Negotiating Personal Relationships and Social Identities Across Contexts* (Cambridge: Cambridge University Press, 2016).

and interestingly, one dialect that gets extended use in two of his short stories, Jewish American English, is not included.

Not only do real people express all their intersecting identity traits (ethnicity, region, gender, class, age) in the way that they speak but they also express different levels of affiliation with those identities (which can and does vary dynamically across contexts), adjusting their speech patterns based on how they perceive the nature of the conversation, the identities of their interlocutors, and the goals they're consciously or unconsciously trying to achieve in the interaction. They may subtly converge with or diverge from the speech patterns of interlocutors within a conversation, to express connection and agreement or a lack of these. The sheer complexity of this system of social signaling could well seem overwhelming to an author trying to encode realistic dialogue, who only has limited conscious awareness of which particular linguistic variables are associated with particular identities, and then also has to contend with which variable will survive the change of medium from face-to-face speech to the written page. To Wallace, on the other hand, the very complexity of this system may have posed an irresistible challenge.

Language has always been used as shibboleth, dividing "us" from "them." The most obvious instantiation of this in Wallace's fiction is the contrast of foreigners with Americans, in portraits ranging from brief, overheard snippets of conversation to the most fully developed ultra-foreigner, Rémy Marathe in *Infinite Jest*. But this constitutes just a tiny portion of Wallace's exploration of language and identity. Is the United States a "melting pot"? Should it be one? Who *wants* to assimilate, who is *allowed* to assimilate, and who does not have that option? Wallace put words in characters' mouths that make readers squirm—but that reaction itself bears deeper scrutiny. As Zadie Smith[95] says about *Brief Interviews with Hideous Men* (BIHM), "it's *our* character that's being investigated" (276); often, Wallace's dialects reflect less on the speaker and more on the readers who have responded to the dialect with automatic negative judgments.

Wallace's "avant-garde" approach to realism (as opposed to what he saw as the "traditional . . . soothing and conservative" American tradition of "big-R realism") aimed "to countenance and render real aspects of real experiences that have previously been excluded from art,"[96] and as someone

---

[95] Zadie Smith, "*Brief Interviews with Hideous Men*: The Difficult Gifts of David Foster Wallace," in *Changing My Mind: Occasional Essays* (London: Hamish Hamilton, 2009), 257–300.
[96] McCaffery, "An Expanded Interview with David Foster Wallace," 38.

whose "real religion was always language,"[97] he must surely have thought about whether his depictions of language were small-r or big-R "real." In cases where he knowingly misrepresented dialects or simply didn't put in the linguistic research that would have been required to capture them in a more big-r-realistic kind of way, it is probable that he had a more small-r-realistic project in mind. It has long been a staple of US culture to mock nonstandard ways of speaking, but Wallace most emphatically was not participating in that tradition. Irony and sarcasm, as he noted in an extended interview on National Public Radio's *Fresh Air*,[98] "are fantastic for exploding hypocrisy and exposing what's wrong with extant values; as far as I can see, they're notably less good at erecting replacement values or coming any closer to the truth." In the case of Wallace's representations of African American English, Jewish American English, and white working-class dialects from different regions, the hypocrisy Wallace was exploding was ours, and the stories he allowed his characters to tell in nonstandard language that slowed readers down and certainly drew their attention provided the necessary ingredients for the empathy he advocated as a "replacement value."

Wallace's dialect portrayals are often fleeting, and they may not always be accurate linguistically, but they are not employed as shorthand "dog-whistles" to evoke particular negative traits supposedly associated with particular communities. Wallace's characters are often in difficult social and economic circumstances, but their use of dialect is never intended to display a lack of intelligence or deficiency of moral character. A few of the drug addicts in *Infinite Jest* are dialect speakers, but many other addicts' speech is portrayed as standard, and Wallace has sympathy and empathy for all of them. The most prominent dialect portrayals in Wallace's work are examined in this book not just in terms of how they contribute to characterizations and themes, but as pieces of "folk linguistics," to see which variables of regional and ethnic dialects were salient enough for Wallace to include and therefore are the features that his readers may come to associate with dialects of which they themselves may have little real-life experience. In an increasingly racially, regionally, socially, and politically divided modern United States, there are many people whose only real encounter with "the other" is through the media. It seems much less relevant now (in the wake of Wallace's death) whether *he* was "capitalist, sexist, racist, xenophobic, homophobic, elitist: unfair" (*CTL* 81) than with whether his work can speak across these divides, whether fans of his work might be encouraged or discouraged in their own

---

[97] Max, *Every Love Story Is a Ghost Story*, 166.
[98] Terry Gross, "*Fresh Air* Interview with David Foster Wallace," National Public Radio, March 5, 1997.

prejudices and unconscious biases. I agree with Joffe[99] that whether or not Wallace was a misogynist is "less interesting than his evident desire not to *appear* as such," and that it is more productive to focus on "the strategies he employs to convince his readers accordingly." Wallace offers his readers not just observations on the social status of particular linguistic varieties but also the complex interrelationship of nationality, ethnicity, regional identity, social class, and gender. Taken together, these portrayals may be seen as one man's ongoing struggle with his knowledge of his own linguistic privilege and his sincere attempt to capture both the diversity of modern American society and the hegemony of whiteness within that society.

---

[99] Joffe, "*In the Shadows*," 38.

2

Foreigners and Foreignness

Figure 2 Wallace's Non-Native Dialects.

Distinguishing the Not-American

Almost all of Wallace's foreigners maintain non-native speech patterns, generally presented in fairly broad stereotypes. When taken on their own, each of these portrayals may seem like a crude caricature, even racist, but Wallace's portrayals of US ethnic dialects and white regional working-class US dialects are equally broad (as will be discussed in later chapters). On a practical level, Wallace seemed to be striving for maximal distinctiveness for all the identities represented. On a more philosophical level, I believe he was deliberately trying to provoke readers' language prejudices, only to then subvert these by forcing the reader into an empathetic response to the character: the stronger the initial reaction, the bigger the potential payoff.

It is a common observation in Wallace criticism[1] that one of the author's main preoccupations was with defining, representing, even cataloguing millennial "America." In a 1996 interview, Wallace said that he wanted to "do something real American, about what it's like to live in America around the millennium."[2] Hayes-Brady calls Wallace "self-consciously American," finding evidence for this in his naming practices and in his (mis)appropriation of elements from his American literary predecessors. Thompson[3] refers to this critical lens as "Wallace-as-national-metonym."

As interested in language as he was, Wallace could not resist exploring what it means to be a dawn-of-the-twenty-first-century American in linguistic terms as well. In Wallace's world, someone who was not born in the United States can become American (or at least their children and grandchildren can), but the reverse path is apparently unthinkable. (There are no expatriate Americans encountered and Wallace's characters seldom set foot abroad, but there is a steady influx of foreigners into the United States.) There are limits to the ability to assimilate for both foreigners and ethnic "others," and Wallace's work shows that "the melting pot" is more a *loss* of community than it is a way to join a new one. Americans are portrayed as having more power and privilege than foreigners, just as whites have more than other ethnicities, but they are no happier or more successful as human beings. Wallace's white Americans are trapped in their solipsism; they do not purposefully seek encounters with and are only peripherally aware of foreign and ethnic others; Wallace seldom gave foreigners or minorities the opportunity to take center stage, but he never let readers forget about them, either.

Hayes-Brady[4] describes a "trajectory in Wallace's work that begins with a preoccupation with language and develops into a more explicit focus on cultural systems, with language as one part of the system, finally culminating in a detailed attention to questions of politics and citizenship, which are intimately and explicitly tied to both language and culture."

She chooses to focus on gender as the main source of "alterity" in Wallace and argues that "by refusing to 'speak for' someone else, Wallace is implicitly

---

[1] Kiki Benzon, "'Yet Another Example of the Porousness of Certain Borders': Chaos and Realism in *Infinite Jest*," in *Consider David Foster Wallace: Critical Essays*, ed. David Hering (Los Angeles and Austin: Sideshow Media Group Press, 2010), 101–12; Lee Konstantinou, "The World of David Foster Wallace," *Boundary 2*, 40, no. 3 (September 2013): 59–86; among others.

[2] Laura Miller, "The Salon Interview: David Foster Wallace," in *Conversations with David Foster Wallace*, ed. Stephen J. Burn (Jackson: University of Mississippi Press, 2012), 58–65, esp. 59.

[3] Thompson, *Global Wallace*, 4.

[4] Hayes-Brady, *The Unspeakable Failures of David Foster Wallace*, 9.

assuming and privileging the identity he *does* speak for—White, American, male." This is undeniable, but it should not be assumed that privileging that identity is celebrating it; rather, Wallace's extreme self-consciousness provides a constant critique of the centrality of that identity.

Araya[5] links "recurrent images of paleness" in TPK with "its implied notions about citizenship. . . . If the United States cannot be strong as a nation, Wallace seems to be asking, how can we be strong as a state? If we do not form a strong, or even viable, community when we are similar, how can we do so when we are different?" Wallace's portrayals of dialects serve both to illustrate individual questions of identity, but also the heteroglossia that exists at the societal level. What does it mean to "sound American"? The positive aspects of linguistic diversity (making room for many voices to co-exist, showing language as a source of playfulness, creativity, and delight) are celebrated, but the multitude of voices may sometimes feel overwhelming, the voices may not easily communicate with or understand each other, and it is clearly the case that the voices do not have equal status or access.

Wallace's foreigners have little in common with each other. They are French Canadian, German (and/or Austrian), Irish, Latin/South American, Haitian/Caribbean, African; they come to the United States for different reasons and have different status within the country. Nativization is not a necessary or inevitable goal; some want what the United States has to offer but are not willing to lose their own identities to gain it. BIHM features several brief fictions titled "Yet Another Example of the Porousness of Certain Borders," which Boswell[6] explains as "situations in which levels of consciousness and/or representation begin to bleed into one another." Benzon[7] and Jansen[8] applied this idea (each using the "porousness of certain borders" phrase in the titles of their respective essays on *Infinite Jest*) to different kinds of systems of categorization that Wallace challenged, with Jansen focusing more narrowly on person/object distinctions and Benzon taking on "boundaries both geographical and social, . . . order and disorder" (103). Benzon's conclusion that in Wallace's fiction "mimeticism exists not on the level of representational 'mirroring'—though detailed descriptions of the material world are a constitutive element," but rather that the narrative itself "assumes the chaotic properties which pervade physical and cultural spheres" (112). I

---

[5] Jorge Araya, "Why the Whiteness?: Race in *The Pale King*," in *Critical Insights: David Foster Wallace*, ed. Philip Coleman (New York: Grey House Publishing/Salem Press, 2015), 238–51, esp. 248.
[6] Boswell, *Understanding David Foster Wallace*, 198.
[7] Benzon, "Yet Another Example of the Porousness of Certain Borders."
[8] Jansen, "On the Porousness of Certain Borders."

make a parallel argument: Wallace's dialects are not mimetic, except for the projection of his own fictional-but-realistic "Dave Wallace" voice.

The only unambiguously foreign-born character Wallace shows speaking indistinguishably from Americans is "Kenyan prorector" Tony Nwangi at *Jest*'s Enfield Tennis Academy (ETA). Tony presumably came to the United States at an early age, so this apparently native command of the language is not just realistic, it is unremarkable; indeed, neither Wallace nor anybody at ETA remarks upon it. It's possible that Audern Tallat-Kelpsa (who may be named for the Lithuanian/Soviet composer of the same surname) is another such example, although it's equally possible that he is a native-born native-US-American speaker. All that readers are told about him is that he is one of the "sub-14 male Eschatonites" (666), that he is "creepily blue-eyed" (118) and "little" (265). The extent of his direct dialogue is five short sentences that sound like all the other ETA boys: "This is early rounds. The kind they give you only two balls. Honor systems. All of a sudden there he is kertwanging on you. It happens" (118). With "foreign" names but indistinguishable speech, the line between immigrant and native is deliberately blurred.

Non-native speakers who come to the United States as adults typically do not lose all their non-native phonological patterns, whatever level of grammatical competency or idiomatic fluency they achieve. Only exceptional adult language learners are able to achieve native-like[9] proficiency, and not all have that goal. One international graduate student Levis[10] interviewed in Iowa "did not want an accent that hid her Russianness, an identity of which she was proud" (4). When characters like Gerhardt Schtitt and Rémy Marathe speak in a noticeably "non-native" way, it is not just because Wallace wanted readers to remember their origins and identities, but because *these characters* are affirming those identities. Wallace's delight in non-native linguistic patterns, his inevitable exaggeration of them, should not be misread as mockery of those patterns or of the speakers—except when readers are meant to recognize a focalizing character's racism, as when *Jest*'s Randy Lenz thinks about Chinese, "Your monkey-languages' exclamatories have an explosive ricocheting sound to them. As in a component of *boing* to every word" (718).

Not all Wallace characters are quite this consciously and explicitly racist or xenophobic. Don Gately's perception of a "cheery young Pakistani M.D." who'd told him "how Teddibly Soddy he was" (912) that his mother's stroke left her permanently incapacitated is no doubt tinged with racism—Gately

---

[9] Alene Moyer, "Exceptional Outcomes in L2 Phonology: The Critical Factors of Learner Engagement and Self-Regulation," *Applied Linguistics* 35, no. 4 (2014): 418–40.

[10] John Levis, "Learners' Views of Social Issues in Pronunciation Learning," *Journal of Academic Language & Learning* 9, no. 1 (2015): 42–55.

is frequently offhandedly racist—but Gately also seems impressed by a foreigner who speaks such impeccable albeit accented English, one who has achieved so much more than Gately has in terms of education and professional success, even though he had to do it in a foreign language. Even in the middle of danger and crisis (the precipitating events that result in his own hospitalization), Gately notices that "Nucks really do pronounce *the* with a *z*"(611)—seemingly surprised and amused that the stereotype is true, but not apparently negatively judging the Canadians for their accent. For readers, this is one of many reminders that the characters' negative views of ethnic and racial others precede any personal contact with them. Racism is more likely to cause bad social interactions than to be caused by them.

The perpetually recurring "English First" or "English Only" political movements that seek to enshrine English as official language of the United States or of individual states have rarely been openly racist and classist, with some proponents claiming to want to help immigrants as well as citizens who speak heritage languages. There is often nevertheless a clear undertone of hostility against foreigners who "don't even try" to learn English. In a meta-analysis of research "that seeks to explain the widespread public support for restrictive language and immigration policies," Schildkraut[11] finds that "the dominant influences on attitudes appear to be conceptions of American identity, education, income, partisanship, ideology, economic perceptions, and identity," and more specifically that "different conceptions of American identity"—for example, one that prioritizes individual freedoms vs. one that prioritizes "civic republican ideals" lead to different attitudes. Rodríguez, Schwartz, and Whitbourne[12] demonstrate that "ethnic minorities felt less American than Whites and believed that, regardless of their citizenship, they are not perceived as American," although fewer than 10 percent of respondents cite language as a key characteristic of being "American."

Linguists have long known that "greater intolerance of immigrants (and their language ability) is attributed to lower-status speakers against whom linguistic prejudices are also strong."[13] For the more economically and socially privileged, mastery of foreign languages is seen as sophistication. When Hal Incandenza thinks that "modern German is better equipped to combining gerundives and prepositions than is its mongrel cousin"

---

[11] Deborah J. Schildkraut, "American Identity and Attitudes Toward Official English Policies," *Political Psychology* 24, no. 3 (2003): 469–99, esp. 470.
[12] Liliana Rodríguez, Seth J. Schwartz, and Susan Krauss Whitbourne, "American Identity Revisited: The Relation Between National, Ethnic, and Personal Identity in a Multiethnic Sample of Emerging Adults," *Journal of Adolescent Research* 25, no. 2 (2010): 324–49, esp. 325.
[13] Niedzielski and Preston, *Folk Linguistics*, 145.

(*Jest* 900), it is intended as a sign of his erudition, as well as an explicit reminder that English, the mongrel cousin referred to, is not "superior" to any other language, despite the pride that many Americans have in speaking such a "hard" language, whose opaque spellings, arbitrary constructions, and vocabulary borrowed from so many sources around the world prove so difficult for non-native speakers to master.

Mediated Representation of Foreignness

The most important feature of most of Wallace's representations of foreign speech is that, apart from the French-Canadians in *Jest*, they are mediated: seen through the eyes of other characters. Gerhardt Schtitt, for instance, is almost always seen through the eyes of Hal Incandenza, who, despite being brilliant, still falls into the trap of overgeneralizing about entire nations: "*Like most Germans outside of popular entertainment*" (emphasis added), Schtitt "gets quieter when he wants to impress or menace" (459). Hal adds parenthetically that "there are very few shrill Germans, actually" (459). Indeed, at times, Schtitt takes on the responsibility of representing "most Europeans of his generation" (82). That the foreigners are seen as caricatures says more about the attitudes of the focalizing characters than it does about the foreigners. When Don Gately refers to "Alfonso Parias-Carbo the totally ununderstandable Cuban" (*Jest* 887), readers may feel smugly superior, as they were perfectly able to understand Alfonso's speech earlier in the novel ("I am drug addict, powerless. I am knowing powerlessness since the period of Castro" [187]). The joke is on Don, not on Alfonso.

This "I-know-that-you-know-better" winking at the reader happens even when the perspective is that (ostensibly) of Wallace himself. The nonfiction "Dave Wallace" narrator develops a "searing crush" (296) on Petra, the cabin cleaner in "A Supposedly Funny Thing," who answers "every question, joke, or protestation of undying love" with either "Is no problem" or "You are a funny thing" (*ASFTINDA* 298). Thompson[14] comments on the "ESL solecisms" of Petra and of the Hungarian waiter, Tibor, but also notes that "Wallace's affection toward them is palpable, and he is clearly kinder to them than many of his fellow cruisers." Thompson misidentifies Petra as "Asian," which is perhaps understandable, as Wallace describes her as "epicanthically

---

[14] Lucas Thompson, "Wallace and Race," in *The Cambridge Companion to David Foster Wallace*, ed. Ralph Clare (Cambridge: Cambridge University Press, 2018), 204–19, esp. 213.

doe-eyed" (297), although he also explicitly identifies her as "Slavonian" in the original *Harper's* essay ("Shipping Out" 46) (unfortunately rendered as "Slavanian" in the *ASTFINDA* collection (298)—an apparent typo). Thompson also mischaracterizes Petra's use of language: "Is no problem" is an elliptical construction (lacking a subject), but so is the equivalent native speakers' formulation ("no problem"), and the grammar of Petra's other stock response is entirely (prescriptively) correct, although its sincerity should certainly be in doubt. The message here is not "haha, foreigners can't speak English correctly," it's that Petra is thoroughly competent and professional, even when harassed by someone she dare not antagonize and whose language she may not understand. Wallace is criticizing himself (and by extension readers who identify with him). Wallace acknowledges the tendency to fetishize the foreign as well as his desire to distance himself from this in an even more blatant example from his fiction: When Lenny in "Say Never" (GWCH) speaks of his South American lover's "utterly deadly accent, a fellation of each syllable" (214), readers are meant to find him ridiculous, not her.

Infinite Jest features frequent passing glimpses of non-native background characters who are not even given names, like the "tired Cuban orderly" (17) who gets the last word in the opening section of the novel, "the Pakistani manager" of Store24 (206), "the Saudi Minister of Home Entertainment" (33), "the Near Eastern medical attaché" and his wife (78), and so on. The foregrounding of foreignness makes it clear that this is a noteworthy part of the social system of categorization, while the frequency of such references normalizes the presence of foreigners in the United States, making it clear that they're just regular people going about their business. Although these are often passing mentions, they are nonetheless generally sympathetic and contribute to Wallace's celebration of heteroglossia in America, at the same time subtly reinforcing the idea that America is dominated by (and for) those of Western European descent. When Gately feels uncomfortable around foreigners, readers understand that his xenophobia is regrettable, an illustration of his own limitations; at the same time, they appreciate that his unconscious racism appears to be in tension with his desire to be a good guy. He understands that it's not okay to be racist; he can't even acknowledge to himself that he is racist; he has to frame it as being "solidly pro-American" (479), not "anti-others."

The Latin Lover: Carlina Rentaria-Cruz ("Say Never")

Readers do not hear Carlina speak directly, but when in a letter her lover Lenny quotes her as saying "I hear this in a club on the Loop," he immediately adds parenthetically "(The Looop)" (*GWCH* 214). This echo of spoken accent in a written letter is an illustration of Lenny's fetishization of Carlina's accent—but also a reminder that Wallace was in the exact same position as Lenny, making the same choices about how to represent her speech. Carlina displays a non-native verb agreement in this quote and elsewhere, and other noticeably non-native syntax (for instance, her formulation "for the screwing in of a lightbulb" in a racist "how many ___ does it take" joke [215]), but Lenny focuses exclusively on her particularly long tense vowels, as seen again when he recalls her saying, "OH LENITO I WILL *EEET* YOU!" (215, all-caps in the original).

The surname Rentaria-Cruz carries the weight of multiple associations. Obviously, there is the cross of Christianity in *Cruz* (she is depicted wearing "Catholic medals" [216]), but an association with "yielding" depends on the reader's knowledge of the Spanish verb *rentar*. The pre-hyphenated part is more apt to be understood by an English speaker as representing a mercenary quality: Carlina—who has dumped the working-class Mikey, who complains about how much money he spent on her, for his older brother Leonard, who can presumably spend more—can be rented. Despite this, Carlina ought to be judged less harshly than Lenny. Without commitment or responsibility, she is free to enjoy her own sexuality. She appears quite independent in other ways, having found secretarial work in a foreign country at the young age of twenty. She appears to be amused by Lenny, and one can hardly blame her for taking advantage of him when he does not seem to take her seriously as anything other than an object of lust. He is the one breaking vows and hearts—she is a young woman having fun. Carlina makes no attempt to "fit in" linguistically, to lose her accent or "improve" her English; she seems to understand that her foreignness is an important part of her appeal. (This relationship will be explored more in the next chapter, with reference to Lenny's dialect.)

The German (Austrian?) Fascist (?): Gerhardt Schtitt (*Jest*)

Thompson[15] refers to *Jest's* ETA head coach Gerhardt Schtitt as "a grotesquely stereotypical, Hollywood-fascist German," and Hering[16] says he's "a caricature of fascist disciplinarianism," although he disagrees with McGurl[17] that "neither Wallace nor Wallace's novel has any serious problem" with Schtitt's implied fascism. Any echo of fascism is embedded in the content of Schtitt's speech, his ideas about discipline, not its form; the treatment of his dialect is no broader nor more stereotyped than that of Rentaria-Cruz or the unnamed "green-card Irishman" to be discussed next. Schtitt's main dialect features

---

[15] Thompson, *Global Wallace*, 204.
[16] Hering, *David Foster Wallace*, 66.
[17] McGurl, "The Institution of Nothing," 40.

appear to be using "yes?" as a tag question, and occasionally exclaiming in German: "Schtitt says *ach*" (82). Lest readers overlook the importance of language, Hal describes the sounds Schtitt makes while exhaling smoke in technical linguistic terms, as "variant in plosivity between P and B" (80). Schtitt's use of actual German words is ironically intended to show his softer side: Endnote 31 (994) reveals that Schitt uses the affectionate term *Lebensgefährtin* for Aubrey deLint, but this note links to Schtitt's use of this term in the plural—indicating that "he now has all these *Lebensgefährtins*" (79), many "life companions." Ortho Stice quotes Schtitt to his "Little Buddies" as referring to ETA students as *mein kinder*, which Stice explains "sort of means my family" (119). "He's not American," Stice scrupulously adds, as if that might be a deal-breaker in the establishment of relationships of affection, "but I tell you straight out right here he makes me proud to be American. Mein kinder" (120).

When the upperclassmen "translate Schtitt into accessible language for the littler kids" (459), it's not his language that is difficult, but his philosophy. It's not even entirely clear that he *is* "German," as he also shares with Mario his "grim childhood experiences" at an "Austrian akademie" (756), "pre-unification" (82), and has an "obscure Austrian blend" of pipe tobacco (80). Either Wallace never made up his mind about this, or Austria and Germany have unified into a larger political unit in the near-future world in *Jest,* or Wallace was spoofing the average American's inability to distinguish these. He admitted to a German interviewer that he had invented the name Schtitt to "sound German-sounding to Americans";[18] he did not remark upon the fact that the name is essentially a blend of *shit* and *tit*.

Thompson[19] sees "Wallace's relentlessly hyperbolic characterization" of Schtitt as conforming to the stereotype of Germans as "stupid, officious, and absurd, but ultimately harmless," but this misses both the respect accorded to his training philosophy, and the depth of emotion that Schtitt inspires in some ETA students. Ultimately, Wallace rejects Schtitt's goal of "self-transcendence through pain" (660) and the idea that people should "get lost in something bigger than them" (660), but does not mock that view as inherently stupid or absurd. Stice is sincere when he tells his Little Buddies that they'd be "privileged to ever get an interface" with Schtitt (119), and that "I'd chew fiberglass for that old man" (120). When one of the ETA students says that "Schtitt just does what he's told like a good Nazi" (104), the locker-room almost explodes into

---

[18] Lucas Thompson, "David Foster Wallace's Germany," *Comparative Literature Studies* 56, no. 1 (2019): 1–30, esp. 22.
[19] Ibid.

violence. Unlike a Nazi caricature, Schtitt "will yield" (268), and has "a soft place inside for anyone who seems even marginally politically repressed" (307). Wallace makes one of his most interesting points about Schtitt through the use of Latin rather than German. Schtitt frequently uses, but refuses to translate, the motto "CONTRARIA SUNT COMPLEMENTA" (713), "allowing prorectors and Big Buddies to adjust their translations to suit the needs of the pedagogical moment" (1054, endnote 298). This openness of interpretation is the very opposite of fascism. In fact, endnote 298 mistranslates the motto as "We Are What We Revile," or "We Are What We Scurry Around As Fast As Possible With Our Eyes Averted"—although it actually refers to complementary opposites, as in a yin/yang symbol, showing not just the slipperiness of language, but its ability to deliberately mislead. This is in contrast to James O. Incandenza's ETA motto "TE OCCIDERE POSSUNT SED TE EDERE NON POSSUNT NEFAS EST" (81), which offered no such ambiguities (albeit quite a bit of irony), and no opportunities for growth. This motto (replaced by new headmaster Charles Tavis after Incadenza's death with a trite "upbeat" English slogan) is translated for readers in endnote 32 as "Roughly, 'They Can Kill You, But the Legalities of Eating You Are Quite a Bit Dicier'" (994)—the "roughness" comes from the hedging on how wrong eating you would be. The Latin makes it quite clear that it would be morally wrong, not just illegal.

The Alcoholic Irishman (*Jest*)

Don Gately briefly recalls hearing a story told at an Alcoholics Anonymous (AA) meeting by a fifty-year-old "green-card Irishman in a skallycap and Sinn Fein sweatshirt, with a belly like a swinging sack of meal and a thoroughly visible ass to back it up" (351), a long-haul trucker whose name Gately didn't catch. The remembered speech is extremely nonstandard, the broadest stereotype of an Irish accent—though Gately is not a reliable narrator on this. Some parts of the representation are plausible (e.g., lexical items like calling the bathroom the *loo* or (less likely) the archaic preposition *twixt*). The avoidance of interdental fricatives (reducing the article *the* to *t'* [e.g., if he can make it part of the onset of the next syllable] or *de* if he cannot, rendering *thought* as *tought*) is a feature of Irish English today.[20] Where most Americans would use a mid-central unrounded vowel, the unnamed Irishman has a *oo* spelling (*hoong* for *hung*, *froom*, *oop*, *troock*, etc.), most likely indicating

---

[20] Raymond Hickey, *Irish English : History and Present-Day Forms* (Cambridge: Cambridge University Press, 2007), 304.

a pronunciation further back and rounded, which as Hickey[21] notes is particularly associated with "vernacular" Irish English speakers. The *oo* spelling in words where most Americans would have the /u/ pronunciation anyway may indicate a degree of vowel lengthening (as in *prodooced*, or *too* for the preposition *to*) and the *ewe* spelling of /ʊ/ may indicate fronting and/ or tensing of the vowel (*stewed* for *stood*). An /o/ pronunciation is indicated for *drop* by spelling it *drope(d)*, and for *lovely* by spelling it *loavely*.

Much of the representation, however, is not systematic or consistent, and doesn't seem to correspond to the phonology or the morphosyntax of Irish English, including the rendering of *you* as *yo*, for instance (with *yo new* for *you know*), or *God* as *Good*, or the frequent lowering of high front vowels /i/ and /ɪ/, as in *confarmed* for *confirmed* and *yars* for *years*, etc.) The representation of the pronoun *I* as *ay* is pure eye dialect, which Ives[22] defined as misspellings that trigger strong awareness of incorrectness (and therefore perceptions of ignorance and lack of education). The nonstandard use of *were* with singular subjects and *me* for possessive *my* evokes nonstandardness, but neither of these was found for Irish English by Szmrecsanyi and Kortmann.[23] I suspect Wallace just enjoyed the sound of *Har Par* for "higher power," *rail tard* for "real turd," and simply could not resist the puns inherent in *Good is me wetness* (351).

Although the heartfelt truth that underlies the Irishman's joy and relief at finally producing a regular bowel movement (after years of drug and alcohol-induced diarrhea) is appreciated by the crowd, Gately also recalls "falling about" and laughing "from the gut," apparently as much at the man and his accent as at the fact that he produced this "ode to a solid dump." The humor in this brief section, and the fact that it is explicitly filtered via the consciousness of a man already known to be racist (and therefore any attitudes expressed are not necessarily those of the author), may have saved it from receiving the same kind of condemnation as the representation of Clenette Henderson considered in the next chapter.

Infinite Jest's "Thinking in French"

Earlier Seeds

Wallace first tried his hand at representing the English of a native French speaker in "Lyndon." President Johnson's assistant has a Haitian lover, René

---

[21] Ibid., 317.
[22] Ives, "A Theory of Literary Dialect," 147.
[23] Benedikt Szmrecsanyi, and Bernd Kortmann, "The Morphosyntax of Varieties of English Worldwide: A Quantitative Perspective," *Lingua* 119, no. 11 (2009): 1643–63.

Duverger, who is not fluent in English; he translates his French word-for-word ("*Elle a tort* . . . She has wrong" because he "had little English he was proud of" (*GWCH* 99). Although French was the language Wallace was clearly the most comfortable playing with, I can find no evidence that he was able to speak it—or any language other than English. Hayes-Brady[24] claims that Wallace "had enough French to read Camus in the original," but Thompson[25] hedges the claim a bit more, saying only that Wallace "was familiar with a wide range of French writers . . . either in the original French or in translation." He also recounts[26] that Wallace signed up for an introductory Russian class at Amherst but dropped it when he discovered he had no talent for it.

Wallace attended the 1995 Canadian Open in Montreal when writing about tennis player Michael Joyce for a 1996 *Esquire* feature, but the extent of the Québécois French included in that article was quoting a couple of billboard advertisement slogans and using the phrase "aller au pissoir" ("go to the public urinal") in a footnote (*ASFTINDA* 247). Wallace acknowledges in this essay that his French was "just good enough" to establish that the stories the local reporters were telling in the Press Box were about sexual adventures and were "tiresome" (*ASFTINDA* 241)—and I suspect he was overstating his receptive competence. It is hard to believe that if he could understand what they were saying, or the conversations of spectators around him, that he would not have incorporated direct quotes overheard. There's no evidence in the essay that he spoke to anybody other than Joyce and Joyce's coach during the several days he spent there. Any French Wallace would have studied in a US classroom would have been Parisian French, but Wallace never featured any characters from France. He was no doubt aware that "for the majority of Americans, French accents are positive ones,"[27] and he may not have wished to accord automatic prestige to a foreign character.

Mistakes, Names, and Slogans

Wallace did not expect *Jest* readers to be familiar with French, mostly arranging for characters to explicitly gloss and/or comment on the language when used, or having his narrator explain via endnotes (with a few notable

---

[24] Clare Hayes-Brady, "'. . .': Language, Gender, and Modes of Power in the Work of David Foster Wallace," in *A Companion to David Foster Wallace Studies*, ed. Marshall Boswell and Stephen J. Burn (New York: Palgrave Macmillan, 2013), 131–50, esp. 149.
[25] Thompson, *Global Wallace*, 121.
[26] Ibid., 92.
[27] Lippi-Green, *English with an Accent*, 72.

exceptions as will be discussed later). The assumed lack of familiarity may also have made him feel comfortable taking liberties, not concerning himself particularly with getting French right. His biggest howler was the "fauteuil de rollent" (88) for "wheelchair," a mistake repeated in the full name of Marathe's terrorist organization "Les Assassins des Fauteuils Rollents" (which drops the unnecessary preposition, but retains the incorrect form "rollent[s]" in place of "roulant[s]"). The full name of the AFR appears over a dozen times in *Jest*, an unfortunate distraction for any Francophone. The *école-spéciale* (481) that the cognitively challenged Lucien Antitoi attended should have been an *école spécialisée*. (Paris has *Écoles Spéciales*, but these are specialized institutes of higher learning, for instance, for architecture or public works.) "Rai Pays" appears to be Wallace's own invention of an in-group designation or slogan for Québec; it may be a deformation of *vrai pays* (real/true country), or some kind of pun that I'm missing. It doesn't make much sense on a literal level, as *rai* means either the spoke of a wheel or a beam or streak of light. As it occurs eight times in the novel (with both *notre* [our] and *leur* [their]), it is clearly not just a typo. A female character is given a male name (Thierry) without any clear motivation. The second acute accent mark in the word *Québécois* is omitted throughout the text. As the then-near-future world of *Jest* was intentionally off-kilter anyway, an easy "out" is always available to explain away errors: either usage in this fictional world had always been a bit different than real-world usage, or it was projected to change in these particulars.

English readers may not notice that Wallace didn't give a French version of "to hear the squeak"—"the very darkest of contemporary Canada's euphemisms for sudden and violent de-mapping" (1056–7, endnote 304), but they might well experience a bit of frustration when there is no English translation of the warning that the AFR embossed "in tiny raised letters" (483) on their read-only copies of the fatal eponymous film *Infinite Jest*: "IL NE FAUT PLUS QU'ON POURSUIVE LE BONHEUR" (483, 722, all-caps in the original). Literally, "it is no longer necessary to pursue happiness" (with correct subjunctive verb form), this might also be rendered as "we should stop pursuing happiness" (a mild judgment), although the all-caps seems to argue for a stronger interpretation: We must no longer seek happiness; we must henceforth avoid the pursuit of happiness. Obviously a response to the offer of "Infinite Jest" (the extreme pursuit of nothing but pleasure that leads to death), this slogan takes direct aim at the US Declaration of Independence's claim to "life, liberty, and the pursuit of happiness" as inalienable rights. Why should one translate a slogan into English that is not just Un- but Anti-American?

Wallace may have been hoping to trigger some deliberate associations in the French surnames chosen for the Canadians in *Jest*. Although Wallace once claimed to know a real-life *Antitoi*,[28] he must have been struck by the felicity of naming a foreign character the equivalent of "anti-you." *Fortier*, the name of a river in Québec as well as of quite a few well-known Canadians, evokes comparative strength: *fort/forte* plus the suffix *-er*, a fitting name for the head of a terrorist organization. Guillaume DuPlessis, albeit undoubtedly named for the two-time premier of Québec, has a surname that—to Anglophone ears—sounds a lot like "duplicity." Poutrincourt is the name of a lake in Québec, but the final syllable (like the English cognate) denotes the space in which ball games such as tennis are played.

Québécois

Wallace went to some lengths to ensure that the same esteem generally given to Parisian French would not attach to Québécois. The derogatory term "Nuck" is used throughout, occasionally with even more dysphemistic variants, such as Pemulis's *nuckwad* (215). Gately observes the "vaguely non-U.S. beards" (609) of the "Nucks" he is fighting with, also thinking of them redundantly as "alien foreigners" (611). Hal admits that he "has never all that much liked [Québécois], particularly sound-wise"; it seems to him "a gurgly, glottal language that seems to require a perpetually sour facial expression to pronounce" (309). The narrator later comments in endnote 222 that Québécois French "is not good old contemporary idiomatic Parisio/European French," and that it "is about on a par with Basque in terms of difficulty, being full of weird idioms and having both inflected and uninflected grammatical features, an inbred and obstreperous dialect" (1036). Undercover as reporter, speaking (ostensibly Parisian) French, Hugh Steeply observes that Thierry Poutrincourt "does indeed sound like the real Canadian McCoy, though her accent is without the long moany suffixes of Marathe" (1052, endnote 274). Steeply's evident command of Québécois—"better than Marathe's English" (89)—is exemplified by his ability to separate "textbook" from idiomatic usage ("the Nuck idiom *réflechis* instead of the more textbook *reflexes*," 1052); this encourages readers to accept his judgments, including his subjective contempt for Marathe. Complicating this somewhat, however, readers had already been explicitly warned that "Steeply barely got an 'Acceptable' in" Québécois "in U.S.O. technical-interview training in Vienna/ Falls Church VA" (1036). The scorn directed at Québécois language and people by both Americans who have little or no direct experience with them and those who

---

[28] Sven Birkerts, "The Alchemist's Retort," Review of *Infinite Jest*, by David Foster Wallace. *The Atlantic Monthly* (February 1996). https://www.theatlantic.com/magazine/archive/1996/02/the-alchemists-retort/376533/.

are presented as expert—is all the more striking as the Quebec separatists' philosophy is ultimately more successful in this novel than the American "pursuit of happiness."

The United States has always had a fascination with Canada, looking across the border as if at an alternate history, fun-house mirror view of the United States. (What if there hadn't been a US revolution? What if the United States now had Canada's system of "socialized" medicine?) Citizens of the United States call themselves "American" (distinguishing "South America" and "Central America" from their presumed default North "America")—yet Canadians are even Northern-er, and must also be peeled away from the referent of "American." The simplest way to make Canada seem strange and alien, linguistically at least, is to focus on Québécois and its status as the official language of Quebec. Whereas US Americans are overly impressed by any white American who can speak a foreign language fluently, or by a foreigner who has "perfect" English, "Francophones are never impressed that anyone else can speak French" (675). When Lucien Antitoi is represented as "one of the very few natives of *Notre Rai Pays* ever who cannot understand French, just never caught on" (480), even though his brother Bertraund ("forever laughing in Québecois," 480) and his mother are Francophones, readers are meant to understand that he has a serious cognitive disability. That the linguistic deficit, specifically, results directly in his death (as he cannot understand or respond to the AFR assassin torturing him) shows again the importance of language. The torture scene contains several untranslated phrases and one stretch of multiple untranslated sentences—perhaps to encourage the reader to empathize with poor Lucien who also cannot understand them.

Perhaps because of his lack of command of other languages, Wallace understood that his non-native characters' comprehensible English was an achievement to be celebrated. Readers are meant to admire the intelligence of Poutrincourt, Fortier, and Marathe, all of whom demonstrate the ability to "simultaneously speak in English and think in French" (91). Although Poutrincourt speaks "nearly accentless English" (682), numerous examples are given of her obviously non-native syntax and lexicon, for instance "You are here to make publicity a child player" (674). She has to ask Steeply for help selecting the right word: "How you say . . . ?" (674). She gets a "little hyphen of wrinkle . . . between her eyebrows when she doesn't follow something and can't quite tell if it's your English's fault or her English's fault" (1057). Her pauses in conversation are tied to her being a non-native speaker, rather than a sign of deliberate reflection: "Poutrincourt always nodded for a while before she replied to anything, as if things had to go through various translation-circuits" (674). Attention is repeatedly drawn to her being "a non-U.S. citizen" (673) and to her status as a speaker of English as a Second Language: "No way Poutrincourt'd have spent the time to E.S.L. her way through U.S. Academese this insufferable" (1056).

Avril Incandenza maintains "Canadian pronunciation of certain diphthongs"(744), but as "the only female academic ever to hold the Macdonald Chair in Prescriptive usage at the Royal Victoria College of McGill University" (64), she maintains prescriptively correct usages at all times; her syntax and lexicon are literally held up as examples for all. As an "expatriate Québecer" (1022) from the "L'Islet region" (191) with a French name (Avril Mondragon, literally *April My Dragon*), known to be involved "with certain members of the Québecois-Separatist Left while in graduate school" (64), Avril is never shown speaking any French; she is presumably native in English, but probably fluent in both. Hal and his brother Orin "made dry fun" (744) of her accent, affirming their own native US identity, while showing their mother some passive-aggressive affection. The absence of Avril's perspective in the novel (which would surely be very different from her husband's or sons' and would be able to answer some important questions left open in the novel) is frustrating, but it is not a loss to Wallace's project of cataloguing dialects; without a visual encoding of the different diphthong pronunciations, Avril's dialect would be indistinguishable from her son Hal's.

Marathe's superiors M. Fortier and M. Broullîme, and other members of the AFR, "young Desjardins" and "the older and valued Joubet" (725), are barely introduced to readers—indeed, their given names are never revealed. On the few occasions when they do speak, they sound much like Marathe. This may have been a deliberate ploy to conceal which "masked A.F.R. leader" tortured Lucien Antitoi so brutally and so pointlessly (forcing readers to attach some of the blame for this to Marathe, whether or not he was there in person); it may also have been intended to show the loss of individual identity that can come about through assimilation into a corporate identity, an idea Wallace would return to in TPK.

Rémy Marathe: The Ultimate (Unmediated) Foreigner

Marathe enters the novel on page 87. The opening of that section cannot be interpreted as Marathe's internal monologue, as he cannot see himself "redly backlit and framed in shale" (87), yet by the end of the third sentence, Marathe's characteristic French syntax begins to take over: "Not yet quite" (88). The first words he speaks out loud are not visibly accented, not notably foreign, but formal and dated: "Stealth becomes you" (88). Steeply's reply, in stark contrast, is current, vulgar, and emphasizes Marathe's foreignness: "Go shit in your chapeau" (89). Wallace gave himself an out in his representation of Marathe's thoughts by stating that Québécois "does not admit of easy coeval expression in English" (1036).

I see no particular significance in the name Rémy Marathe, other than the phonaesthetic association of murmuring in the sequence of sonorant /r/ and /m/ sounds, but Kate Gompert begins to "Americanize" Rémy's given name as she warms up to him (or perhaps as she gets drunker), calling him "Ramy" several times (777, 778, 779), nativizing the pronunciation, before finally settling upon "Ray" (780, 781), presumably more acceptable because less foreign. Although Marathe does not claim an American identity for himself, and his speech is notably non-native, she would appear to insist upon projecting this onto him, not understanding that somebody might not want to be American.

Marathe does not claim to speak very good English: After acknowledging that Steeply's Québécois is better than Marathe's English, he nonetheless deems Steeply's pronunciation "horrid," and voices his suspicion that Steeply deliberately mangles his syntax to irritate Marathe (529). When Marathe attempts to infiltrate Ennet House, posing as an addict, Pat Montesian offers him the backhanded compliment that "in the years I've been on Staff here, we've had aliens, resident aliens, E.S.L.'s whose English was worse than yours by a long shot" (749).

Marathe does not fall into the stereotype of the non-native who speaks better than the natives, or the one who is incapable of adjusting his style; he is shown speaking both formally and informally (and vulgarly), and makes both lexical and morphosyntactic errors. For instance, he frequently uses the progressive aspect ("*-ing*") suffix with stative verbs, where native speakers would use simple present tense (marked *-s* for third-person singular, otherwise unmarked) (e.g., "you are knowing this" [94, cf. 317, 319 inter alia]). When Marathe uses "recircling" for "recycling"(643), Wallace draws extra attention to the usage with an endnote that stresses that this in no way diminishes Marathe's comprehensibility: "*Sic*, but it's pretty obvious what Marathe means here" (1046). Likewise, readers are informed in another endnote that Pat Montesian does not actually refer to Ennet House's "living" staff (754), that this is just "Marathe's malentendu of *live-in*" (1062). Note, however, that the mistakenly umlauted first vowel of *Bröckengespenstphänom* (641) is unlikely to be a deliberate error inserted to reflect on Marathe's competence in German; given US-Americans' general ignorance of languages other than English and the obscureness of this particular lexical item, Wallace would have known that he would need to be much more obvious to trigger such an interpretation. He may, however, have been spoofing Pynchon, who also included a few examples of faux German in his works.

Even readers unfamiliar with French will intuit that Marathe's frequent use of sentence-initial "thus," "we too," "but yes" and sentence-final "so" are word-for-word translations of French discourse markers *donc, nous aussi, mais oui,* and *alors*. Some of the idioms Marathe uses appear to have been translated to French and back, as in "We have, as one will say, larger seafood to cook" (91). Marathe is fond of the double-subject construction that places an accusative case personal pronoun outside the syntactic frame, as in "Me, I. . ." (94, 748, 749, 775), "Us, we . . ." (318, 508), another feature quite familiar to French speakers (*Moi, je . . .*). He often uses awkward periphrastic possessive constructions: "of you" instead of *your* (420, 423), "pacemakers of the heart" (470), "his blanket of the lap" (528). He occasionally throws in an actual French word or phrase: "c'était la guerre" (89), "c'est ça" (490), "Annulateur" (490), and the realistically abbreviated "'n sûr" (93).

Despite the pervasive and heavy-handed depiction of Marathe's nonnative dialect, there is no altered orthography to indicate his apparently strong accent; this is not revealed until much later in the novel, through the mockery of other characters. Presumably, Marathe brings what Steeply describes as his "moany" pronunciation of Québécois to his performance of English. When Kate Gompert (who has a long and increasingly drunken conversation with Marathe after being mugged) mistakenly thinks he is making a pass at her, she replies to his question ("You would reply to me what?") with derisive mimicry: "*I voot make ze hreply zat* I've heard that one before, asshole" (782).

Realistically, Marathe's English gets worse as he gets tired ("He had the great fatigue, a time at which English was straining" [747]), occasionally can't find the word he needs ("How does one say?" [108]) or needs to ask for a definition of a word ("But what does this U.S.A. expression want to mean, this *Buckeroo?*" [320], and "What does this wish to mean, this *bonking?*" [426]). When residents of Ennet House helpfully advise Marathe to "pet the dogs" to win Pat Montesian's approval, he does not understand that they mean this literally: "This idiomatic expression was not in Marathe's knowledge of U.S.A. English" (731). Like most speakers (native or non-native), Marathe can often infer the meaning of an unfamiliar expression from context: "There was no way Marathe was going to touch the evident U.S.A. childhood expression *Mummykins*" (639).

Marathe knows that Americans will find his non-native dialect amusing, but instead of passively accepting condescension or mockery, he uses this to his advantage, exaggerating his non-native command of the language when he wants to lighten the mood. For instance, when recounting a troubling story of his youth, Steeply refers to his "kid sister," and Marathe feigns ignorance of the term: "You are not meaning your sister was a goat.... Steeply was not provokable into some different emotion, however" (643).

Readers' stereotypes of foreign speech (and foreigners) are exaggerated to brilliant effect, forcing readers to consider what it means to sound American, while holding up a not-usually flattering mirror, a glimpse of the United States through these foreign eyes. Marathe comments repeatedly on "U.S.A. English" (88, 89, 423), and the briefest section in the book bears particular scrutiny: a single sentence, only fifteen words long, and not triggered by a change of date, time, location, or characters, yet with its own header to make the section stand out: "Several times also Marathe called U.S.A. to Steeply 'Your walled nation' or 'Your murated nation'" (127). Lest readers miss the importance, Wallace had Marathe later repeat this phrase, explaining the irony: "For your walled-up country, always to shout 'Freedom! Freedom!' as if it were obvious to all people what it wants to mean, this word" (320). Kelly[29] argues that Steeply's position on the value of negative liberty (freedom *from*) is "paradigmatically American," whereas Marathe (as non-American) argues for the superiority of positive liberty (freedom *to*); Kelly points out that Wallace himself appears to have espoused a position closer to Marathe's in his commencement speech at Kenyon College (*This is Water*).

Wallace's prescience here is eerie: *Infinite Jest* was published two decades before "Build the Wall!" became a rallying cry across the United States and helped to elect TV star Donald Trump as president in 2016—a frighteningly similar tale to that of *Jest*'s Johnny Gentle, a phobic former Las Vegas singer, elected president as the head of the "Clean Party," who tries to solve the nation's waste problem by catapulting it into Canadian territory, thus setting off potentially catastrophic geopolitical warfare. In addition to Trump's nationalistic stance on immigration and "The Wall," the 2020 election is shaping up as a referendum on negative versus positive liberty: freedom from (gun control regulations, government control of health insurance, increased taxation, regulation in general) versus freedom to (enjoy life without fear of being shot, access to health care and education).

Wallace's playful representation of non-native dialects (with hypothesized borrowing and interference from the speaker's native language) is further support of Hayes-Brady's observation that "for Wallace, literalization is part of a process of investigation";[30] he used dialects to make social fault lines in US society not just visible but audible. As such, the non-native representations are just the tip of the linguistic iceberg.

---

[29] Kelly, "Development Through Dialogue," 274.
[30] Hayes-Brady, *The Unspeakable Failures of David Foster Wallace*, 12.

3
Ethnicity and Segregation

Readers have mostly accepted Wallace's exaggerated sketches of foreigners' speech, understanding these as archetypes of the nations those foreigners represent; his depictions of US ethnic dialects, however, have met with greater unease. Race and ethnicity are even more fraught issues in the United States now than when Wallace was writing, with the marked rise in white supremacy, nationalism, and hate crimes associated with the Trump presidency, which makes it even more important to deconstruct the way these are presented in literature and other media. The current generation of sociolinguists tends to avoid pre-categorizing speakers into supposed identities, not assuming that any particular perceived identity will correspond to a speaker's internal self-perception, not assuming that any particular category will explain someone's linguistic behavior, seeing identity as both more performative and more fluid.[1] Fiction, however, is not real life; authors do often label characters' identities or encode identities via identifiable dialects. Wallace did both.

Platt and Upstone[2] place Wallace's treatment of race in context as "heir to an earlier generation of white postmodern writers, attempting to speak about race as part of a broader commitment to ending postmodern cynicism in favor of a reworked 'humanism,'" wondering "whether postmodern fiction might play a role in gesturing towards a displacement of racial categories." Witzling[3] notes that "a certain ambivalent critique of the privilege accorded to white masculinity is part of the appeal of the sometimes cool, sometimes incoherent, and sometimes seemingly

---

[1] Norma Mendoza-Denton, *Homegirls: Language and Cultural Practice among Latina Youth Gangs* (Malden, MA: Blackwell, 2008); Mary Bucholtz, *White Kids: Language, Race, and Styles of Youth Identity* (New York: Cambridge University Press, 2011); Rob Drummond, *Researching Urban Youth Language and Identity* (Basingstoke: Palgrave Macmillan, 2018); inter alia.
[2] Len Platt and Sara Upstone, *Postmodern Literature and Race* (New York: Cambridge University Press, 2015), 8.
[3] David Witzling, "Postmodern Prose and the Discourse of the 'Cultural Jew': The Cases of Mailer and Foer," in *Postmodern Literature and Race,* ed. Len Platt and Sara Upstone (Cambridge: Cambridge University Press, 2015), 160–76, esp. 387.

atonal affect of postmodernist writing." Engles[4] posits that in the fiction of Don DeLillo, one of Wallace's acknowledged influences, "the subsumed white collective commonly seeks an illusory redemption in self-serving, identity-bolstering nostalgia." Thomas Pynchon, to whom Wallace has also been frequently compared, portrays white men recognizing their own complicity in a system that has privileged them at the expense of others: "Unquestioned in *Gravity's Rainbow* is the need for white guys to change."[5] Wallace's work may be read in some ways as a sad acknowledgment that not much *has* changed with respect to race since the 1950s setting of *Gravity's Rainbow*, nor since its 1973 publication. "The Man" *still* "has a branch office in each of our brains."[6]

Wallace, who described himself in A&AU as "resoundingly and in all ways white" (*CTL* 102) was too young to have directly experienced most of the civil rights movement or the race riots that occurred in inner cities far from Bloomington, or the assassination of Dr. Martin Luther King, Jr., but like all Americans, he bore some of the psychic scars of these events. In "A Supposedly Fun Thing I'll Never Do Again," he admits that "I'm always suddenly conscious of being white every time I'm around non-white people" (310). His limited attempt to get inside the heads of a few African American characters may represent a compromise between his linguistic abilities and his anxiety over cultural appropriation, but it was most certainly a conscious attempt to challenge and provoke his (imagined white) readers.

Citizenship is an objective and verifiable fact, but ethnicity is more abstract, based on both self-identification and identities projected by others due to perceived physical characteristics, including one's speech. It is often intertwined in US discourse with more essential/biological conceptions of race, which remains a stark dividing line in many areas of American life, despite so many Americans' blended heritage. As Wolfram and Schilling-Estes[7] point out, regional dialect markers may be seen as quaint or charming, but "the stakes are much higher when it comes to socially and ethnically related differences. On the basis of these differences, speakers may be judged on capabilities ranging from innate intelligence to employability and on personal attributes ranging from sense of humor to morality." Charged with drafting a statement on language and race for the Linguistic Society of

---

[4] Tim Engles, "White Male Nostalgia in Don DeLillo's *Underworld*," in *Postmodern Literature and Race*, ed. Len Platt and Sara Upstone (Cambridge: Cambridge University Press, 2015), 195–210, esp. 208.
[5] Patrick McHugh, "Cultural Politics, Postmodernism, and White Guys: Affect in *Gravity's Rainbow*," *College Literature* 28, no. 2 (Spring 2001): 1–28, esp. 11.
[6] Thomas Pynchon, *Gravity's Rainbow* (New York: Viking, 1973), 172.
[7] Wolfram and Schilling-Estes, *American English*, 2006.

America, Charity Hudley et al.[8] note that "while language can be somewhat predictive," predicting culture is "a slippery slope that leads into stereotyping."

The Terminology for Ethnicity and Ethnic Dialects

Americans' discomfort with race and ethnicity is reflected in the inadequate vocabulary used to address these topics, especially as the "minority" population approaches the demographic majority. The linguistic designation "Hispanic" has fallen out of favor; "Latino" and "Latina" now seem unnecessarily gendered, and the gender-neutral "Latinx" has not yet gained wide currency. And people aren't sure of the proper referents of these terms: Are they interchangeable? If someone tells you they prefer the term "Mexican-American" to "Chicano," are they just correcting your terminology, or are they making a different identity claim? Is there any commonality among Mexican-Americans and Cuban-Americans and Puerto Rican-Americans (and so on) that warrants the use of an umbrella term rather than a more specific designation of cultural heritage? White people know they can't say anything that even sounds like "the N-word," but is it okay to call African Americans *black*? (Or should that be *Black*?) Frequent change in terminology about race and ethnicity is not superficial linguistic fashion—although like fashion, not everybody buys it, and trends may cycle back around—but rather a symptom that racism is still a powerful force in the United States. Any word that becomes attached to a stigmatized community itself becomes stigmatized over time, leading the group to either claim a new label which allies adopt to show respect or to reclaim the stigmatized term for its own purposes, as some African Americans have adopted an AAE pronunciation of the "N-word" as a term of in-group solidarity, although its use across group lines remains an act of provocation.

It is difficult to have a national conversation about race and ethnicity in the United States without general agreement of which terms are acceptable and to whom they refer. The white California high school students studied by Bucholtz[9] talked "around rather than about race," lest they be thought racist, alluding instead to unspecified "difference." Avoidance strategies may be well

---

[8] Anne H. Charity Hudley, Christine Mallinson, Mary Bucholtz, Nelson Flores, Nicole Holliday, Elaine Chun, and Arthur Spears, "Linguistics and Race: An Interdisciplinary Approach Towards an LSA Statement on Race," *Proceedings of the Linguistic Society of America* 3 (2018): 8:1–14, esp. 2. https://journals.linguisticsociety.org/proceedings/index.php/PLSA/article/view/4303. doi: http://dx.doi.org/10.3765/plsa.v3i1.4303.
[9] Bucholtz, *White Kids*.

intentioned, but they "do not in fact serve to diminish racial awareness, as the colorblind ideology advocates. On the contrary, because these strategies are so highly marked in interaction they call greater attention to race and to the speaker's hyperawareness of racial topics."[10] For an author, using ethnic labels not only activates stereotypes in the reader's mind but also dates the fiction rather rapidly. The term "Hispanic" appears five times in *Infinite Jest*, mostly in sections focalized by Hal, who doesn't seem to know any people in that category; Kate Gompert refers in passing to "Latino males" (699). The narrator, summarizing and universalizing "exotic new facts" that "you may find out" if you ever spend time in (any) recovery halfway house notes both that "black and Hispanic people can be as big or bigger racists than white people, and then can get even more hostile and unpleasant when this realization seems to surprise you" (200) and that "female chicanos are not called chicanas" (202). This latter point, of course, depends on which "female chicano" you ask.[11]

Hal's foregrounding of racial and ethnic descriptions—"the black girl" (633), "so black she's got a bluish cast" (527), and "the tired Cuban orderly" (17)—illustrates how uncomfortable he is with anybody outside his own limited and fairly homogeneous social circles. Thompson[12] points out that although Wallace puts racist epithets in the mouths and minds of his characters, the author distances himself from this overtly. After one use of "nigger" in *Infinite Jest* (857), the associated endnote says (in its entirety) "*Sic*" (1026). Gately's use of this as a "private term" is explicitly disparaged as a sign of ignorance: "unfortunately still all he knows" (1026). He also refers to an "Oriental kid" as a "Chink" in his thoughts, and even describes him "squatting chinkishly" (977), which the narrator does not comment on.

As the terminology for races and ethnicities keeps changing in the United States, there have likewise been many names for what I call AAE here, following Green,[13] whose textbook remains the most complete descriptive source for the common traits that can be abstracted from "the varieties of AAE spoken in the United States" ([1]). Wallace called the abstraction "Standard Black English (SBE)" in A&AU, a term that has also been used in

---

[10] Ibid., 174–5.
[11] Diane Rios, "Chicana: A Negative Connotation?" *La Prensa San Diego*, October 13, 2000. http://www.laprensa-sandiego.org/archieve/october13/chicana.htm; Karen Wisel and Joel Zapata, "Why I Call Myself Chicana." Video clip from oral history interview with Lilia Escajeda. Amarillo, TX: Civil Rights in Black and Brown Interview Database July 6, 2016. https://crbb.tcu.edu/clips/2533/why-i-call-myself-chicana; inter alia.
[12] Thompson, "Wallace and Race."
[13] Green, *African American English*.

academic descriptions,[14] emphasizing that it is rule-based.[15] A footnote that made it into the second round of typeset proofs for A&AU before it got cut (apparently just for length) was attached to Wallace's use of the term "SBE" with the parenthetical comment "(this SNOOT can't yet stomach Ebonics)" (HRC Wallace Papers, container 30.7). (Note that this refers to Wallace's distaste for that particular *name*, not a comment on the palatability of the dialect itself.)

Erasure versus Evocation of Difference

An effort to bring one aspect of identity into focus may have the effect of "erasing" other aspects—at least temporarily. As Irvine[16] discusses, this is at the heart of the very definition of "style": In order for a style to be meaningful, it must be distinctive (otherwise it would not be noticed, and no meaning could be attached). Once a meaning has been attached to a style, it becomes very easy for anybody perceiving that style to overlook other, competing identities that may simultaneously be indexed.

Thompson[17] finds that it is now "a critical commonplace" that "Wallace had serious blind spots and failings when addressing matters of race," and posits that that Wallace's "problematic representations of race and culture speak to a deeper strain of American insularity underlying [his] writing" (205). Hayes-Brady[18] agrees that "Wallace's engagement with diversity is (at best) mostly implicit." I respectfully disagree with both of these formulations; Wallace explicitly engaged with diversity in his linguistic representations, and these often serve as explicit critiques of insularity. Thompson also argues that Wallace's "reluctance to explore the specific racial positions

---

[14] Arthur K. Spears, "The Black English Semi-Auxiliary *Come*," *Language* 58 (1982): 850–72, for example.
[15] AAE has also been called "Black English Vernacular" (Labov, *Sociolinguistic Patterns*), "Black Vernacular English" (Baugh, "Steady: Progressive Aspect in Black Vernacular English."), "African American Language" (Geneva Smitherman, "Language and African Americans: Movin On Up a Lil Higher," *Journal of English Linguistics* 32, no. 3 (2004): 186–96; Laneheart 2015), "African American Vernacular English" (AAVE) (Walt Wolfram, "The Grammar of Urban African American Vernacular English," *Handbook of Varieties of English* 2 (2004): 111–32.), "Black Street Speech" (Baugh, 1983), and many other names.
[16] Judith T. Irvine, "'Style' as Distinctiveness: The Culture and Ideology of Linguistic Differentiation," in *Style and Sociolinguistic Variation*, ed. Penelope Eckert and John R. Rickford (Cambridge: Cambridge University Press, 2001), 21–43.
[17] Thompson, "Wallace and Race," 204.
[18] Hayes-Brady, *The Unspeakable Failures of David Foster Wallace*, 12.

occupied by various characters" was due to his desire to erase differences—that the "attempt to address broadly defined human problems—boredom for instance, along with suffering and solipsism" (216) made him take a somewhat utopian view that race was irrelevant, echoing Aubry,[19] who says that "Wallace underscores problems that afflict individuals across class and racial boundaries, thus furthering a desire, which he voices in multiple essays and interviews, to portray universal forms of suffering." This comforting interpretation is bolstered by Wallace's praise of Cynthia Ozick's "utter erasure of difference, which does not happen to me with a lot of writers from different cultural backgrounds. I can appreciate the peering across the chasm at another culture, but with Ozick that chasm just vanishes."[20] As Toni Morrison[21] points out, however, "A criticism that needs to insist that literature is not only 'universal' but also 'race-free' risks lobotomizing that literature, and diminishes both the art and the artist." Wallace's choice to encode different ethnic dialects shows that he was still "peering across the chasm," but that he had no desire to lobotomize his fiction by ignoring painful social rifts.

It is not very surprising if *Broom* and TPK, both set in the Midwest, are dominated by white characters. When Lipsky commented that he hadn't seen any black people in Bloomington, Wallace explained, "The racism here is very quiet, very systematic."[22] Peoria's lack of ethnic diversity is one of the first things Claude Sylvanshine notices when he arrives; the irony is that the very terminology he uses in observing the absence of "any sort of black or Latin person" (49) shows that he "isn't very acquainted with the people he refers to."[23] Characters in these novels are less obviously racist, as they aren't often confronted with racial or ethnic differences, with the notable exception of *Broom*'s patriarch Stonecipher Beadsman, who refers to his daughter's supervisor, Walinda Peahen, as "a charming negress" to her face. Joffe[24] says that "no one in the room flinches" at this, but in fact, as will be seen later, Walinda responds forcefully, as anybody who knew her would predict. (It is a particularly chaotic scene, however, and it has already been established that

---

[19] Timothy Aubry, "*Infinite Jest* and the Recovery of Feeling," Chapter 3 of *Reading as Therapy: What Contemporary Fiction Does for Middle-Class Americans* (Iowa City: University of Iowa Press, 2011), 97–126, esp. 102.

[20] Mark Schechner, "Behind the Watchful Eyes of Author David Foster Wallace," in *Conversations with David Foster Wallace*, ed. Stephen J. Burn (Jackson: University Press of Mississippi, 2012), 104–9, esp. 108.

[21] Toni Morrison, *Playing in the Dark: Whiteness and the Literary Imagination* (Cambridge: Harvard University Press, 1992), 12.

[22] Lipsky, *Although of Course You End Up Becoming Yourself*, 45.

[23] Araya, "Why the Whiteness?" 238.

[24] Joffe, "In the Shadows," 59.

Lenore is ignoring much of what her father says.) Araya[25] outlines several examples of characters in TPK approaching race in a "seemingly unintentional insensitive or offhand way" (249). As Bucholtz[26] notes, "the hegemony of whiteness" in American literature, television and film is "typically exerted not by calling attention to white racial dominance but instead by treating whiteness as unremarkable—even unnoticeable."

When, in the title essay of *A Supposedly Funny Thing I'll Never Do Again*, Wallace observes that some people standing near him "look Jewish to me," he reports feeling "ashamed to catch myself thinking that I can determine Jewishness from people's appearance" (272). Thompson[27] attributes Wallace's sharing of this "racist moment in flagrante delicto" to his desire "to lay bare one's own cognitive processes in an honest exchange with the reader," suggesting that "Wallace's dramatization of such moments—in both his fiction and nonfiction—[has] the potential to prompt similar self-examinations on the part of his readers . . . by making whiteness visible and thus raising it as an object for analysis" (208). In his 1998 essay "The Nature of the Fun," Wallace explains that writing fiction is "a way to go deep inside yourself and illuminate precisely the stuff you don't want to see or let anyone else see, and this stuff usually turns out (paradoxically) to be precisely the stuff all writers and readers share and respond to, feel" (*BFAN*, 198). Internalized racism—even by those who consciously disavow it—may be one of those private points of shame that all Americans share, regardless of skin color or ethnic heritage. "The most obvious, ubiquitous, important realities are often the ones that are hardest to see and talk about," Wallace later reiterated (*Water* 8), urging this for everyone, not just writers.

Wallace was less successful at exploring implicit, unconscious racism in his description of the cloggers at the Illinois State Fair: "There's an atmosphere in the room—not racist, but aggressively white. . . . It's not like if a black person came in he'd be ill-treated; it's more like it would just never occur to a black person to come in here" (*ASFTINDA* 125). It was, of course, sheer speculation on Wallace's part that black people stayed away by choice, and that they would not be "ill-treated" if they attempted to join; this borders on every attempt to justify all-white or all-male (or other such exclusionary) spaces. He would have done better here to appreciate his own advice on the goals of a liberal arts education: "to be just a little less arrogant, to have some 'critical awareness' about myself and my certainties . . . because a huge percentage of the stuff that I tend to be automatically certain of is, it turns out, totally wrong

---

[25] Araya, "Why the Whiteness?"
[26] Bucholtz, *White Kids*, 15.
[27] Thompson, "Wallace and Race," 207.

and deluded" (*Water* 35). Coughlan[28] argues that "Wallace's desire to make us aware of, and question, who and why we are judging is part of what makes him such an ethical writer." It is not surprising that someone who had very lofty goals occasionally fell short of them.

"Democracy and Commerce at the U.S. Open" has a somewhat similar anecdote to the ASFTINDA one recounted earlier, in which Wallace mistakenly guesses the ethnicity of a well-dressed Greek-American man after chatting with him. Seeing his name on his business card, Wallace realizes (with no apparent shame) that "he's not Italian after all" (BFAN 162). It is left ambiguous whether this latter story is a commentary on his not-so-perfect-after-all ear for how people speak or on the tendency of white populations to assimilate linguistically, losing the markers that facilitate ethnic identification. Apparently, he did not deem it shamefully racist to stereotype people based on accent.

Wallace's representations of African American speech have received more condemnation than anything else that he wrote. Clearly, he was not just identifying speakers as African American, which he could have done in a variety of other ways; equally certainly, he was not mocking them, as many nineteenth-century authors did in their dialect depictions. Nor was he trying to encode "physical signals of 'substandard' morals," as Twain did by differentiating Jim's speech from the other "Negro" characters in *Huckleberry Finn*.[29]

Signifying Rappers, the book Wallace wrote with his friend Mark Costello, "vividly displays Wallace's anxieties over assuming an identity that is not his own," according to Hayes-Brady.[30] The book directly interrogates what right two white guys have to explore an art form invented by and dominated by African Americans, great fans or not. Cohen[31] describes that work as characterized by "two main emotional tones, . . . enthusiasm and apology," adding that Wallace "wrote out of an anxiety surrounding race that despite its best intentions may have expressed itself in his work." McGurl[32] agrees, and

---

[28] David Coughlan, "'Sappy Or No, It's True': Affect and Expression in *Brief Interviews with Hideous Men*," in *Critical Insights: David Foster Wallace*, ed. Philip Coleman (New York: Grey House Publishing/ Salem Press, 2015), 160–75, esp. 173.
[29] David Carkeet, "The Dialects in Huckleberry Finn," *American Literature* 51, no. 3 (1979): 315–32, esp. 332.
[30] Clare Hayes-Brady, "'Personally I'm Neutral on the Menstruation Point': David Foster Wallace and Gender," in *Critical Insights: David Foster Wallace*, ed. Philip Coleman (New York: Grey House Publishing/Salem Press, 2015), 63–77, esp. 65.
[31] Samuel Cohen, "The Whiteness of David Foster Wallace," in *Postmodern Literature and Race*, ed. Len Platt and Sara Upstone (Cambridge: Cambridge University Press, 2015), 228–43, esp. 234.
[32] McGurl, "The Institution of Nothing," 43.

adds, perhaps as a direct consequence of this anxiety, that Wallace "did not feel empowered to ground his fiction in the cultural capital of ethnically or racially marked experience."

In A&AU, Wallace offers a hypothetical scenario in which he, a white guy, were to approach a group of black guys using AAE terms of address ("yo," calling them "brother," asking "'s'up, s'goin'on, pronouncing *on* with that NYCish . . . diphthong that Young Urban Black English deploys for a standard *o*." In such an instance, Wallace rightfully argues, he would be seen as mocking them or "simply out of my mind" (192). Nonetheless, aware of these risks, he *did* slip into the "voice" of African Americans in his fiction, just as he attempted to inhabit the minds and hearts of foreigners, of Jewish Americans, and of speakers of multiple regional dialects other than his own. Morrissey and Thompson[33] discuss "Wallace's often curious depictions of race and racial issues" (12), and three years later, Thompson is still "coming to terms with the racial content of Wallace's work."[34] He asks, "Do we give Wallace the benefit of the doubt, . . . as the product of a certain cultural moment . . .? Or do we instead take a harder line, wondering why Wallace . . . never seemed to devote a great deal of thought to the racial politics of contemporary U.S. culture?"

Although default whiteness is the norm in Wallace's work, it is clear that he in no way saw this whiteness as any kind of superiority. BIHM is almost all direct dialogue—Boswell[35] says the book "positively brims with talk and more talk"—but Wallace did not take the opportunity to play with dialect in that work, leaving readers to read all the hideous men as "(likely white)."[36] In the absence of an overt narrator who could have described the men either physically or shared details about them that the men themselves would not have chosen to reveal, in the absence of speech from the redacted interviewer (whose questions might have been likewise revelatory), the use of dialect would have helped trigger all kinds of implicit social knowledge about these men. Yet Wallace (who loved playing with language) did not saliently differentiate the language of the nineteen men interviewed in terms of dialect; they are designated by number and location (all over the United States), but it is unclear whether the interviewees are natives of these areas or merely incarcerated there. Each of the interviews "conjures up an individual

---

[33] Tara Morrissey and Lucas Thompson, "'The Rare White at the Window': A Reappraisal of Mark Costello and David Foster Wallace's *Signifying Rappers*," *Journal of American Studies*, 49, no. 1 (2015): 77–97.
[34] Thompson, "Wallace and Race," 206.
[35] Boswell, *Understanding David Foster Wallace*, 184.
[36] Coughlan, "Sappy Or No, It's True," 163.

speaker through distinctive speech patterns and verbal tics,"[37] but nothing about their speech is regionally or ethnically marked, apart from one hideous man in Roswell GA calling his interviewer "darlin," and another in Nutley NJ who begins a couple of sentences with "Alls I'm saying [sic]." Nor do the vignettes sandwiched between the interviews contain any overt dialect markers. Coughlan[38] refers to "the seemingly unvarying pitch of the writing." This absence of dialect features was clearly intentional and motivated: The psychopathy that makes such men hideous has nothing to do with heritage, race, ethnicity, social class, native language, ethnic or regional dialect; the hideousness derives, as Frantzen[39] points out, from their "zero sense of empathy."

Wallace's teaching materials (HRC Wallace Papers, container 32.8) contain his handwritten notes on a photocopy of an essay by Willie Morris ("The Ghosts of Ole Miss," *Inside Sports*, May 1980). By the end of the opening paragraph, which ends with a direct quote, Wallace wrote "Why put this in other guy's voice?" He comments, too, on the use of dialect ("Who dat . . . who dat . . ."), circling the /d/s and asking: "?! What year?" He seems to have used the Morris piece both as an example of bad writing in general (as evidenced by further marginal notes: "Lame," "Weak," "Low Point," "Bad prose," "Who cares?"), but also to focus on the inappropriateness of the writer making assumptions about the women and African Americans discussed in the essay ("How does he know this?"). Ironically, Wallace didn't seem to have a lot of empathy for Morris, even though he faced many of the same challenges in his writing.

Wallace's Misunderstanding of AAE Grammatical Rules

In A&AU, Wallace discusses the regularization of the AAE present tense verb paradigm: "Using 'He don't' makes me a little more uncomfortable. . . . Standard Black English is way out on the cutting edge of English with its abandonment of the 3-S present in 'to do' and 'to go' and 'to say'" (*CTL* 100). Almost all of his African American characters feature leveled third-person

---

[37] Simon de Bourcier, "'They All Sound Like David Foster Wallace': Syntax and Narrative in *Infinite Jest, Brief Interviews with Hideous Men, Oblivion* and *The Pale King*," *Orbit: A Journal of American Literature* 5, no. 1 (2017): 1–30, esp. 12–13. https://doi.org/10.16995/orbit.207.

[38] Coughlan, "Sappy Or No, It's True," 163.

[39] Mikkel Krause Frantzen, "Finding the Unlovable Object Lovable: Empathy and Depression in David Foster Wallace," *Studies in American Fiction* 45, no. 2 (2018): 259–79, esp. 265.

singular present tense verb forms, although some of them are realistically inconsistent with respect to this feature. It is also common for Wallace's African American characters to use "narrative present," to recount past stories as if they are happening now, giving him more opportunity to use this feature and to emphasize the nonstandardness of the speaker.

Even though he acknowledged that "SBE and SWE conjugate certain verbs in totally different ways" (*CTL* 108), Wallace clearly did not have command of AAE's complex verbal morphology. He never had an AAE speaker use near future (*finna*), future perfective (*be done*), *I'ma* for first-person singular future tense, or *had* + *V-ed* (*had finished, had ate*) with a simple past tense interpretation, showing a lack of familiarity with AAE verb tenses. With verb aspect he fared worse still, not just failing to represent, but actually mispresenting the use of invariant (unconjugated) *be*, the function of which he apparently continued to misunderstand years after his fictional portrayals of AAE were published. In the same "interpolation" to A&AU mentioned earlier, Wallace "praised" SBE for "its marvellously streamlined six identical present-tense inflections of 'to be.' (Granted, 'he be' always sounds weird to me, but then SBE is not one of my dialects)" (*CTL* 100). This is an erroneous description of AAE grammar, in which *be* does *not* function as a present tense verb, neither as grammatical copula (in constructions expressing identity or description such as "X is Y") nor as auxiliary verb for progressive aspect (e.g., *he was thinking* vs. *he thought*), but rather as a marker of habitual action. For example, "he be working" would mean that he works regularly, that he has a regular job, as opposed to the zero-copula construction "he (Ø)[40] working" (right now). Both Ronkin and Karn[41] and Rickford and Rickford[42] discuss the frequent misunderstanding of this feature of AAE, and its incorrect inclusion (in nonhabitual grammatical contexts) in many representations that mock "Ebonics." Wallace's intent was not to mock, and he would likely have been mortified to discover his error—which makes it all the more ironic that he did not read any linguistic studies of AAE (which would not have been difficult to access, even before the days of easy computer searches, for instance Labov's 1972 *Language in the Inner City*[43] or Baugh's 1983 *Black Street Speech*).[44]

---

[40] A null sign is used to show that an expected element does not occur.
[41] Maggi Ronkin and Helen E. Karn, "Mock Ebonics: Linguistic Racism in Parodies of Ebonics on the Internet," *Journal of Sociolinguistics* 3, no. 3 (1999): 360–80.
[42] John R. Rickford and Russell John Rickford, *Spoken Soul: The Story of Black English* (New York: Wiley, 2000).
[43] William Labov, *Language in the Inner City: Studies in the Black English Vernacular*, Vol. 3 (Philadelphia: University of Pennsylvania Press, 1972).
[44] John Baugh, *Black Street Speech* (Austin: The University of Texas Press, 1983).

AAE has a more complex system of verbal aspect than SWE (which only explicitly marks progressive and perfect aspects), but these are examples of what Wolfram and Schilling-Estes[45] call "camouflaged forms," as they "bear surface resemblance to constructions found in other varieties of English even though they are used differently." Apparently, Wallace was able to listen obsessively to AAE in the lyrics of rap songs without understanding these forms; it is inconceivable that he would not have included at least some of the aspect markers if he had been even passingly familiar with them. When Roy Tony refers to himself "coming over feeling comfortable" (*Jest* 506) he is apparently not using the AAE aspectual *come* (which would indicate speaker indignation over an unwarranted action),[46] just using the verb as SWE would. Nor does Wallace ever use the remote past *been* (which is always stressed and not equivalent in meaning to the similar SWE verb form, so many scholars of AAE prefer to write it in all-caps (*BIN*) or with an accent mark (*bín*) to avoid potential confusion), which would apply to an action or state that began a long time ago, but also continues into the present.[47] Baugh[48] details the use of *steady* for progressive aspect, and Wolfram and Shilling-Estes[49] cite also the AAE construction *call X-self +ing* (as in "He call himself dancing") "to indicate that someone is attributing qualities or skills to themselves which they do not really possess." AAE use of *it* as existential pronoun (vs. SWE *there*) is conceptually very simple yet is "little recognized by nonspeakers of AAVE"[50] because unlike the more complex verb aspect markers, it is unstressed in normal discourse. Wallace does not include any of these forms in his representations.

Wallace perceived that relative clauses without a relative pronoun (or what Green[51] calls "zero relative pronoun") are allowed in a greater number of syntactic environments in AAE than in SWE, but he was clearly fuzzy on the details. In SWE, the relative pronoun is required when it is the subject of the relative clause, but AAE does not require it when the relative clause modifies a noun in object position or in the predicate nominative position.[52]

---

[45] Wolfram and Schilling-Estes, *American English*, 216–7.
[46] Lisa J. Green, *African American English: A Linguistic Introduction* (Cambridge and New York: Cambridge University Press, 2002); cf. Spears, "The Black English Semi-Auxiliary *Come*."
[47] Ibid., 54.
[48] John Baugh, "Steady: Progressive Aspect in Black Vernacular English," *American Speech* 59, no. 1 (1984): 3–12.
[49] Wolfram and Shilling-Estes, *American English*, 217.
[50] Bucholtz, *White Kids*, 134.
[51] Green, *African American English*, 89.
[52] Gunnel Tottie and Dawn Harvie, "It's All Relative: Relativization Strategies in Early African American English," *Language In Society-Oxford* 28 (2000): 198–232; Ibid.

So sentences like "I have a manager (Ø) don't share the needle" and "He a manager (Ø) don't share the needle" would be grammatical in AAE, but when Too Pretty uses "a manager (Ø) don't share the needle" (94) as the subject of a larger sentence, this violates the AAE rule. Again, it would seem that Wallace simply got this wrong.

It is not surprising that someone who immersed himself in rap music would nonetheless be unable to produce original strings of grammatical AAE. In addition to the issue of "camouflage," Preston[53] explains that people who display detailed awareness of other dialects may still lack imitative control over those dialects (and some who are able to mimic them perfectly have little to no ability to describe them). Bucholtz's[54] study of white high school students in California who consider themselves members of the "hip-hop" community finds that they routinely incorporated only the most salient morphosyntactic marker of AAE, multiple negation (a sociolinguistic marker shared by many white working-class dialects), although they freely borrow AAE lexical items and prosody. Of course, they are not attempting to *pass* as African American, just to signal affiliation. (Cf. Pichler and Williams,[55] who find similar behavior in London hip-hop fans.)

Wallace once famously admitted that he imagined his readers as "pretty much like myself... mostly white upper middle class or upper class, *obscenely well-educated*."[56] This would come as no surprise to Toni Morrison,[57] who observes that "until very recently, and regardless of the race of the author, the readers of virtually all of American fiction have been positioned as white" (xii). It is hard to determine now whether Wallace's lack of linguistic research when crafting his AAE passages was due to overconfidence in his ability to mimic other dialects, or whether his disregard for potential African American readers was such that he did not care whether or not these were plausibly realistic performances. As Mura[58] points out, "White writers can and do remain unconscious of readers of color; writers of color must be conscious of white readers, even if, ultimately, they decide not to write to accommodate white readers."

---

[53] Preston, "Language with an Attitude," 50–1.
[54] Bucholtz, *White Kids*.
[55] Pia Pichler and Nathanael Williams, "Hipsters in the Hood: Authenticating Indexicalities in Young Men's Hip-Hop Talk," *Language in Society* 45, no. 4 (2016): 557–81.
[56] Lipsky, *Although of Course You End Up Becoming Yourself*, 82.
[57] Morrison, *Playing in the Dark*.
[58] David Mura, "White Writing Teachers (or David Foster Wallace vs. James Baldwin)," *Journal of Creative Writing Studies* 1, no. 1 (2016): 1–7, esp. 4, footnote 2. http://scholarworks.rit.edu/jcws/vol1/iss1/7.

Wallace's African American Dialect Depictions

Very seldom, in Wallace's works, do people of color play major roles or even have the opportunity speak for themselves—but that makes the rare dialect performances I discuss next stand out against a very white background. Although I do not agree with McGurl[59] that the depictions in *Jest* "have difficulty differentiating themselves from the long tradition of disrespectful racial mimicry in US culture," it is important to recognize that such a tradition exists, and that its "most obvious victim of misrepresentation was black language."[60] Morrison[61] identifies a pattern of representation of dialect in American literature featuring "patterns of explosive, disjointed, repetitive language. These indicate a loss of control in the text that is attributed to the objects of its attention rather than to the text's own dynamics." Yet it is precisely in the amount of "control" that Clenette Henderson's traumatized internal monologue differs from the confident self-expression and swagger of the character Londell ("Too Pretty") Tyson in the early short story "Solomon Silverfish." Walinda Peahen, despite some shouting, is seen to be clearly in control of her (well-justified) anger, and Yolanda exhibits control over her language by style-shifting.

It is unlikely, given the anxieties Wallace expressed elsewhere, that he was naïve about how negatively these dialect sketches would be received; these must be viewed as part of his strategy of frequently making readers uncomfortable and self-conscious, to make them interrogate their own reactions to questions (and people) they might prefer to ignore. The way Wallace distinguished the speech of his African American characters shows that he recognized AAE as a continuum, not a single uniform dialect. Even though individual performances are flawed by Wallace's misunderstanding of particular aspects of AAE, they still serve to showcase linguistic variation among African Americans and—most importantly—to show that there is no isomorphism between the use of African American dialect features and any particular social or moral attribute.

Not included in this chapter's brief survey is a story shared by an African American member of Cocaine Anonymous in *Jest* (707–11), because it is recounted from the perspective of Joelle van Dyne, who (as endnote 293 points out) "was acculturated in a part of the U.S.A. where verbal attitudes toward black people are dated and derisive" (1054). The narrator adds that Joelle "is doing pretty much the best she can," but where Gately seemed to

---

[59] McGurl, "The Institution of Nothing," 43.
[60] Jones, *Strange Talk*, 11.
[61] Morrison, *Playing in the Dark*, 69.

exaggerate the unnamed Irishman's dialect features in his thoughts, Joelle largely uses her own voice to re-tell this man's tale of his wife and child going hungry because he spent their food money on drugs, and how he then abandons them, honestly believing they will be better off without him. As Jackson and Nicholson-Roberts[62] note, the passage "arguably never develops an extended relationship between the voice of the speaker and the narrator without an interjection from Joelle." Araya[63] nevertheless deems this story one of the most moving in the novel, although he is under the misapprehension that the man's name is Jim, rather than understanding that this name is used generically, like "Holmes," which Joelle notes is "apparently the current colored word for other coloreds" (1054). Ennet House staffer Johnette Foltz shows her knowledge of this, using every term of address she can think of to get Roy Tony's attention (and deflect it from Erdedy): "Yo Roy T., man, easy there Dude, Man, Esse, Bro, Posse, Crew, Homes, Jim, Brother" (507). Like *Jack* before it (more common in the 1970s), *Jim* appears to be a "form of address among black males (used emphatically or as verbal punctuation)."[64] Although *Holmes* and *Homes* likely have different etymologies, with the former coming from a Sherlock reference and the latter coming from *homeboy/homegirl*,[65] the difference between these would likely have been opaque to Wallace as well as Joelle.

Walinda Peahen (The Broom of the System)

Though she remains somewhat two-dimensional, Walinda Peahen is Wallace's only middle-class African American character. She is a working mother with two jobs, one of which is a supervisory position. She takes no crap from anyone, but rather than being just a stereotype of "an angry black woman" (as Joffe[66] calls her), Walinda is described as "the kind of woman whose bad moods tended to be made worse by people around her behaving as if she were in a bad mood" (*Broom* 403). Thus, she, like protagonist Lenore, is something of a "linguistic construct," although in her case, it's less innocuous, reflecting a destructive cycle of social and racial stereotyping: she's specifically a black

---

[62] Edward Jackson and Joel Nicholson-Roberts, "White Guys: Questioning *Infinite Jest*'s New Sincerity," *Orbit: A Journal of American Literature* 5, no. 1 (2017): 1–28, esp. 21. DOI: https://doi.org/10.16995/orbit.182.
[63] Araya, "Why the Whiteness?," 245.
[64] Edith A. Folb, *Runnin' Down Some Lines: The Language and Culture of Black Teenagers* (Cambridge: Harvard University Press, 1980), 243.
[65] Ibid., 253, 242.
[66] Joffe, "In the Shadows," 59.

women who is always angry because the white people who surround her always assume that a black woman will be angry.

Walinda has a variety of other good reasons to be angry, reasons why she might have "put her hands on her hips and glared" (515): she was kept overtime at her other job, her "subordinate" showed up to work hours late, but Walinda knows she can't do much about it other than fume, as Lenore is the lover of one of the named partners of the firm and daughter of an even more powerful executive. Walinda *says* "you gone, you done" (90) but her words have no illocutionary force—as opposed to when Lenore says "I quit" later in the novel, which does have real-world effect. Walinda is in an impossible situation: a supervisor who has no power of enforcement, a woman who, no matter how forcefully she expresses herself, will not be able to make the world conform to her words, yet she stubbornly refuses to cave to the pressure to make her words conform to the unjust world around her. This is a different kind of strength—an admirable resilience, persistence against all odds, self-assertion in the face of power. Despite all her legitimate grievances, Walinda is able to enjoy her conversations with white co-worker Candy Mandible, to listen to Candy's stories and laugh.

When Lenore's father calls Walinda a "perfectly charming negress" (515), it's clear that he's being ironic about the charming part and apparently deliberatively provocative (not just tone-deaf) in his choice of terminology. Walinda, who knows that he is the most powerful man in town (her boss's boss, the CEO of the largest industry in the area, and the son of the man who literally built the town), responds, "Boy, I'm gonna kill you for that" (515), using the informal, but non-ethnically marked future tense. Everybody, including Walinda and the readers, knows that she will not, that her words are exaggerated because she understands the emptiness of her threat—yet it is important that she responds with strong protest, that she doesn't simply accept such blatant disrespect.

Walinda does not overtly attempt to assimilate to the white language around her. She uses *ain't*, perfective *done* ("you done played the last time" [90]), counterfactual *like to* ("he like to die" [403]), null copula and auxiliary ("what [Ø] these messages for you?" [89], "if I think somebody [Ø] workin' and they [Ø] not" [90]). Alim[67] argues that the null copula, one of the most extensively studied sociolinguistic variables for AAE, has become a conscious marker of identity for black Americans. As noted earlier,

---

[67] H. Samy Alim, *You Know My Steez: An Ethnographic and Sociolinguistic Study of Styleshifting in a Black American Speech Community* (Durham, NC: Duke University Press/The American Dialect Society, 2004).

Wallace was apparently unaware of AAE existential *it*, so Walinda uses the SWE existential *there*, and maintains the copula after it: "There's messages for you" (89). Walinda has a couple of utterances that could plausibly be interpreted as habitual aspect ("that crap be *nasty*" [403], "you (Ø) the chump be makin' that nasty food" [515]), but he presumably intended these as present tense. Walinda has a past tense *give* (403), and always pronounces *-ing* verb suffixes with the alveolar nasal (*workin'*, *talkin'*, *makin'*, etc.), though the "-ing" spelling in the gerund "writing" (89) and the noun "Building" (404) presumably indicates the velar pronunciation prescribed by SWE. She frequently uses mild profanity (*goddamn* [90], *crap* [403], *foulass* [403], *damn* [511]), addresses subordinates and superiors alike with infantilizing terms of address (*boy* [515], *girl* [406, 511], *child* [405]), or (when angry) derogatory ones implying lesser intelligence (*fool* [513], *chump* [516]). Apart from terms of address, the only salient AAE lexical item is the verb "play" to signify posing, making unjustified claims, perpetuating a fraud (as exemplified in Morgan[68]), which Walinda repeats: "You can't play. You done played the last time" (90).

Notably, however, Walinda has no multiple negation (despite frequent use of negation), no nonstandard relative clauses or unmarked possession, even though Wallace used all of these features with other African American characters. Even more extraordinarily, all of her third-person singular present tense verbs are marked with the *-s* suffix, as SWE prescribes. African American speakers studied by Rickford and Rickford[69] used the suffix in as few as 3 to 4 percent of their third-person singular verb forms. It is perhaps significant that Walinda is shown interacting only with white characters, enacting her professional role, circumstances in which many African Americans would use fewer AAE variants. Alim[70] found that "third-person singular *-s* variability appears to be fundamental in Black American styleshifting," echoing findings from Baugh.[71] Despite her apparent responsiveness to these circumstances (avoiding certain stereotypical features of AAE), however, she maintains a number of distinctive AAE features, as if she is drawing a line in the sand, meeting white interlocutors only partway.

---

[68] Marcyliena Morgan, "'Nuthin' But a G Thang': Grammar and Language Ideology in Hip Hop Identity," in *Sociocultural and Historical Contexts of African American English*, ed. Sonja L. Laneheart (Amsterdam and Philadelphia: John Benjamins Publishing, 2001), 187–210, esp. 204.
[69] Rickford and Rickford, *Spoken Soul*.
[70] Alim, *You Know My Steez*, 161.
[71] Baugh, *Black Street Speech*.

Londell "Too Pretty" Tyson ("Solomon Silverfish")

Too Pretty is initially presented (through the eyes of Solomon Silverfish's brother-in-law) as "the loathsome and very lowlife Londell 'Too Pretty' Tyson, a young shvartzer of the pimping profession" (72). A few pages later, Solomon's wife Sophie thinks more kindly of him: "Such a nice and deep-down polite young man, you could tell, even if he did wear a purple hat with a pink feather from an ostrich and use language who a mother of a son who talked that way would cut her heart out from her body" (75). Although nonspecific, Sophie's complaint about language appears to refer to his frequent unmarked swearing—not in anger, but as part of his regular means of self-expression— rather than his grammar per se. "Too Pretty" is the name the character uses for himself in his internal monologue; he is amused when Solomon refers to him as "Schwartz" (93), undoubtedly recognizing this as a Jewish name, but oblivious to its Yiddish meaning, *black*. That he is destined to play a larger role in the story is foreshadowed when a section is headed "/Everyone Except Too Pretty/" (79), even though the scene at the police station includes only Solomon, his two brothers-in-law, and the district attorney. It is nonetheless surprising when the narration later switches to Too Pretty's point of view and remains there for the rest of the story (92–6).

Thompson[72] calls Too Pretty's narration "flamboyantly ungrammatical," which says as much about his own views of AAE as it does about Too Pretty's speech, though this is certainly the Wallace character who incorporates the greatest quantity of AAE features. According to Hayes-Brady,[73] he "speaks in the kind of argot associated with stereotyped black characters"—adding that "this vernacular also appears at times in *Infinite Jest*," and that it is "problematically rendered," which is somewhat ironic, given her assertion that "small slippages of language are never accidental in Wallace's writing" (152). Too Pretty, Walinda, and the African American characters in *Infinite Jest* do share a few linguistic features used to signal African American identity, but they do not speak at all alike, differing in both morphosyntax and tone. The comparison Hayes-Brady and others have made between Too Pretty and *Jest*'s Clenette Henderson may have been influenced by the recurring character names Wardine and Reginald. It is unlikely that Wallace meant to refer to the same characters, as Skokie is quite some distance from Boston, and Too Pretty would probably have mentioned if one of his "bitches" had serious back scars, as *Jest*'s Wardine would. Wallace particularly liked the name Wardine, which he also used in "Lyndon" for the "black servant in

---

[72] Thompson, "Wallace and Race," 213.
[73] Hayes-Brady, *The Unspeakable Failures of David Foster Wallace*, 171.

black stockings and a doilied apron" (81) in the Johnson White House, clearly a different person in a different era.

From the first line of his internal monologue, Too Pretty is confident and intentionally humorous, expressing an unlikely sympathy for and appreciation of the title character (who, among other things, brought Too Pretty to dinner at his country club): "Yall want to play, just don't play with my man S.S." Unlike Walinda (who is also quite confident), Too Pretty tends to be amused by everything he sees, although he is also rather philosophical, making several general abstract pronouncements as well as reflecting on his own thought processes: "This set my ass thinkin" (93). One of the reasons that Too Pretty "be likin the big honky bastard" (92) is because "my man know some shit" (93); he appreciates not just Solomon's sincerity, but the rightness and rareness of Solomon's wisdom: "He open his mouth to say shit no white bastard got no right to know" (96). The "Everyone Except Too Pretty" scene was the accusation and interrogation of Solomon; Too Pretty is clearly a character witness for the defense, although his testimony (unlike Sophie's passionate defense of her husband) is made known only to the readers. Despite the fact that half of Too Pretty's monologue is narrated under the effect of heroin, with the last few pages a single, increasingly chaotic paragraph, he comes across as a very credible witness. (I will return to this dynamic in the discussion of "Solomon Silverfish" in the next chapter.)

Too Pretty uses stereotyped vocabulary (*my man, honky, crib*, use of *jim* and *jack* as generic terms of address), and frequent but inconsistent use of unmarked third-person present tense verbs (*he get, [he] like, [he] look* (all 92), and so on, but *dude knows,* [it] *slides,* [it] *melts* [all 94]). There are a couple of uses of modal *gots to* (which Morgan[74] argues highlights necessity) with an implied second-person subject: "Gots to do it to see" (93), "Gots to see" (94), and although he is mostly recounting past events, does use one future verb complex with auxiliary *gone* (which AAE scholars Smitherman,[75] Green,[76] Alim,[77] inter alia render as *gon*, to avoid confusion with the SWE/AAE past participle). He uses a null copula (*He* [Ø] *wild, his bitch* [Ø] *his life*), except after presentational pronouns (e.g., *heres* [92]), and sometimes Wallace has him incorrectly use invariant *be* in that same context ("Name be Sophie. Bitch be pretty, too" [93]). Folb[78] argues that in AAE, "bitch" is a "designation for female (positive or negative)," not implying disrespect.

---

[74] Morgan, "Nuthin' But a G Thang," 204.
[75] Geneva Smitherman, *Talkin and Testifyin: The Language of Black Americans* (Detroit: Wayne State University Press, 1977).
[76] Green, *African American English*.
[77] Alim, *You Know My Steez*.
[78] Folb, *Runnin' Down Some Lines*, 229.

Wallace also has Too Pretty incorrectly use invariant *be* to express narrative present tense, not habitual aspect, as in the narrated sequence of events "I be thinkin . . . Solomon Silverfish be there . . . I be waitin" [96]). His use of apostrophes is inconsistent, but he does consistently use the *-(')s* marker on possessors (*folks ass, Wardine's high ass, the bitchs tourniquet*). Unmarked second-person pronominal possession (*you ass* [92 et seq], *you head, you balloon* [94]) may indicate some r-lessness, although this is not seen in other lexical items. Too Pretty prefers reflexives formed with *-ass* rather than *-self*: *my ass, you ass, his ass*, except when using the intensifying infix *-own-*,[79] as in "my own self" (93, 94), "you own self" (94), and "her own self" (95).

Too Pretty frequently (but not consistently) uses multiple negation (for instance, "I aint never seen" [93]) and one instance of negative inversion with a negative indefinite subject, although this is embedded in a relative clause: "That what his lady really be cant no sickness lay its cold white hand on" (93). (To "translate" to SWE: no sickness can lay its cold white hand on [the essence of] what Solomon's wife really is. Too Pretty is ostensibly paraphrasing Solomon's explanation of why he still finds his wife attractive; the "cold white hand" phrase is presumably Solomon's.) One instance of a double modal seems out of place ("they might could earl" (93), where *earl* is presumably based on *hurl* as a synonym for *vomit*. Phonologically, he almost always has alveolar pronunciation of *-ing* suffixes (*gettin, likin, walkin*, etc. vs. *flying* [92]), and even uses the alveolar pronunciation in the compound noun *somethin*. He drops the unstressed initial syllable of *(be)fore* (92) and *(ap)prove* (94).

Wallace put almost every AAE feature he was familiar with into Too Pretty's speech, and this may well coincide with readers' worst stereotypical notions of a pimp in a ghetto, although I would argue that the main effect is to show Too Pretty's freedom. He is unapologetic, unafraid, unconcerned about the image he projects—he is one of Wallace's most joyful creations. As he asks rhetorically, "whose black ass I gone love if not Too Pretty?" (93). Even if Wallace lacks the familiarity with AAE grammar to pull it off, the intention is clearly for Too Pretty to be seen as "keepin' it real."

Clenette Henderson *(Infinite Jest)*

Wallace's representation of the stream of consciousness of a very young Clenette Henderson (37–8) has received harsh criticism, although Thompson[80] points out that "Wallace was extraordinarily proud of this extract," which

---

[79] Green, *African American English*, 22–3.
[80] Thompson, *Global Wallace*, 204.

he asked his agent to send to various literary magazines. Clenette is mostly thinking about her friend Wardine, so this brief section is sometimes misleadingly referred to as "the Wardine section." For instance, the "Infinite Summer" website (which was originally put together in the summer of 2009 by a group of Wallace fans reading *Infinite Jest* together, posting their questions, comments and discoveries, but which has continued to expand over the last decade) has a list of tips on "How to Read *Infinite Jest*."[81] Tip #3 mentions "several popular way stations on the road to abandoning *Infinite Jest*," but mentions only the "Wardine" section specifically, saying that it is written in "a tortured, faux-Ebonics type dialect. . . . Potentially offensive (if one wants to be offended), and generally hard to get through."

Clenette's disordered and strange internal monologue has been almost universally vilified, but seldom placed in context with the language depicted for other African American characters later in the novel. Cohen[82] says this section is "badly done in a particularly simplistic way," but adds that it "is no proof of racism. It may only be evidence of a flaw in the technique of a still-young writer, and maybe an inherent absence of *sprachgefühl* or innate feeling for a language, or in this case a dialect." Araya[83] concedes that "Wallace may have stumbled in the Wardine section." Alexander[84] nevertheless finds purpose in the section's disruption of the novel's flow, "providing a moment of discontinuity for us to analyse," in order to force readers to confront taboo topics they are otherwise loath to consider, specifically the sexual assault and emotional traumatization of young girls.

Clenette's unique voice jumps out of the text, demanding attention, with no other focalizing character to describe her, about six years and hundreds of pages before she appears again as a recovering addict living at Ennet House, with a job up the hill at the tennis academy. The earlier section is interior monologue; although a lot of speech is reported in this section ("Wardine say," "Reginald say"), Clenette does not speak. She reports Wardine asking her a question, but does not reveal if she answered. Wardine begs Clenette not to tell Clenette's mother of her abuse, and Clenette keeps the secret ("I aint tell"). Later in the novel, Clenette appears only as a background character, and readers are not privy to her thoughts. In fact, she speaks only two words in the entire novel (albeit each several times). When Gately notes

---

[81] Matt Bucher, Nick Maniatism, and Kathleen Fitzpatrick, "How to Read *Infinite Jest*," Infinite Summer website. June 17, 2009. http://infinitesummer.org/archives/215.
[82] Cohen, "The Whiteness of David Foster Wallace," 237.
[83] Araya, "Why the Whiteness?," 245.
[84] Matthew Alexander, "David Foster Wallace and Repressive Taboos: Clenette Henderson, Yrstruly and the Identity Politics of Representation," *FORUM: University of Edinburgh Postgraduate Journal of Culture & the Arts*, no. 24 (2017): 1–10, esp. 2.

that "most of the residents [of the halfway house] are mingling satisfactorily," he specifies that "the couple of residents that are black are mingling with other blacks. . . . Clenette Henderson clutches another black girl and laughs and says "Girl!" several times" (363). Later, when Canadian attackers come for Randy Lenz, only Gately is willing to intervene; once Gately has been shot, however, all the Ennet House residents join the fight. This is a particularly powerful moment in the novel, and one in which readers rejoice to see the recovering addicts coming together across all the social fault lines that normally divide them. During the fight, Clenette and Yolanda (or, as Erdedy thinks of them, "the Afro-American girls" [614] or "the black ladies" [615]) repeatedly say "mutha-*fu*cka," "landing solid high-heel kicks. . . each time they get to *fu*" (614). The obscenity is gleefully cathartic for both the speakers and the readers. In her earlier interior monologue, Clenette had no hope for her future, and readers had no hope for her—which makes her reappearance later in the novel so heartening, as she is then sober, employed, owns a car, has a good friend and a supportive community. She has not just found her voice, she has developed full agency—she is literally fighting back, and working together, the community prevails.

Joffe[85] argues that Wallace intended readers to see parallels between Hal and Wardine (that he frames the emotional "abuse" of Hal as the equivalent of the physical abuse of Wardine), but I read this as Wallace honestly trying to work through how white people may sincerely believe they are "victims." The equation of emotional and physical abuse (most overtly propounded by Marlon Bain as proxy for his friend Orin Incandenza) is not mocked, but readers are surely meant to understand that statements equating horrific physical abuse with "excessive criticism or disinterest" (1050) are patently absurd. The more realistic and important association would appear to be the contrast between Hal and Clenette. Hal, who was given so much, falls prey to narcissism, solipsism, and ends up lost and silenced; Clenette's trajectory is exactly the reverse.

Readers are certainly meant to quickly recognize that the mind encountered in this section is African American. Her thoughts include stereotypically AAE lexical items (i.e., *crib*, *double dutch*, as well as the more local reference to an urban housing development, the *Brighton Projects*), and unmarked third-person present tense verbs forms (*Wardine say, he live*, etc.). Other recognizably AAE features of Clenette's monologue are unmarked possessors (as in *Wardine momma, Reginald crib), gone* as future tense auxiliary (as opposed to the more widespread and non-ethnically marked *gonna*), and multiple negation with

---

[85] Joffe, "*In the Shadows*," 76.

and without *aint* (lack of apostrophe in the original, as in *Wardine aint never let . . .*). Although she has one negative indefinite subject in the last line, she avoids the AAE negative inverted structure ("don't nobody know") in favor of the non-inverted (SWE) structure "nobody know except me" (38). She uses only one relative clause, and it follows the AAE rule discussed earlier, using zero-relative pronoun in a clause that modifies the object of the sentence: "He got some thing on his ankle [Ø] send radio signals to Parole" (38).

Thomas and Bailey[86] note that the "putative metathesis" of /sk/> /ks/ in "ask" (pronounced [æks]) which occurs in so many mocking depictions of AAE is not specific to that dialect, and in fact is presumably a preservation of the original consonant order from the Old English verb *acsian*. Interestingly, although "Too Pretty" alternates between *ax* and *ask*, Wallace's other AAE representations do not use the nonstandard variant; in fact, in Clenette's interior monologue, this verb form is the only example in which a third-person singular verb occurs with the standard suffix: "asks" (38).

The typed manuscript which Wallace asked his agent to submit for publication as an independent story titled "Las Meninas" shows that he at least considered representing additional phonological differences to the Clenette section. A couple of *-ing* forms without the final g are corrected by hand, and Wallace changed the typed "close" back to "clothes" (HRC Wallace Papers, container 15.7), although the published version in *Jest* avoids that term altogether, referring instead to "shirts." It's possible these were simple typos, but they would have been prompted by his familiarity with AAE phonology, and upon seeing them, he made the conscious choice not to let them stand.

Staes[87] suggests that the Clenette section gets AAE wrong because it is channeled through the perspective of Hal Incandenza, assuming that he may have heard her recount her story at Ennet House or at a twelve-step meeting after the timeline of the novel ends. Not only is there no evidence to support such an interpretation, but it also requires readers to believe that Hal was interested enough in Clenette to remember her story in great detail, but not interested enough to remember the actual words she used, although he is portrayed as a language prodigy with an impressive memory. It certainly doesn't explain why he would represent *aint* without an apostrophe—the one bit of "eye dialect" Wallace incorporates into this representation.

---

[86] Erik R. Thomas and Guy Bailey, "Segmental Phonology of African American English," in *The Oxford Handbook of African American Language*, ed. Sonja Lanehart (Oxford, UK: Oxford University Press, 2015), 403–19, esp. 409.

[87] Toon Staes, "Rewriting the Author: A Narrative Approach to Empathy in *Infinite Jest* and *The Pale King*," *Studies in the Novel* 44, no. 4 (Winter 2012): 49, 409–27.

Although readers identify Clenette as African American, her ethnicity is less important than her evident panic and despair. Neither Hal (whose consciousness dominates the first sixteen pages of the novel) nor Ken Erdedy (whose internal monologue occupies the next ten) seems as helpless or as trapped as Clenette, whose world is so much smaller and whose problems (unlike those of the white male characters) are clearly not of her own making. Hal and Erdedy have squandered the privileges they were born into, but Clenette had no such advantages to begin with. Wallace presents depression (in Kate Gompert, among others) as characterized not just by obsessive loops of thought, but as a loss of "any sense of the other."[88] Clenette's empathy for Wardine is a clear illustration that she is not depressed; that objective hardship and trauma do not necessarily result in clinical depression. Clenette would have "better" reasons to be depressed and suicidal than Kate Gompert or Joelle van Dyne did, but her internal monologue is a cry in the dark from someone who very much wants to live and be heard. A clinically depressed person "is incapable of empathy with any other living thing" (*Jest* 696), but Clenette is terrified not for herself, but for Wardine and Reginald.

Wallace sets readers up to think that Clenette is simply witness to Wardine's physical abuse. Readers such as those represented on the "Infinite Summer" website who have negative knee-jerk reactions to this young girl due to her "bad" language but who nevertheless push through it to understand what she is saying should feel ashamed of their feelings being triggered by what Cameron[89] dubbed "verbal hygiene" concerns when they *should* be horrified by the details of emotional, physical, and sexual abuse. If they are not already floored by this, there's a final "sucker-punch" in the revelation that closes the section, "And I am gone have a child," which forces the realization that Clenette herself has been *equally* victimized, though she appears to have much less concern for herself than she does for her friend.

This section would seem to be part of the same project Boswell[90] identified for BIHM, testing "the boundaries of our willingness to empathize." Wallace knew that Clenette's use of language would trigger negative judgments accompanied by a reflexive lack of empathy on the part of white readers, and attempted to nevertheless jar them into it, in the space of two short pages. Young Clenette is a total innocent—there is no way even the most racist readers can blame her for the terrible things happening around her and to her. White readers presumably do not compare themselves to Clenette—they compare what their reaction was to what it should have been.

[88] Frantzen, "Finding the Unlovable Object Lovable," 260.
[89] Deborah Cameron, *Verbal Hygiene* (London and New York: Routledge, 2003).
[90] Boswell, *Understanding David Foster Wallace*, 196.

African American readers—and anyone else who recognizes the misrepresentation of AAE—must read the Clenette passage differently. The errors in representation would trigger negative judgment, but as this would be of the author rather than the character, Clenette's story would not then lead to re-evaluation of that response. Realizing that Wallace was trying to evoke empathy for Clenette might somewhat mitigate readers' impression of him as racist or simply ignorant, but would not necessarily reverse the initial reaction, and would not impel such readers to interrogate their own internalized racism.

Yolanda Willis *(Infinite Jest)*

An unattributed piece of dialogue on page 180 that features multiple negation with negative inversion and epenthetic pronoun ("they didn't none of them start till 11," in which both the indefinite noun phrase and auxiliary are obligatorily marked for negation as described by Green[91]) and the invariant negative auxiliary *ain't* ("if I ain't been trying") might come from either Yolanda Willis or Didi Neaves, both identified as "black girls" at Ennet House. Didi does not have any dialogue attributed directly to her in the novel. The short speech cites Clenette as a potential source for confirmation ("Go on and ask Clenette"), ruling her out as speaker. Contrastive stress is marked with italics, but this does not seem to be dialect-specific; it does not indicate nonstandard placement of stress within words, for instance.

Yolanda has a short conversation with Don Gately (565), shown in medias res, complaining about the inappropriate behavior of her Alcoholics Anonymous sponsor. At first, Yolanda's speech has no ethnic markers ("I didn't even tell you yet how he suggested I should thank the Higher Power at night"), but when Gately asks her to reveal the sponsor's identity, she code switches abruptly into AAE ("I ain't use no names in here. All I say . . ."), expressing heightened emotion. She finds sexual harassment unsurprising, but the implication that she is snitching triggers strong indignation.

Another AAE feature in this speech is relativization with null relative pronoun, when Yolanda refers back to "this dude [Ø] I ain't say no name." Her pronunciation of "anonymous" as "nomonous," may be a solecism, but could also be intended as a deliberate reference to AAE phonology (dropping an unstressed initial syllable) and therefore another sign of her indignation. One of her past tense verbs drops the final *-ed* suffix (i.e., *say* for *said*), which may be interpreted either as a morphological feature (the narrative present

---

[91] Green, *African American English*, 78.

tense, although other verbs in the same sentence have past tense suffixes) or as phonological, as pronunciation of the past tense -*ed* suffix is more variable in AAE than SWE.[92]

Yolanda expresses herself clearly and confidently in both SWE and AAE. Code-switching the way she does, at the precise moment she does, is very plausible—a beautiful illustration of Bucholtz's observation that "individuals do not passively inhabit identity categories to which they have been assigned; rather, they negotiate and navigate these categories in a variety of ways within social interaction."[93] Yolanda is, in Giaimo's[94] terms, "talking back through 'talking Black.'" None of the critics who panned Wallace's representation of Clenette have found any fault with his treatment of Yolanda. They might, in fact, wonder why Gately refers to her in passing as "the deeply whacked-out Yolanda W" (601), when readers have only seen her sober and completely sane. If the earlier unattributed speech is interpreted as coming from Yolanda, it reinforces the impression of her as someone who speaks up for herself, and who will use more AAE when doing so. If readers do not associate that snippet with Yolanda, they nonetheless interpret it as another African American speaker showing resilience as well as warranted emotion.

Roy Tony *(Infinite Jest)*

Roy Tony is identified early in *Jest* as a particularly vile character. He is labeled a murderer and would-be incestuous child molester by Clenette (37–8), and appears in the narrative of yrstruly (129–31) as the leader of a gang of drug-dealing "nigers." It would have been easy (and lazy) for Wallace to trigger negative evaluation of him by giving him the broadest, most fully developed AAE dialect, but Roy Tony does not speak directly until years (and hundreds of pages) later, when he is sincerely invested in his recovery and sobriety (505–6). Despite his despicable past, Roy Tony is more likeable in this scene than the insincere white middle-class recovering addict Ken Erdedy.

Although his "What it is" greeting (already dated when the book was published in the 1990s) is ethnically marked and stereotypical so there can be no confusion as to his ethnicity, his speech contains fewer dialect markers than Clenette's or Walinda's. His speech is all first and second person, so he has no opportunity to display unmarked third-person possessors or

---

[92] Green, *African American English*, 110.
[93] Bucholtz, *White Kids*, 1.
[94] Genie Giaimo, "Talking Back Through 'Talking Black': African American English and Agency in Walter Mosley's Devil in a Blue Dress," *Language and Literature* 19, no. 3 (2010): 235–47, esp. 235.

unmarked third-person singular present tense verbs. (Of course, Wallace *could* have given him such opportunities, if he had wanted to emphasize the nonstandardness of his speech.) As with Yolanda, though, the use of AAE features seems to increase when he gets angry. In this case, the trigger for emotion is Erdedy's refusal to engage in the Narcotics Anonymous ritual of members hugging one another at the end of a meeting. In addition to frequent italics marking stress shifts, there are nonstandard verb complexes, including use of completive *done* ("We done motherfucking *surrendered* our wills in here"), and future tense with *gone*. Roy Tony's speech is affirmed as righteous by "one of the Afro-American women who was looking on," who claps her hands and shouts "*Talk* about it!"(506). Although Wallace didn't show any real familiarity with AAE speech events and verbal genres, this evokes the well-known pattern of call-and-response in which the members of the traditional black church respond to the preacher, falling specifically into Smitherman's[95] "co-signing" category, affirming what Roy Tony has said.

The upshot of the story is that Roy Tony terrifies Erdedy into complying with the ritual. Like the unattributed dialogue on page 180 which I have associated with Yolanda, Roy Tony's speech contains some italics to indicate unusually heavy stress, but it is marked on entire words or on the syllable for which SWE prescribes primary stress in any case, so this doesn't seem to be dialect-specific, just an expression of his emotion. It is remarkable that Roy Tony's criminal, anti-social, and immoral behavior early in the novel is entirely divorced from his use of AAE, indeed from his use of language at all; like Clenette, he only speaks directly when he is working for a greater good. In this case, he is not only teaching Erdedy a much-needed lesson but also reinforcing the group norms for the good of the larger community (including across ethnic and class divisions).

Individuation of Characters vs. the (Missing) African American Community

Morrison's study of the treatment of race in American literature[96] described and decried how the dialogue of black characters "is construed as an alien, estranging dialect made deliberately unintelligible by spellings contrived to disfamiliarize it." For the most part, Wallace did not attempt to capture AAE phonology, except where he could use visual conventions already familiar to his audience (such as Walinda's *-in'* suffixes or the use of italics to indicate

---

[95] Smitherman, *Talkin and Testifyin*, 106.
[96] Morrison, *Playing in the Dark*, 52.

stress added to a syllable). Wallace's decision not to engage in such visual "disfamiliarization" may have been an attempt to avoid the scathing critiques he nonetheless received for these dialect sketches.

As noted earlier, Wallace does indulge in one small piece of visual manipulation in Clenette's internal monologue, consistently using *aint* without an apostrophe. Presumably, this is meant to reinforce the "strangeness" of her speech, and her lack of education (although she uses commas in the standard way). Even this allows for differentiation, however: Too Pretty uses apostrophes inconsistently, and they appear according to SWE conventions in the represented speech of both Yolanda and Roy Tony. Although Ives[97] deemed some use of eye dialect "inevitable, even in the most carefully done literary dialect," Wallace seems to have been particularly sparing of it—certainly using it less for his ethnic characters than for a couple of regional dialect speakers.

As a longtime fan of rap music with a supposedly good ear for mimicry, Wallace should have been on more familiar ground with the sound of the dialect, even if he occasionally misunderstood (or at least lost some meaning from) the lyrics. Green[98] and Thomas and Bailey,[99] among others, detail how AAE phonology is distinct in many ways from SWE: speakers use monophthongal $\bar{aɪ}$ in words like *I, high*, typically devoice final /d/ (as in *wicket* for "wicked"), put primary stress on the initial syllable of polysyllabic words (either performing stress shifts as in *pólice*, or by deleting unstressed initial syllables as in [a]*'bout* or [re]*'member*), do not allow word-final consonant clusters (as in *jus'*[t] or *min'*[d]), substitute stop consonants (/t,d/) or labiodental fricatives /f,v/ for interdental fricatives (/θ,ð/ both spelled "th" in SWE) in particular phonetic environments (as in *toof* and *mouf*), while retaining θ word-initially, substitute [skr] for [str] word-initially, and vocalize liquids after vowels /r,l/ (as in *mo'* for "more" and *ba'* for "ball"), especially in unstressed syllables. As illustrated in this (admittedly incomplete) list, these features are numerous and complex, but not difficult to represent on the page, nor would they render the writing particularly difficult to read. Not only does Wallace not include any visual indication of such pronunciations, he even avoids switching *-ing* suffixes to *-in'* for the African American addicts and former addicts in *Infinite Jest*, even though Green[100] says the phonetic realization of the suffix as (n) in AAE occurs "in most contexts." Niedzielski

---

[97] Ives, "A Theory of Literary Dialect," 147.
[98] Green, *African American English*.
[99] Thomas and Bailey, "Segmental Phonology of African American English," 403–19.
[100] Green, *African American English*, 121.

and Preston[101] discuss "the loss of g in -ing endings" as "a common folk preoccupation . . . attributed to laziness." This perception is demonstrably incorrect, since one sound is simply substituted for the other—there is no "savings" in time or effort—but it may have been a factor in Wallace's choice to avoid this judgment for Clenette, Yolanda, and Roy Tony.

As Table 1 shows, Wallace chose different constellations of mostly grammatical features for each of his African American speakers, with just a few lexical and phonological items included. Of course, the choice of grammatical structures, like the choice of particular words, very much depends on what meanings a speaker is trying to express. It cannot be asserted whether Yolanda, who never expresses a future intention, would use future *gone, gonna, going to, will,* or *I'ma*. Likewise, Roy Tony uses little negation, so it is unclear whether he would have consistently used single negation, consistently used multiple negation, or varied. What is clear is that Wallace did not assume that ethnic identity would erase other forms of difference between these characters (although many critics have failed to see the differences that he encoded), and that he viewed both identity and associated use of dialect(s) as more complex than he has been given credit for. Roy Tony in recovery is terrifyingly earnest (and just plain terrifying), Walinda is justifiably angry, Yolanda is more quietly pragmatic—and all are depicted only talking to white people. Not only is there no access to their interior monologue, but readers understand that they are constrained both linguistically and socially. Direct access to Clenette's and Too Pretty's thoughts allows more AAE features to emerge, but Wallace took care to distinguish those performances, as the personalities and circumstances were completely different (Table 1).

Wallace's inability to deploy African American aspectual markers significantly detracts from the realism of the speech of his African American characters—but only in ways that those who have (at least receptive) command of AAE would recognize. Many critics were, in fact, misled into thinking Wallace was more knowledgeable about AAE than he really was. Thompson[102] refers to Wallace's "extensive knowledge of what he labelled 'Standard Black English' and its dialectal variants." In Wallace's "spiel" to black students (discussed in A&AU) about why he expected them to use SWE in their essays, he offered to recommend and discuss with a student "great books by scholars of Black English" (*CTL* 109). Notably, however, the scholars he actually named and praised are those who use what he called

---

[101] Niedzielski and Preston, *Folk Linguistics*, 261.
[102] Thompson, "Wallace and Race," 201.

Table 1 Features of AAE in Wallace's Dialect Representations

	Roy Tony (Jest)	Yolanda (Jest) + unattributed	Walinda (Broom)	Clenette (Jest)	Too Pretty ("Solomon Silverfish")
Ain't	+	+	+	+	+
Null copula/auxiliary	+	+	+	+	+
Invariant be			+	+	+
Counterfactual like to			+	+	+
Nonstandard relativization		+		+	+
Future gone	+		Ø	+	+
AAE lexicon (crib, to play, etc.)	Ø	Ø	+	+	+
Multiple negation	Ø	+	Ø	+	+
Yall			+		+
Perfective done	+		+		+
Unmarked 3-S present verbs		+	Ø	+	+
Negative inversion		+		Ø	+
Deletion of unstressed syllables	Ø	Ø	Ø	Ø	+
-in'	Ø	Ø	+		+
Intensifying -own- in reflexives					+
Gots (narrative present -s)		Ø			+
Ax (vs. ask)				Ø	+
Unmarked possessors			Ø	+	Ø

KEY: + AAE variant attested; Ø AAE variant avoided (despite opportunity to use); left blank (no opportunity to use, meaning not expressed).

"totally ass-kicking SWE ['standard white English']" (109). His observation that "some of the cultural and political realities of American life are themselves racially insensitive and elitist and offensive and unfair, and that pussyfooting around these realties with euphemistic doublespeak is not only hypocritical but toxic to the project of ever really changing them" (109) presupposes that everyone shares in that project of changing racist linguistic ideologies. Wallace may sincerely have believed that he did share that goal, but there's little evidence that he did much to advance the cause. Mura[103] has a particularly trenchant response to Wallace's tone-deaf "spiel": "He's the type of white guy who thinks he's thought it all out in terms of race, and there's nothing I could say to him about what I know or my experiences that would ever cause him to doubt . . . Deep inside, I know he's not on my side; he doesn't want the best for me."

The "Dave Wallace" narrator in TPK observes "the way two unconnected black people will often go out of their way to nod at or otherwise specially acknowledge each other if everyone else around them is white" (305–6). As Araya[104] points out, although this comment "might seem to point out the community *between* African Americans, it is one that only exists *in opposition to* 'everyone else around.'" The "evidence notebook" Wallace was keeping for that novel puts the chasm between black and white even more starkly: "Why black kids scare white kids just with their presence: it was their otherness and the force with which they asserted it" (HRC Wallace Papers, container 43.1, p. 39 of the notebook).

Clenette, Roy Tony, and Too Pretty are from "the Projects," but Walinda and Yolanda may well have come from more comfortable backgrounds. (It is, of course, possible that they too came from poverty, but that Walinda managed to work her way into the middle class.) There is no blame attached to Too Pretty or Roy Tony for their criminal behaviors, just as there is no judgment of those who succumb to addiction. Forming communities in opposition to whiteness (including criminal gangs, but also the more prosaic tendency to stick to "one's own kind") may provide some degree of protection and comfort, but Wallace implies that it is healthier to form larger communities that transcend race and ethnicity, as the recovering addicts at Ennet House eventually manage to do.

In Martínez's[105] terms, Wallace does not offer African American readers many available inputs for blended "self-schema storyworld possible selves."

---

[103] Mura, "White Writing Teachers," 9.
[104] Araya, "Why the Whiteness?" 240.
[105] María-Ángeles Martínez, *Storyworld Possible Selves: Applications of Cognitive Linguistics*, Vol. 37 (Berlin: De Gruyter Mouton, 2018), 124.

In this sense, he undoubtedly falls into the tradition Morrison[106] identifies of using "Africanist language practices . . . to reinforce class distinctions and otherness as well as to assert privilege and power." Clearly sensitive to all of these dimensions, Wallace may have been asserting that privilege and power distinctions continue to exist, but it would appear that he was (perhaps clumsily) trying to show the unfairness of the systems that continue to segregate and disadvantage people like Clenette. Wallace's white characters are in no way more virtuous or intelligent or successful than his racial others.

When Hal repeatedly notices Clenette working at the tennis academy, but never feels comfortable engaging directly with her, it is not simply a personal failing, it is a societal failure. Had Wallace not let her speak for herself, he would have appeared to validate and endorse that segregation. His anxiety about writing African American voices may have limited his ability to dip into some characters' perspectives, but it is also quite possible that he was limiting his attempts at this in order to illustrate the very limited opportunity that many Americans have to actually get to know people of different ethnicities. Wallace's belief that it should be possible for his white readers to empathize across racial lines, even when given very limited glimpses into racial and ethnic others' experiences, can be read as optimism and confidence in a shared sense of humanity, despite the social structures that continue to keep populations separate.

It is valid to criticize Wallace for featuring so few African Americans and for so seldom letting them speak for themselves (not to mention making them all drug users and/or dealers, although to be fair, this is true of most of the white characters in *Jest* as well); it is not accurate, however, to say that they all sound alike. Although the color of someone's skin may be the first thing that the white focalizing character notices, it is, in fact, their voices that readers will recall. An explicitly raciolinguistic reading of Wallace's work—that is, a sociolinguistic study that does not just describe ethnic dialects, but actively pushes back on the hegemony of white linguistic practices being imposed on nonwhite communities, rejecting the "melting pot" goal[107]—should be less concerned with the individual dialect depictions (which *should* contain a lot of individual variation) and more concerned with the absence, in Wallace's writing, of any healthy African American or multiethnic communities.

---

[106] Morrison, *Playing in the Dark*, 52.
[107] Cf. H. Samy Alim, "Introducing Raciolinguistics: Racing Language and Languaging Race in Hyperracial Times," in *Raciolinguistics: How Language Shapes Our Ideas about Race*, ed. H. Samy Alim, John R. Rickford, and Arnetha F. Ball (Oxford: Oxford University Press, 2016), 1–30; Jonathan Rosa, *Looking Like a Language, Sounding Like a Race: Raciolinguistic Ideologies and the Learning of Latinidad* (New York: Oxford University Press, 2019).

With the exception of the Clenette section of *Jest* (which is a horror show of poverty, addiction, physical and sexual violence), black people are only seen hovering around the fringes of white America, unable to be integrated. There are no depictions, in Wallace's work, of black people talking to each other; only trying (and usually failing) to be heard by white people. (The white characters *see* Clenette and Yolanda talking to each other, but all readers *hear* is the occasional "Girl!") Part of the misapprehension that Wallace's African American characters sound alike may be due to reflexive reactions to any use of language perceived as nonstandard, but some may be an unconscious perception of salient absences in their speech: African Americans in Wallace's work are not given access to the regional identities that white people may use to gain a sense of working-class community, nor are they granted access to the social identities ("jock," "nerd") that would provide a pathway for upward mobility.

4

Ethnicity and Assimilation

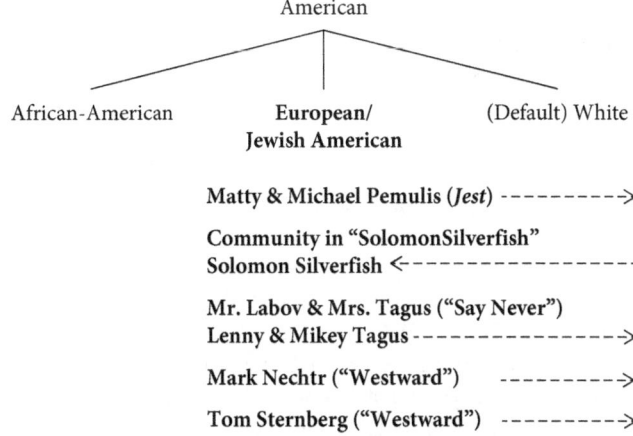

Figure 3 Wallace's European and Jewish American Dialects.

Whereas African Americans remain separate from the rest of the population, denied the chance to assimilate, European and Jewish immigrant communities are swallowed whole, at the cost of losing their languages and cultures. White ethnic heritage is reduced by Wallace to an idealized memory, a catchy slogan on a button to wear at parades, words and foods that have been "Americanized" and now belong to all. There is an inverse relationship in Wallace's work between ethnicity and regional identity: only white people are perceived as regional; anyone with a regional identity must be white. Whiteness is the construed as the *absence* of ethnicity—it is the "unmarked" identity, in linguistic terms, and therefore the default, with no particular cultural or identity traits predicated upon it.

Although this is just one minor thread among many in *Jest*, where it may be overwhelmed by other themes, Wallace explored the issue of "assimilation" of immigrant populations more explicitly in some of his earlier work. There is a long tradition of American literature tracing "the evolution of European nationals and ethnics into white Americans"[1] of which Wallace was certainly aware, mostly "written by immigrants who, though white by appearance, were still marginalized by class, language, religion, and ethnicity."[2] "White" and "black" seem like fairly distinct categories in Wallace's worldview, but what of other people of color? There are very few Asian American characters in Wallace's works (or foreigners from Asia), but those who do appear tend to have "American" given names, ethnically marked family names, and no trace of ethnic dialect. LaMont Chu, who is compared directly to the real-life professional tennis player Michael Chang, does not speak directly the first dozen or so times he appears in *Jest*, but when he finally does (388–9), his speech is entirely standard. This same phenomenon is seen in "Church Not Made with Hands" (*BIHM*) in the character Eric Yang, and in TPK, with the presumably Japanese Keith Sabusawa. It is not limited to those of Asian descent, however. There is also the Kenyan (presumably black) Tony Nwangi in *Jest*. The first names of TPK's Persian F. Chahla Neti-Neti and *Jest's* "Petropolis" Khan are not given, but the use of first initial and/or nickname are different ways of Americanizing their names. Araya[3] calls Khan "charming and hilarious," which is a bit of a stretch, though his speech is certainly depicted as standard in a casual, teenage boy kind of way. Only a few of Khan's words are reported by Hal, first "asking what was all this brooha upstairs" and then reporting that "the scuttlebutt on breakfast was sausage-analog and OJ with palpable pulp, he said" (989).

Hybrid names given to people who presumably are visibly not white could be read as a sign that, no matter how standard their speech may be, they cannot assimilate entirely to a default white American identity. On the other hand, Wallace makes a more complex statement about the interrelationship of national origin, race, and ethnicity by including the white family at the heart of *Jest* in the same pattern. The surname Incandenza is recognizable as an abridged version of the Italian word for "incandescence" (*incandescenza*), but although a distant "Umbrian" ancestor is mentioned (101), the Incandenzas in no way identify as Italian. Hal's father, James, was said to take after "a great-grandmother with Pima-tribe Indian S.W. blood" (101), and Hal himself is said to "look ethnic" in the same way (101)—"radiantly dark," although his eyes are blue—and his skin color is explicitly noted as a weird genetic fluke. His brother Orin "had got the Moms's Anglo-Nordo-Canadian phenotype" with "lighter-blue eyes" (101). It is never suggested that they have any cultural

---

[1] Valerie Babb, *Whiteness Visible: The Meaning of Whiteness in American Literature and Culture* (New York: New York University Press, 1998), 9.
[2] Ibid., 5.
[3] Araya, "Why the Whiteness?," 244.

inheritance from the more distant progenitors. If this is the "success" story of assimilation and intermarriage of European Americans, the main result appears to be emptiness and depression.

Jest, set in the Boston area, offers the greatest variety of ethnic voices, but Wallace's main characters are all white, and there are notable ethnic gaps even in scenes that should, realistically, have more diverse populations, such as the halfway house, the twelve-step meetings, bars, crowded street scenes, and so on. In the 1990 census, black people accounted for over a quarter of the population of the city of Boston, "Hispanic origin (of any race)" just over 10 percent, with almost half of the Hispanic population Puerto Rican, and Asians just over 5 percent, with more than half of the Asian population Chinese.[4] *Jest* contains no reference to Puerto Ricans, and although there are multiple references to Chinese restaurants and to the country of China, the only Chinese Americans who appear in the novel are the elderly ladies carrying shopping bags whom Lenz stalks and then mugs. Lenz's racism is apparent in his use of not just "Oriental," but the adjectival form "Orientoid" (718) and "Chinkette" (728). Although a neighborhood in Cambridge is designated "Little Lisbon" (479), and there is a "Portuguese grocery" opposite Antitoi Entertainment (483) and a "Portuguese Restaurant" (682), there are no people of Portuguese descent featured in the text—they have been completely assimilated. In a kind of postcolonial revenge, the neighborhood is now populated by Brazilian immigrants, seen only in passing, who will also presumably soon be assimilated.

Araya[5] sees TPK as embodying whiteness. Mura's "manifesto" (his article is so labeled)[6] places Wallace within a tradition in which "most white fiction writers don't ever think consciously about identifying their white characters as white; lacking a racial marker, characters are still to be regarded by default as white." Bucholtz[7] observes that for the European American high school students she studied in California, "whiteness was not readily available as an ethnicity or culture but rather was often viewed as an absence of culture."

Embodying whiteness is emphatically not the same thing as celebrating it, however. Araya[8] notes that not only are people of color relatively absent in TPK but the white characters are also relatively homogeneous (239). Wallace was certainly able to differentiate characters linguistically in terms of social

---

[4] "Race and Hispanic Origin," *1990 Massachusetts Census*, Table 6: 24. https://www2.census.gov/library/publications/decennial/1990/cp-1/cp-1-23.pdf.
[5] Araya, "Why the Whiteness?"
[6] Mura, "White Writing Teachers," 1.
[7] Bucholtz, *White Kids*, 234.
[8] Araya, "Why the Whiteness?"

and regional identities when he wanted to, as will be detailed in the next few chapters. The absence of such differentiation in TPK was likely no oversight, but rather a warning. Choosing to affiliate oneself with a group that one is not born into does not have to erase the identities that one already has. The "melting pot," as presented in TPK, reduces the humanity of all involved, making them indistinguishable cogs in a machine; their identity as IRS agents supplants all previous identities. The "stew" metaphor represented by Alcoholics Anonymous in *Jest*, on the other hand, allows everyone to retain their separate identities while also accepting a new common identity as recovering addicts.

Rosa[9] points out that "the ethnoracial status of Latinx identity is widely debated in both scholarly and popular discourses, often from the perspective of spectrum-based racial logics that problematically imagine Latinxs as an intermediary 'brown' population located between Blackness at one end and Whiteness at the other, or as a phenotypically heterogeneous group that is better understood ethnically (i.e., stereotypically defined culturally or nationally) than racially (i.e., stereotypically defined physically)." Wallace acknowledges various "foreign" Hispanics (Carlina, Alfonso) as discussed in Chapter 2, but there are no extended portrayals of native-born Latinx in his work. Eugenio Martinez, a recovering addict and volunteer counselor who calls himself "Gene," makes several appearances in *Jest*, but is never allowed to speak for himself. The (false) implication of this absence is that Latinx populations are fully "assimilated."

More surprising still, there are virtually no blended or hybrid identities, no mention of multiracialism, no black Jews, no children of Vietnamese mothers and US GI fathers. In this, Wallace does reflect the census data of the time, as the census did not allow people to indicate more than one "race" until 2000. Neighborhoods in the Boston area are identified as "mixed" (i.e., "Watertown from east to west is Catholic, Armenian, and Mixed" [811]), but not people—except for the white-on-white "Dutch-Irish" identity Joelle van Dyne claims in her pre-suicide monologue (234), but which in no way informs her character.

Araya[10] argues that the absence of multiracial characters in TPK "is not linked to a judgment about their place in society. Rather, Wallace presents the reader with a simplified, more homogeneous version of society, and traces that society's inability to live up to the ideals on which it was founded." Wallace undoubtedly simplifies the categorization of race and ethnicity, but does not

---

[9] Rosa, *Looking Like a Language, Sounding Like a Race*, 2–3.
[10] Araya, "Why the Whiteness?," 248.

allow readers to ignore racial tensions and complex questions of identity for long. Voices pop out of the text, all the more starting against the homogeneous background. Readers are reminded that those who cannot assimilate live segregated, separate lives, resulting in a failure of empathy across group lines. The ethnicity of European and Jewish Americans that have assimilated is reduced to tropes that then belong to all Americans, as all of America can feel a bit Irish on St. Patrick's Day or feel a bit Jewish eating bagels.

Thompson[11] points out that in the notes for TPK, Chris Aquistipace is referred to "at various points as being of wildly different races and ethnicities, with the point being that he is racially othered, rather than occupying a particular identity position that Wallace is keen to explore" (216). Indeed, the concept of "othering" is central to understanding Wallace's representations of race and ethnicity. To what extent *are* we really different, and can we nonetheless connect with and understand one another across these differences? To what extent can ethnic groups assimilate, and is this even desirable? In addition to his African American depictions, Wallace explores these ideas via depictions of Irish Americans in *Infinite Jest*, but explored it more fully with Jewish Americans in earlier stories.

Irish Americans: *Infinite Jest*'s Pemulis Family

Although the ethnoracial landscape of *Jest*'s fictionalized then-near-future is simplified, almost literally reduced to black and white, Wallace could hardly avoid dealing with Irish Americans in the Boston-based novel. McGurl[12] talks of Wallace identifying with "his ancestor" in *Braveheart*, but he acknowledges that Wallace only seems to have considered his Celtic heritage in private, not in his writing. Even in the impressively large cast of characters of *Infinite Jest*, there are no Scottish characters.

Wallace's treatment of the anonymous Irishman discussed in the previous chapter and the Pemulis family seems to have been influenced more by his own observations of the status of the Irish Americans in Boston, perhaps particularly informed by his close friendship with Mark Costello, who is "from a large Irish-Catholic family,"[13] than by a tradition in American literature. Fanning[14] surveys 250 years of Irish American authors, but many

---

[11] Thompson, "Wallace and Race."
[12] McGurl, "The Institution of Nothing."
[13] Max, *Every Love Story Is a Ghost Story*, 19.
[14] Charles Fanning, *The Irish Voice in America: 250 Years of Irish-American Fiction*, 2nd ed. (Lexington: University Press of Kentucky, 2000).

are little remembered today, and it would not appear that Wallace was particularly influenced by them, if indeed he had read some of the more successful, such as Finley Peter Dunne or James T. Farrell. Even if Wallace had not read any of Farrell's trilogy, he might still have been aware of the thuggish Chicagoan Studs Lonigan character from the 1960 film or the 1979 miniseries based on the novels (with Studs played by Frank Gorshin and Harry Hamlin, respectively). He would likely have been aware of racist portrayals of Irish Americans written by writers who were not themselves Irish American, including T. S. Eliot's awful Sweeney, or by early portrayals of Irish Americans in the media more generally.

Jest features several racist narrators, as discussed in the previous chapter, and although their attitudes toward the Boston Irish are more offhandedly racist than toward African Americans, there are multiple references to "Irish luggage" (541, 823, meaning garbage bags, with specially reinforced ones upgraded to "Irish Guccis" [542]). The "tough blue-collar Irish lads" Tiny Ewell recalls being "bussed in from the East Watertown projects" are clearly not foreigners, but Irish Americans, who are described in starkly unflattering terms: with "runny noses, home-cut hair, frayed cuffs, quick with their fists" (810). The presumably also Irish American women who are part of the tennis academy's custodial staff are described only as "thick-ankled Irish women" (152). The derogatory term "Paddy" is used multiple times in the section focalized by yrstruly (rendered there as "Patty"), and although some readers might not be aware of the etymology of the term "paddy wagons," Wallace certainly would have been.

The members of the Pemulis family illustrate the pressures to assimilate into default whiteness, as well as the obstacles inherent in this. "Matty's Da'd come over on a boat from Louth in Lenster in 1989" (683) when Matty was "three or four." (Wallace undoubtedly meant "Leinster," in the Republic of Ireland.) Pemulis, Sr., a dockworker who raped his elder son repeatedly (until his death, when Matty was seventeen), has notably accented speech in that son's memory: "A fook in t'boom" (684), for example, although his speech is much less accented than the Irish immigrant at AA discussed in the previous chapter whose every word is re-spelled. Da Pemulis only has a few words adjusted, mainly the words that index his relationship with Matty, both as father (*Da, sone*) and as abuser (*fook, fookin, boom*). He elides an occasional vowel, and has some phrasings that sound Irish-inflected, as in "what are we scared of then?," "to be scared so," "nought on his mind but a fook," "why then so I've a mind to give you just what you're thinking t'fear" (all 684).

Matty, whom we meet as a 23-year-old prostitute, came to the United States young enough to become fully nativized; he has no traces of Irish in his adult dialect, except for referring to his father as "Da." Matty's younger brother is Michael Pemulis, whom Matty always thinks of as "Micky," but who is never called that by his classmates. Michael's ethnicity is referred to in passing—but only to make the point that it isn't accepted ("he's barred by DeLint and Nwangi from shirts that mention the Sinn Fein" [266]), or isn't normally evident. Hal comments during the Eschaton game that "the combination of several Tenuate spansules plus Eschaton-adrenaline bring his blue-collar Irish right out" (334). Hal needs to mention this for readers, because the actual utterance supposedly illustrating this does not encode any sort of ethnic dialect: "It's only real-world snow if it's already in the *scenario!*" (334). The "Irish" in him must be normally very well controlled, if it takes a combination of game-fuelled adrenaline and an amphetamine-like drug to allow it to surface. The extent of his "Irishness," linguistically, appears to be his vowel pronunciation in "*Jay*sus" (334, 338)—but there has long been a deleterious stereotype of Irish temper, as evidenced by the idiom "getting one's Irish up." When Pemulis says "Jaysus" with good humor during a poker game with his "Little Buddies" (117), nobody comments on his "Irishness."

Although Wallace could not avoid Irishness completely with a novel set in a town with the largest Irish American population in America, this heritage did not particularly interest him, presumably because the anti-Irish sentiments that prevailed in the nineteenth century are no longer common in the United States. Negra[15] calls Irish heritage today "enriched whiteness," arguing that it has become "the ideal guilt-free white ethnicity of choice." I will nonetheless return to Michael Pemulis in Chapter 8, as he illustrates a different aspect of identity, the association of regional dialect with the white working class, and limits on opportunities for upward mobility.

The Assimilation of Jewish Americans

Although Wallace once self-identified as "the goyest gentile anybody's ever met"[16], he repeatedly wrote tales featuring the assimilation of Jews into default whiteness. There may have been some personal reasons for this, based on his own relationships with and observations of Jewish people in his life, but he was undoubtedly also responding to a tradition in American literature with which he was known to be familiar, and the absorption of a part of Jewish linguistic and cultural heritage into general US culture.

Wallace's appreciation for Cynthia Ozick's ability to effect "an utter erasure of difference" was noted in Chapter 3; he called her "an immortally good

---

[15] Diane Negra, "The Irish in Us: Irishness, Performativity, and Popular Culture," in *The Irish in US*, ed. Diane Negra (Durham, NC: Duke University Press, 2006), 1–19, esp. 11.
[16] Schechner, "Behind the Watchful Eyes of Author David Foster Wallace," 109.

pure prose writer."[17] He was a fan of Philip Roth, but thought Alan Lelchuk "embodied the clumsiness of mainstream realist fiction."[18] Wallace had a very close relationship with longtime agent Bonnie Nadell, and although they were only a few years apart in age, described her as his surrogate Jewish mother, and not the first such in his life: "I have this thing, the nearest Jewish mother, I will simply put my arms around her skirt and just attach myself."[19] The affection between Wallace and Nadell is evident in their correspondence, archived at the Harry Ransom Center in Austin, Texas. With this kind of personal connection, Wallace may have trusted his ear even more than he did when attempting to capture other dialects.

"Solomon Silverfish" and "Say Never" both center around Jews in the Chicago area, but are complementary in their exploration of assimilation and the performative nature of identity. The speech of Mrs. Tagus's two adult sons in "Say Never," neither of whom retains their mother's linguistic markers of Jewish identity, is portrayed without commentary, apparently as natural and unsurprising; the assimilation from Jewish immigrant to a default white identity is complete within a single generation. On the other hand, the discovery that the title character Solomon Silverfish is not "actually" Jewish comes as a shocking revelation to his longtime friends and family. Solomon, identified in the opening line of the story as a "secret Saxon, closet Celt" (67), has chosen to go against the social pressures that would find Jewishness marked, deviant, and less worthy than a default white identity. This story is more overtly about the connection between language and identity, about which identities people are allowed to claim, including who has the right to use which dialect. This makes it somewhat ironically awkward for Hayes-Brady[20] and Thompson[21] to criticize the dialect portrayed as overly stereotyped, as they recognize, although Thompson nevertheless labels the dialogue in this story "like the most grotesquely stereotypical Jews from Hollywood entertainment" (213).

Witzling[22] argues that "cultural Jewishness in postmodernity can only be understood in comparison to constructions of other 'ethnic' and 'racial' minority cultures subject to some complex of social prejudice and politico-

---

[17] Ibid.
[18] Max, *Every Love Story Is a Ghost Story*, 39.
[19] David Lipsky, "The Lost Years and Last Days of David Foster Wallace," in *Conversations with David Foster Wallace*, ed. Stephen J. Burn (Jackson: University of Mississippi Press, 2012), 161–83, esp. 167.
[20] Hayes-Brady, *The Unspeakable Failures of David Foster Wallace*,
[21] Thompson, "Wallace and Race."
[22] David Witzling, "Postmodern Prose and the Discourse of the 'Cultural Jew': The Cases of Mailer and Foer," in *Postmodern Literature and Race*, ed. Len Platt and Sara Upstone (Cambridge: Cambridge University Press, 2015), 160–76, esp. 161.

legal discrimination. Many individuals of Jewish descent and Jews as a group have benefitted from the expansion of whiteness in the United States to include them during the middle decades of the twentieth century" (161). He demonstrates that Norman Mailer and Jonathan Safran Foer "articulate ways that Jewishness can disappear into invisibility or even render itself wholly absent" (162). The fictional character who bears the author's name in Foer's *Everything Is Illuminated*[23] is described by his Ukrainian taxi driver as "not a Jew with a large-sized letter J, but a jew, like Albert Einstein or Jerry Seinfeld" (104).

Wirth-Nesher[24] details "representation of accented speech" by Jewish American writers, "from the striding Yiddish-American dialect in Abraham Cahan's work to accented speech restricted to non-Jewish American characters in Saul Bellow's novels." She traces the use and portrayal of language(s) in different generations of Jewish American writers, from foreign-born, non-native-English speakers to native-born bilinguals, to members of the third generation who do not speak Yiddish or Hebrew. The next logical extension of this would logically be someone like Wallace, who has no Jewish heritage, but has absorbed part of Jewish language and culture from common cultural references. Spinner[25] shares an anecdote of running a book club ("a few years ago," presumably in the 2010s) focused on Yiddish literature in translation, in which most of the members were "well-educated American Jews," but "none of them knew more than a few words" in Yiddish. In that sense, Wallace was not at a linguistic disadvantage in representing a Yiddish-influenced American dialect, although he might still be at a cultural one, and still left himself open to claims of cultural appropriation and/or anti-Semitic mockery.

There are no obvious errors in the representation of Jewish American speech in these stories; it is likely the frequency with which the dialect features occur that gives rise to the perception of stereotyping. It is possible that common cultural access to Jewish American discourse instantiated in the work of (e.g., among many others) Woody Allen, Mel Brooks, and Neil Simon made Wallace think that a thick Jewish accent would feel like a "familiar friend" in Oster's[26] terms. When Solomon's friend Zero Kretzman accuses him of speaking "the way a person speaks when he tries to imitate a

---

[23] Jonathan Safran Foer, *Everything Is Illuminated* (Boston: Houghton Mifflin, 2002).
[24] Hana Wirth-Nesher, *Call It English: The Languages of Jewish American Literature* (Princeton: Princeton University Press, 2006), 4.
[25] Samuel Spinner, "Reading Jewish," *Publications of the Modern Language Association* 134, no. 1 (2019): 150–6, esp. 151.
[26] Judith Oster, *Crossing Cultures: Creating Identity in Chinese and Jewish American Literature* (Columbia: University of Missouri Press, 2003).

Jewish person" (81), it's funny not just because readers get the metalinguistic joke that Wallace was engaged in that very task as he wrote those very words (and would, like Solomon, be accused of cultural appropriation), but because there is no apparent difference between Kretzman's way of speaking and Solomon's (which passed successfully as Jewish for thirty years).

The Affirmation of Community in "Solomon Silverfish"

"Solomon Silverfish" takes place in "Skokie, a certain part of Chicago" (67). Skokie was home to thousands of Holocaust survivors and was predominantly Jewish when a Nazi march was planned there in the late 1970s, leading to a protracted and very public legal battle over freedom of speech when Wallace was still a teenager in Illinois. As the Holocaust survivors have died off, and the descendants of the immigrants have assimilated linguistically, Chicago is now much less associated with Jewish identity in popular culture, although the Jewish population of the city (and larger metropolitan area) has continued to grow.[27] *Ethnolinguistic Chicago*[28] has chapters on African Americans, Greek-, Arab-, Nigerian-, Italian-, Swedish-, Chinese-, and Japanese-Americans, but no mentions of Jewish people even in passing. Nonetheless, one of the important distinctions between this story and "Say Never" is that "Solomon Silverfish" depicts a large and vibrant Jewish community holding on to its heritage, resisting assimilation, and absorption—even presenting an appealing alternative (in Solomon's eyes at least) to a default white identity.

"Solomon Silverfish" includes direct borrowings of Yiddish words such as *klotz* (68, clumsy person),[29] *shaygets* (82, a derogatory term for a male who is not Jewish), *Schwartz/shvartzer* (as discussed in the previous chapter), going far beyond what Wallace might have expected average Americans to recognize. When Solomon's mother-in-law tells his wife Sophie that Solomon has "pretended" to be Jewish ever since he first met her, the mother-in-law code switches into Yiddish for an entire sentence: "a goy bleibt a goy" (82), meaning "a gentile remains a gentile," an instantiation of a common Yiddish

---

[27] Jacob B. Ukeles, Ron Miller, Peter Friedman, and David Dutwin, *2010 Metropolitan Chicago Jewish Community Study*. Berman Jewish Databank. https://www.jewishdataban k.org/databank/search-results/study/576.

[28] Marcia Farr, ed. *Ethnolinguistic Chicago* (Mahwah, NJ: Lawrence Erlblaum Associates, 2004).

[29] Yiddish words and phrases are spelled here as Wallace had them in the manuscript. Yiddish was traditionally written using the Hebrew consonantal alphabet, and different authors have chosen different transliterations, more or less phonetic. Bernstein (2006: 253) prefers "klutz." This is one of the large number of Yiddish words she cites that "have spread from Jewish English into more general American usage."

derogatory formula, as in "a chazer bleibt a chazer" (a pig remains a pig), "a nahr bleibt a nahr" (a fool remains a fool). Sophie responds to her mother incredulously, "You're here before dawn in the morning to say my husband is a non-Jewish non-goyish demon of a Chaim Yankel?" (82), using the Yiddish equivalent of "average Joe," but one that is often portrayed in jokes as a trickster who gets the last laugh. This level of borrowing seems appropriate for a story in which Jewish identity is sought and affirmed; it is also redundant enough with the English that a reader who doesn't understand a word or phrase does not miss the intended meaning.

The Jewish characters in "Solomon Silverfish" all sound alike, but this is motivated by the story's central question of whether someone can simply decide to claim Jewish identity. When Solomon is accused of having been "so identity-less in your life that you made up an identity for yourself" (84) and having spoken "so as to imitate and mislead" (85), he replies, "I spoke as friends of mine spoke. I was in Rome I spoke as the woman-who-I-love-and-who-has-made-me-me-for-thirty years spoke. I spoke like my wife" (85). Rather than manipulating orthography to represent the phonological features most commonly associated with Jewish English—the raising of pitch and emphatic pronunciation of /t,d/, slight lisping of /s,z/, pronunciation of a hard /g/ in -*ing* suffixes, and exaggerated intonation[30]—Wallace relies more on recognizable discourse features. Jewish conversational style has been analyzed as overlapping, loud, high-pitched, fast, and featuring exaggerated gestures,[31] sociable disagreement that is actively sought rather than avoided, and competition for turns,[32] all of which are on ample display in the lively arguments in "Solomon Silverfish."

The uniformity of Jewish American voices within the story makes the internal monologue of Too Pretty, the African American pimp discussed in the previous chapter, all the more startling when it takes over the narration at the end. Too Pretty corroborates the sincerity and extraordinary depth of Solomon's love for Sophie, not just testifying directly ("But my man love his bitch? I see my man like to die with love" [92]), but by illustrating the social and even criminal risks Solomon was willing to take to get marijuana to ease Sophie's nausea after her cancer treatments. Too Pretty serves as an unwitting character witness for Solomon, all the more credible because he is

---

[30] Cynthia Bernstein, "More Than Just Yada Yada Yada (Jewish English)," in *American Voices: How Dialects Differ from Coast to Coast*, ed. Walt Wolfram and Ben Ward (Malden, MA: Blackwell, 2006), 252–7, esp. 254.
[31] Deborah Tannen, "New York Jewish Conversational Style," *International Journal of the Sociology of Language* 30 (1981): 133–50.
[32] Deborah Schiffrin, "Jewish Argument as Sociability," *Language in Society* 13, no. 3 (1984): 311–35.

unaware that Solomon stands accused. Solomon's brother-in-law (who had Solomon followed by an investigator) accuses him of "carrying on" in the cemetery, "assorted kinds of shtupping. With a young woman" (86). Solomon does not dignify this with a response—but readers learn from Too Pretty that the "carrying on" was with Sophie (in her chemo wig), both of them high on the dope Too Pretty gave them.

Perhaps more importantly (since Solomon's love for Sophie was never in doubt), Too Pretty provides concrete evidence that Solomon can connect meaningfully with someone from another ethnic identity without changing anything about himself ("And I be likin the big honky bastard too. He wild" [92]). Even referring to Solomon as "my man" is an indication of the depth of their relationship: Folb[33] defines this as a "form of address between black males that connotes positive feelings between the two." The strength of this unlikely friendship confirms that Solomon did not need to "pretend" to be Jewish to win Sophie or to be accepted by her community; rather, he chose to be Jewish, and in making that choice, became Jewish. This included taking on all the anti-Jewish prejudice: Too Pretty calls him "this hebrew cracker" (94). Unlike Sophie's parents and brothers, Too Pretty (like Sophie) understands that Solomon can be "lots of things at one same time" (94). The most important proof of Solomon's "real" identity is that the dialect is maintained when the free indirect discourse narration dips into his thoughts. (Whether one can choose to be one of "the chosen people" is a matter for Talmudic debate; notably, the story does not deal with religion at all, as is typical for Wallace.)

Part of the critical uneasiness with "Solomon Silverfish" may come from the name of the character: both "Silverstein" and "Fishman" are common Jewish surnames (both derived historically from occupations, jeweler, and fishmonger, respectively); combining them into "Silverfish," however, inevitably conjures up images of the insect and appears to be insulting (although the term is also applied to actual silver fish). But if readers see "Silverfish" as anti-Semitic mockery, then what do they make of the revelation *in the first line of the story* that Solomon was not born Jewish? Wallace wasn't trying to be subtle, but he was having fun: "Schoenweiss," Sophie's maiden name, is hardly less markedly Jewish—and literally means "beautiful white" in German. (Wallace uses the same surname again, in passing, in "Say Never.")

During his famous road trip with David Lipsky, Wallace discusses a story he wrote "about a WASP who passes himself off as Jewish. Even with his

---

[33] Folb, *Runnin' Down Some Lines*, 246.

wife,"[34] in which he says he was trying to "show off in various technical ways. Like to do really good, a kind of really good kitschy Jewish voice and dialogue" (174). Wallace's biography recounts that when Wallace submitted this story during his MFA program at the University of Arizona, his conservative Jewish professor was "mildly offended," and that the other students in the program "assumed it was Wallace's attempt to get under the skin of a professor who was not giving him the praise he expected."[35] This may be true, but it does not make the story any less interesting in its own right, especially when it can be put in context of Wallace's other dialect portraits. It appears to have intrigued Wallace that, even though the loss of religion, culture, and ethnic dialect among American Jews is perfectly commonplace, assimilation to a Jewish identity would be seen as astonishing and highly contested. Wallace's returning to Jewish Americans in "Say Never" to further explore the concept of ethnic identity shows that this wasn't just a private joke or a personal grudge, but a topic of genuine interest.

The Fraying of Community in "Say Never"

"Say Never"—which Ellerhoff[36] dubs "a Roth-or-Lelchuk 'old-Jews pastiche'"—takes place on Chicago's North Side and portrays many of the same dialect features. The older generation (Mr. Labov and Mrs. Tagus) continue to perform Jewish identity, but see their community shrinking as their spouses and friends die off and the younger generation moves toward complete assimilation. It may be stereotypical that the elder generation complain despite claiming not to complain and refer to people by profession (e.g., "Schoenweiss the dentist" [217]), but the elderly characters are portrayed with sympathy and dignity. They display an exaggerated politeness that evokes an old-world courtliness, as when Mr. Labov refers to his life-long friend as "Mrs. Tagus" throughout, and asks to be excused for expressing an opinion. (It may be purely serendipitous coincidence that Wallace chose the surname of the most famous sociolinguist in the United States, William Labov, to use in a story that so prominently illustrates linguistic variation. He had no books by Labov in his library nor did he cite him in A&AU, but it seems implausible, given his amateur interest in the field of linguistics that he would not have heard the name.)

---

[34] Lipsky, *Although of Course You End Up Becoming Yourself*, 173.
[35] Max, *Every Love Story Is a Ghost Story*, 64.
[36] Steve Gronert Ellerhoff, "Proteus Bound: Pinning *Girl with Curious Hair* under Short Story Theory," in *Critical Insights: David Foster Wallace*, ed. Philip Coleman (New York: Grey House Publishing/Salem Press, 2015), 112–27, esp. 124.

Salient features of the dialect shared by Mr. Labov and Mrs. Tagus—upon which neither Wallace nor any character in the story comments—include initial pronoun "this" to refer back to a topic expressed in the previous sentence (or sentence fragment), as in "Anger from me at her Lenny, however? This I could not manage" (217), "Lenny Tagus is a nice boy. This is a thing I know" (217); rhetorical questions embedded in relative clauses, as in "in a print so tiny who could read it?" (208); "from this girl who who would want to hurt her?" (209); nonstandard placement of adverbs and adverbial prepositional phrases, as in "who is too deaf now to converse about weather with *even*" (219); "yellow bruises I can still *with my eyes closed* see" (219); object pronouns in compound subjects, as in "Her husband and *me* were like this, we were so close" (210); "*Us* and Mike and Bonnie and this person should just sit down and talk like old friends?" (218); loan translations from Yiddish resulting in nonstandard phrasal verbs, as in "she is *making with* the fist with her hand in the air again" (211); "You *know from* warmth?" (218); and frequent use of *such* as both determiner and comparative, as in "such discomfort . . . such worry" (205), "for such a dinner" (218).

This is a long list of nonstandard features, so the judgment that Wallace overdid it here may seem reasonable, but he did not actually throw in every feature he could have. There was no use of the productive nominalizing suffix *-nik,* describing a practitioner or devotee of a particular practice,[37] for example, even though he was apparently familiar with this one since he was a young boy, as it features in one of the possible interpretations for his family term "SNOOT," as mentioned earlier. (The Yiddish use is itself a borrowing from Slavic, and it's possible that Wallace associated the suffix more with Russian, as in *Sputnik*.) Nor was there any use of the affectionate diminutives *-chik,* or *-el(e)* (which may also be combined, as in *boychikel* for a little boy).[38] One of the most common stereotypes of "Yinglish"[39] is the partial-reduplicative *shm-* (as in "fancy-shmancy") (also mentioned in Gold[40]), which minimizes the importance of whatever is referred to, but that is also notably absent in these stories.

Stereotype or no, the elderly Jews portrayed in both "Solomon Silverfish" and "Say Never" sound very much like my maternal Ashkenazi grandparents and their (dozen) siblings. As Gold[41] points out, the linguistic characteristics

---

[37] Bernstein, "More Than Just Yada Yada Yada (Jewish English)."
[38] Ibid.
[39] Ibid., 251.
[40] David L. Gold, "The Speech and Writing of Jews," in *Language in the* USA, eds. Charles A. Ferguson and Shirley Brice Heath (Cambridge and New York: Cambridge University Press, 1989), 273–92, esp. 290.
[41] Ibid., 276.

of the Ashkenazi Jewish immigrants to the United States have largely disappeared, which may make a portrait of such speech seem less realistic to current readers. One reason the story may have struck a chord with me is because it reflects the story of my own family's linguistic and cultural assimilation so well.

With such a strong constellation of marked dialect features in the older generation, it is all the more striking that none of these is maintained by Mrs. Tagus's two sons. The originally unmistakably Jewish *Leonard Shlomith Tagus* and *Michael Arnold Tagus* have turned into the default white *Len(ny)* and *Mike(y)*. Lenny, a professor at Northwestern "who wrote a book about Germans before Hitler . . . that got called Solid and Scholarly in a Review" (208–9), has academic and pompous speech with no ethnic markers even in his internal monologue (e.g., "to describe, probably via the time-tested heuristic pentad" [212] and "I will wait for the arrival of those whose orbits I've decayed" [223]). Becoming a successful academic does require some assimilation into the "Academese" Wallace reviled—though for many academics, this results in bidialectalism, code-switching between the home style and school style. (As more linguistic minorities attain status within higher education, the more "pushback" there is on these linguistic gatekeeping practices.) Becoming "fluent" in Academese did not force Lenny to lose Jewish American speech patterns; he has made a choice about who he wants to be, and how he wants others to see him.

His younger brother Mikey speaks like a working-class white Chicagoan, using *ain't* and negative concord ("She just said how she didn't want to go out no more. . . . And it ain't the brakes, either" [223]). Having dropped out of college, Mikey now works for "the Softball Department of the Chicago Park District" (218–9). As a high school football player, Mikey is reported to have swallowed his tongue (211)—a rather obvious symbol of his loss of his heritage dialect. The class distinction that has opened up between the two brothers is palpable; Mikey notes that his older brother "talks down" to him (215).

The precipitating action in "Say Never" revolves around Lenny's affair with Mikey's girlfriend, Carlina Rentaria-Cruz (a South American discussed in Chapter 2). Lenny is unable to resist the "cinnamon girl" (208), as he repeatedly calls her, despite his full awareness that the relationship is not just hurting his family, but him as well: "She is *wrong* for me" (216, emphasis in the original). On the surface, this sentence is very simple—one short clause with a simple words and an obvious meaning, which the reader, along with everybody in the fictional world, already knows to be true. Yet readers are given multiple clues that the apparent simplicity is deceptive. Not only is the sentence given its own paragraph, but it's perfectly symmetrical in its structure: the five monosyllabic words begin and end with rhyming pronouns, the second and fourth positions are occupied by grammatical function words (copula and preposition), and the adjective at the heart of the sentence, the only content word, the longest word orthographically, has italics for added emphasis, even though it would normally take primary stress in the sentence anyway. (The sentence/paragraph is also placed at the midpoint of the story, the end line of the seventh of thirteen sections, though this centrality would not be apparent in a first reading.)

Why would Wallace apparently work so hard to bring attention to this one sentence? It is certainly possible for a reader to take it at face value and to think no more about it, but any one of the earlier bits of patterning might catch a reader's attention, allowing them an extra moment to really hear those five simple words and think about them. Hayes-Brady[42] mentions Wallace's "tactic of slowing a reader's progress through the narrative," and Shapiro[43] gives a detailed linguistic analysis of how Wallace does this for a phrase in another story, to underline particularly important themes. McGurl[44] reports experiencing a similar moment of pause when he encountered a short sentence amid longer, "amusingly agonized" ones whose "zigzags" take "considerable mental energy to follow," finding that the short sentence that popped out ended up being nonetheless "more obscure in its meaning" than the longer ones. Wallace applies this technique on multiple levels: lexically (establishing a certain register or tone, and then startling readers with a lexical item that distinctly does *not* belong to that register), syntactically (establishing an expectation for long, tortuous sentences, to draw attention to occasional well-placed short simple ones), and (as this monograph argues) with respect to dialects (with many similarly voiced narrators creating a default background against which his nonstandard dialects can stand out sharply).

In this particular case, a momentary pause gives readers time to register a whole host of potential ambiguities: *Wrong* can mean incorrect or mistaken (without any intention behind it, without necessarily even being aware of the mistake), but it can also mean unfair, immoral, even criminal in ways that may be intentional. The adjective primes recognition of the related verb, which would place blame on an associated subject/agent. Carlina *wronged* Mikey; Lenny *is wronging* Bonnie; Lenny knows Carlina will eventually *wrong* him. He later thinks of "that inevitable day" when she will leave him "for a man the color of a fine cigar" (224). The preposition *for* is even more ambiguous.

---

[42] Hayes-Brady, *The Unspeakable Failures of David Foster Wallace*, 140.
[43] Mary Shapiro, "The Poetic Language of David Foster Wallace," *Critique: Studies in Contemporary Fiction* 60, no. 1 (2019): 24–33. DOI: 10.1080/00111619.2018.1441121
[44] McGurl, "The Institution of Nothing," 36.

In the most obvious idiomatic interpretation, Lenny is simply acknowledging that he and Carlina are not well-matched, that their relationship will not last. This attributes no blame, but it does seem to reduce Carlina to a described object. (Although subject of the sentence, she is not an agent, and the only important thing described about her is her effect on Lenny.) *For* can also be used to express an opinion or belief (as in "For me, I think/believe."): Lenny views himself as unable to resist, passive, and therefore in some sense blameless. In his view, she is the one who is (doing) wrong. Similarly, *for* can mark surrogate agency, indicating someone acting instead of the expected or appropriate actor; Carlina's very foreignness represents a level of "wrongness" (Un-Americanness) to which the fully assimilated Lenny can feel superior: she is wrong in place of him. Finally, *for* can indicate the beneficiary of an action: she is doing wrong, but it is for his benefit, his gain. For a thoughtful reader, recognition of any of these ambiguities raises questions of agency, responsibility, and blame, not just with respect to the making, keeping, and/or breaking of commitments to individual people, but also to entire cultures.

The Jews portrayed in this story have none of the "friendly dissociability" that gives "Solomon Silverfish" such a strong sense of community. In that story, characters confronted each other directly, shouting and talking over each other, accusing and counter-accusing, and finally settling on an interpretation that the entire community will accept. It is, ultimately, a joyful story of people coming together, whereas "Say Never" is a very lonely one in which already fragile ties are broken, leaving everyone estranged. Lenny sends a letter to his mother and Mr. Labov to explain the situation (which Mr. Labov does not even receive, and is not even personalized, but Xeroxed), Mikey vents to his friend Louis instead of confronting his brother, and every phone call (Bonnie to her mother-in-law, Mrs. Tagus to Lenny) is portrayed as one-sided. "She is *wrong* for me" makes it perfectly clear that there is no "us" that unites Lenny and Carlina. "She" isn't just different from "me," she's literally on the other side of *wrong*, the two are not just distinct, they are distant.

Although the assimilation of both Mikey and Lenny into default whiteness is seen as natural (indeed, unremarkable), the loss of community is not yet complete. Leonard's wife Bonnie does not get a chance to speak for herself in this story, but when quoted by her husband sounds much like the older generation ("he's about to cry almost the poor love" [214]). Bonnie embodies the Jewishness that Lenny now finds unappealing and suffocating, even as he admires her fundamental goodness. Carlina, on the other hand, represents his total abandonment of that tradition—in fact, she represents total abandon. Readers cannot fail to find Lenny's fetishization of the young woman creepy. He describes her as "silk in a bed of mail-order satin. Complete and seamless, an egg of sexual muscle" (216), and claims that her lips "*manufacture their own moisture*" without help from her tongue (213, emphasis in the original). It is clear that they do not have a real and meaningful emotional connection, that he is causing everyone a great deal of pain in exchange for what can only be temporary sexual pleasure.

Despite the symbolic contrast between Bonnie and Carlina, it is not ultimately the abandonment of Jewish tradition that is presented as problematic. At no point does Mikey's assimilation cause anybody any discomfort or concern. (He has presumably found a new community, as he never appears in the story without his friend Louis.) Lenny's crime is not that he is moving away from Jewishness—it's that he has broken commitments to his wife and three children, betrayed them as well as his brother, which in turn hurts his mother, and even their old friend Mr. Labov, who feels caught in the middle. People matter more than abstract ideas. Although "Solomon Silverfish" shows assimilation *to* a Jewish identity and this story shows movement away from it, they are nevertheless both about how we define ourselves *in relation to* those to whom we have committed ourselves. (There are numerous echoes of this across Wallace's work, perhaps most prominently with Marathe, whose ultimate allegiance in *Jest* is not to any abstract nation or state, but to his wife.) Lenny recognizes that "you're bound up with people" (216). His anxiety is not prompted by abstract ethical or moral concerns, but by the fear that he can never be forgiven for this affair by people he loves. Carlina asks him "who it was who first said never say never," and Lenny replies that "it must have been someone alone" (216).

Total Assimilation

"Westward the Course of Empire Takes Its Way" also exemplifies the "naturalness" of ethnic assimilation into default whiteness, although this is somewhat obscurely buried under the weight of the novella's metafictional playfulness and intertextuality. The story telegraphs its intention to play off Barth's *Lost in the Funhouse* by quoting it as an epigraph and harking back to it in multiple comments such as "Central Illinois is, by no imaginer's stretch, a Funhouse" (242); it features young creative writing students whose teacher is *Funhouse*'s own alter ego for Barth, Ambrose. Boswell[45] discusses the name of the "hero," Mark Nechtr, as containing coded references to Barth (and "nectar" may plausibly trigger associations with "ambrosia"), but it also codes as Jewish, with the common Yiddish "cht" cluster, and the reference in the

---

[45] Boswell, *Understanding David Foster Wallace*, 105.

second paragraph to "health-club franchises" disrupting the "ancient Aryan order," allowing those "who were inherently meant to be pale and weak to appear dark and strong" (233).

Mark's traveling companion, writing program alumnus Tom Sternberg, is clearly identified as Jewish, although his name is more ambiguously Germanic. His mother's (remembered) speech bears traces of Yiddish syntax, as well as the stereotype of the comedically put-upon Jewish mother: "Such as like for example crosses his eyes just to hurt a mother." She has "whatever resources orthodox mothers with lapsed sons access" (280). As in "Say Never," the next generation—in this case, Tom and Mark—is easily assimilated into whiteness, with no linguistic markers of ethnic identity.

Despite its massive size and enormous cast of characters, there are no Jews identified in *Infinite Jest*, a surprising absence in a text in which the entertainment and film industry plays a large role. It's a bit of an uncomfortable truth that there have been few well-known Jewish tennis players (apart from Renée Richards, who was more famous for her gender realignment surgery at a time when transgender identity was seldom discussed publicly than for her tennis prowess), so the absence of Jews at the tennis academy is not so salient, but the absence of Jewish stories at all of the twelve-step meetings for addicts is less understandable. Jewish people must, logically, be there; by the same token, since we cannot distinguish them, they must be fully assimilated.

Infinite Jest features only a little bit of "lower-case jewishness," the common cultural stereotypes that have become part of American culture, not necessarily attached to Jewish bodies or to the practice of Judaism. At a "'Big Buddy' powwow" at the tennis academy, two of the younger boys "rock and bob Hasidically" to stay alert (67). Gately, who is never shown to interact with anybody Jewish, nonetheless unselfconsciously uses *kosher* in his own thoughts (606), and *yutz* in a conversation with Yolanda (565), clearly expecting her as an African American to be equally familiar with the Yiddishism. Hal, talking to Michael Pemulis in the midst of crisis, thinks "I was trying to make my intonation Jewish-motherish, that melodic dip-rise-dip" when he says, "All week: not a call, not a card. Now I should hear this about urgency?" (908). It's interesting that he does not project this intonation pattern onto all, or even most American Jews—it's specifically "Jewish-*motherish*," that is, an older generation fulfilling a specific social role.

In the throes of withdrawal, Poor Tony Krause is "haunted by the word *Zuckung*, a foreign and possibly Yiddish word he did not recall ever before hearing. The word kept echoing in quick-step cadence through his head without meaning anything" (302). (It is, readers learn hundreds of pages later, the sound of his heartbeat: "*zuckungzuckungzuckung*" [721]). In fact, it the *German* word for convulsion or spasm, but it is interesting that Poor Tony is more conscious of Yiddish than German as a general cultural resource, even though he has direct access to neither. Marathe notes that Steeply's undercover assignment as a woman reporter is in keeping with his organization's "latent and sadistic" cover personae, including "casting . . . women as longshoremen or Orthodox rabbinicals" (419), among other unlikely pairings. It was perhaps the persistence of visible ultraorthodox Jewish communities that captured Wallace's imagination—the contrast between the choice to remain separate (as with the Hasidic communities in Brooklyn), the total assimilation of people of Jewish descent, and every intermediate stage in between.

In Wallace's worldview, if someone is holding on to a cultural heritage—such as Jews who have chosen not to assimilate—then by definition, they are not prioritizing membership in the local community; regional identity will therefore not be a major part of their self-identity and will not be manifested in the way they speak. This results in a deliberately blurry distinction between foreigners who have no desire to become American, immigrants who are trying to assimilate (but have not yet fully achieved this), and Americans who are trying to maintain a cultural heritage instead of blending in to a "melting pot." Apart from a couple of short stories built around them, these are minor background characters, yet that does not mean that they are unimportant to Wallace's thematic preoccupations and to his portrait of millennial America.

Regionality and the White Working Class

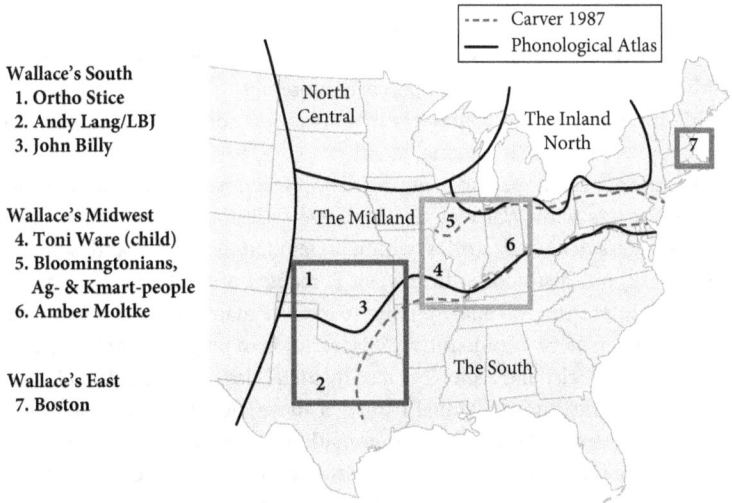

Figure 4 Wallace's Regional Dialects, Situated on the University of Pennsylvania's National Map of US Dialects (Labov, William, Sharon Ash, and Charles Boberg. "A National Map of the Regional Dialects of American English" 1997. https://www.ling.upenn.edu/phono_atlas/NationalMap/NationalMap.html).

Quinn[1] and Foster[2] explored geographical locations in Wallace's work (both real and man-made), making it clear that "the environmental landscape is reflective of the cultural landscape,"[3] but neither includes a discussion of the

---

[1] Paul Quinn, "'Location's Location': Placing David Foster Wallace," in *A Companion to David Foster Wallace Studies*, ed. Marshall Boswell and Stephen J. Burn (New York: Palgrave Macmillan, 2013), 87–106.

[2] Graham Foster, "A Blasted Region: David Foster Wallace's Man-Made Landscapes," in *Consider David Foster Wallace: Critical Essays*, ed. David Hering (Los Angeles and Austin: Sideshow Media Group Press, 2010), 37–48.

[3] Ibid., 47.

linguistic landscape. The speech of Wallace's regional dialect speakers is, like that of the ethnic dialect speakers, differentiated, so that they are never just monolithic representations of some abstract idea, but appear to be real people whose suffering is put on display. At the same time, there is again reductive simplification, with just a few categories illustrating and exemplifying regionality. The Boston setting of *Infinite Jest* essentially stands in for the East Coast (with no prominent characters specifically from New York, New Jersey, etc.), and the main contrast for this is a geographically fuzzy concept of the South Midland dialect area, with a couple of brief forays into the heart of Texas. "The porousness of borders" of named regions is illustrated by Midwestern characters whose speech is more apt to trigger stereotypes of Southernness, and with characters who live on a border, fighting any easy characterization of their regional identity.

The use of actual, specific linguistic dialect features does sometimes evoke real places (as with Wallace's use of Boston-area words and references), rooting characters and stories within a familiar linguistic and semiotic framework, not just adding to the Big-R realism of his fiction, but also—and most interestingly—allowing him to explore many different ideas about individual versus group identity. Wallace's idiolect portrayals are informed not just by ethnicity and region but also by social class and aspirational social roles. The quirky and individual nature of these "not-me" voices stand out contrastively from the pervasive domination of his sound-alike alter ego characters and narrators. Even when brief, they are salient and memorable.

In Wallace's work, ethnicity effectively erases the perception of regional identity and vice versa, as clearly demonstrated through the depiction of characters' dialects. Like some of his characters, Wallace understood that the relationship between ethnic and regional identity is only partially a matter of individual psychology and conscious, deliberate affiliation. The system is also realized and reinforced (if not imposed) at the societal level, as a strategy to ignore and erase "problematic realities," in order to support a dominant ideology.[4] Wallace's portrayal of default, hegemonic whiteness does not appear to celebrate this, but rather points to problematic rifts in US society, illustrating how institutional structures as well as internalized belief systems keep African Americans trapped in ghettos and excluded. His occasional brief sketches are painful reminders of this—periodically poking at wounds that one should not ignore, which will not heal on their own.

---

[4] Judith T. Irvine and Susan Gal, "Language Ideology and Linguistic Differentiation," in *Regimes of Language Ideologies, Politics, and Identities*, ed. Paul V. Kroskrity (Santa Fe, NM: School of American Research Press, 2000), 35–84.

Social Class and the Possibility of Upward Mobility

White characters do not have an ethnic identity to claim, having given up their specific heritages in order to blend into a more default whiteness, but of course they are not all alike. Quite a few regional dialects appear in Wallace's fiction, but it is clear that regional identity is largely a proxy for socioeconomic class in his work. Having regional identity always co-occur with whiteness may have been a deliberate strategy on Wallace's part, but it may also have been influenced by an unconscious internalization of US stereotypes. The disentangling of region and ethnicity has always been difficult for observers. Laferriere[5] finds that Bostonians attribute a phonological feature used most often by Italian-Americans in the region to an Irish accent, hypothesizing that this happens because they have a stereotype of "Boston Irish," but have no equivalent stereotype of "Boston Italians." As Niedzielski and Preston[6] argue, it doesn't really matter what linguists can demonstrate in terms of actual speech production: "What nonlinguists believe constitutes precisely that cognitive reality which needs to be described—one which takes speech community attitudes and perception (as well as performance) into account." In fact, the very idea of a "speech community" was defined by Labov[7] as a group of people who do not necessarily share a particular way of speaking, but who share a set of norms for how various ways of speaking should be judged.

Apart from a very few exceptions, regional dialect tends to be associated in popular culture with the working class, and all the stereotypes associated with poverty. Haugen[8] observes that "it is less customary to speak of 'London dialect' or 'Boston dialect,' except in reference to the lower-class speech of those cities." Fictional representations have bolstered this stereotype, mostly ignoring the regional norms to which the speech of educated characters conform. In the absence of marked dialect patterns, the typical writer "would assume that a reader would take his conventional spelling to mean only that the character spoke according to the commonly accepted standards for educated persons of his own region."[9]

---

[5] Martha Laferriere, "Ethnicity in Phonological Variation and Change," *Language* 55, no. 3 (1979): 603–17.
[6] Niedzielski and Preston, *Folk Linguistics*, 43.
[7] Labov, *Sociolinguistic Patterns*, 158.
[8] Einar Haugen, "Dialect, Language, Nation," *American Anthropologist* 68, no. 4 (1966): 922–35, esp. 924.
[9] Ives, "A Theory of Literary Dialect," 152.

Matched-guise experiments, developed by Lambert et al.[10] and replicated many times in different locations with very consistent results (e.g., Ryan and Giles,[11] Campbell-Kibler,[12] and others discussed by Niedzielski and Preston[13]) have shown that in general, speakers of regional varieties find speakers of their own varieties warm, friendly, honest, sympathetic, and trustworthy (high marks for solidarity), but also as slow, unintelligent, uneducated, and unsuccessful (low marks for social status and prestige). "Standard" speakers, not surprisingly, are judged as cold, dishonest, and unsympathetic (low on solidarity), but quick, intelligent, and ambitious (high on status). These judgments are made on the basis of voice alone, from audio recordings, where what is said is held constant, and with some of the same voices judged under different dialect guises, controlling for physical qualities of the voices. Wallace was certainly aware of the kinds of judgments that get attached to regional dialects, but often, as he did with ethnic dialect representations, deliberately subverted them. In his work, regional dialect is typically associated with lower socioeconomic status, but more often signals rural identity. It is usually associated with a lack of education, but never with lack of intelligence.

That working-class speakers incorporate a higher proportion of stigmatized local features into their speech has long been a staple of regional dialectology; more recent work in quantitative/variationist sociolinguistics has only served to confirm this. This is not a failure of the educational system (as has often been decried) but a predictable consequence of the systems of rewards available to rational speakers. The rewards average people receive from sounding like those around them—social solidarity, in-group acceptance—far outweigh any "status" they would receive from sounding more standard. On the contrary, by orienting toward a presumed "standard" (i.e., an upper-class sociolect), working-class speakers would seem to reject affiliation with friends and family, thus losing the social capital they don't just value but often need to survive. The concept of social class isn't merely "the objective, economic measures of property ownership and the power and control it confers on its possessor," it is also shaped by "the subjective measures of prestige, reputation, and status."[14]

---

[10] Wallace E. Lambert, Richard C. Hodgson, Robert C. Gardner, and Samuel Fillenbaum, "Evaluational Reactions to Spoken Languages," *The Journal of Abnormal and Social Psychology* 60, no. 1 (1960): 44.

[11] Ellen Bouchard Ryan and Howard Giles, eds. *Attitudes Towards Language Variation: Social and Applied Contexts* (London: Edward Arnold, 1982).

[12] Kathryn Campbell-Kibler, "Accent, (ING), and the Social Logic of Listener Perceptions," *American Speech* 82, no. 1 (2007): 32–64.

[13] Niedzielski and Preston, *Folk Linguistics*, 43–4.

[14] Sharon Ash, "Social Class," in *The Handbook of Language Variation and Change*, ed. J. K. Chambers, Peter Trudgill, and Natalie Schilling-Estes (Malden, MA: Blackwell, 2004), 402–22, esp. 403.

Wallace underlined the "Class Distinctions" section of Garner's *Dictionary of Modern American Usage* (124–6), in which Garner quotes American writer Paul Fussell saying that "proles... unselfconsciously engage in poor usage such as double negatives (*I don't have no butter*) and subject-verb disagreements *(he don't have no butter)*." The upper-middle and upper classes, Fussell claims, have "a plain-speaking style." It is the "insecure middle class" whose "language is often inflated." Garner comments that "most usage books are silent on the subject of class," but "typically reflect upper-middle-class preferences, as this book generally does." His rationale for this preference is that "that is the class into which most even modestly intellectual achievers fall, and the class to which the ambitious members of the middle class most aspire."

The linguistic insecurity of the middle class has been amply documented in sociolinguistic literature for the last fifty years (with Labov[15] prescribing research methods that would be used in hundreds of subsequent studies), with research demonstrating not just socioeconomically stratified use of stigmatized dialect variables, but clear patterns of hypercorrection of these among middle-class speakers. (That is, because the actual difference between middle and upper classes is typically a small quantitative difference, middle-class speakers aiming for an upper-class pronunciation will typically overshoot the mark.) Niedzielski and Preston[16] attribute the linguistic insecurity to awareness "that the local variety will not serve extra-regionally"—specifically, it "will not convince some outside listeners that the intelligence, education, and authority of the speaker or writer are high, and it will not, therefore, inspire confidence in the content of some messages."

Araya[17] points to Wallace's "sincere effort to engage with" economic inequality in the contemporary United States, saying this is "perhaps portrayed most painfully in descriptions of Toni Ware's childhood in a trailer park." Cohen[18] refers to this same section of TPK and to the inner dialogue of Lane A. Dean, Jr., in that same novel, saying that "both characters are also arguably as distant from Wallace's own experience as rappers and other speakers of AAVE are. Neither, however, is subject to reproduction of their dialect." Lane appears to come from a middle-class background and is orienting himself toward upward mobility, majoring in business and accounting in college; his language (in so far as it is "heard" in the free indirect discourse narration of sections six and thirty-three) reflects this. (He also quotes from scriptures; the language of religion dominates his thoughts in these sections.) The

---

[15] Labov, *Sociolinguistic Patterns*.
[16] Niedzielski and Preston, *Folk Linguistics*, 44.
[17] Araya, "Why the Whiteness?" 249.
[18] Cohen, "The Whiteness of David Foster Wallace," 240.

choice not to directly represent the dialects of these characters may reflect Wallace's "increasing inclination to use a more subtle free indirect discourse in his fiction,"[19] although it seems more symbolic of Dean's assimilation into corporate upper-class blandness. Eckert[20] notes that the suppression of regional features (and local slang) is commonplace in people aspiring to upward mobility, to positions of the middle-class establishment.

In two different sections of the novel, Toni Ware recounts events from her youth that occurred in Missouri as she and her mother were traveling back to Peoria, after her mother's "succession of bad-news men in the US Southwest" (439). Wallace may have deliberately chosen Missouri in order to focus more on class than regionality per se; Missourians themselves argue about whether the state is Midwestern or Southern. Toni digresses, "somewhere in eastern Missouri" (440), to explain that the word "holler" is used "in the rural sense . . ., which is almost a special kind of art form; it used to be the way that people who lived way out in hill country out of sight of each other would communicate" (440). Section eight of the novel ends with Toni recalling being in a diner "in Plepler MO," overhearing direct dialogue from the waitress and "the workingmen whose names she knew." Apparently, the fictional Plepler (a distinctly uneuphonious name) falls into the "South Midland" dialect region Wallace felt most comfortable with, with the verb "set" for "sit," and sentence-initial *why* (as non-interrogative discourse marker): "What are you settin' in a dirty booth for? . . . Why you could have set over right there and been closer yet" (65). When the woman behind the counter comments on the weather ("Still tootin' out there I see"), Ware responds with the common Southern counterfactual *like to*, indicating something that almost, but did not, occur: "Like to blow me right off the road comin' in" (513). The "counter woman," it is noted, "seemed unaware that Toni Ware was affecting the exact accent and cadence of her own speech" (513–4). Again, it is important to realize that Toni was not local to this area—the younger woman is able to connect with the older one because of their shared *working-class* identities. Williams[21] points to other examples of "Toni's literal embodiment of polyglossia" in the novel, astutely noting that this "seems to perfectly encapsulate and validate Wallace's own attempts at polyphony, and his belief that it was constituent of authentic art."

Both Toni and Lane become IRS agents, and as noted previously, the linguistic assimilation of all the IRS agents is purposeful. Joining this powerful

---

[19] Ibid., 240.
[20] Penelope Eckert, *Linguistic Variation as Social Practice: The Linguistic Construction of Identity in Belton High* (Malden, MA: Blackwell, 2000).
[21] Iain Williams, *"Something Real American": David Foster Wallace and Authenticity*. Ph.D. Dissertation, University of Edinburgh, 2016, 198. https://www.era.lib.ed.ac.uk/bitstream/handle/1842/31007/Williams2016.pdf.

organization has allowed these characters upward mobility, but it has come at the cost of their individual identities, preserved only in the flashbacks to their youth. The often-invoked "American dream" is a rags-to-riches story, but part of the magical transformation necessarily involves speech: someone who sounds "lower class" (i.e., whose speech incorporates regional nonstandard features) will not receive the same respect and acceptance. And thus the hierarchy of identities illustrated in Figure 1 is complete: (1) There are Americans and not-Americans (who can become American); (2) Americans are divided into African American, European and/or Jewish Americans (who can become white), and white; (3) whites are divided into upper class and working class; (4) the working class is divided into regional identities. There is a possibility, however, for upward mobility: the children of the working class who can excel as jocks or nerds can use those identities to recreate themselves, and can do so at an early enough age to easily acquire the upper-class ways of speaking, so that they can "fit in," moving at least from blue collar to white collar, if not to stardom.

The most important caveat about this system of categorization is that none of these distinctions is a moral one in Wallace's work. All of the categories represent the human, and all are worthy of respect and empathy; belonging to one social category as opposed to another is primarily an accident of birth. Social pressures push people from the left side of the diagram to the right side, but the people who are born on the right side or who end up there via assimilation are in no way presented as superior to those on the left side, who may choose to resist the significant assimilatory pressures. In fact, characters who refuse to relinquish their identity (Gerhardt Schtitt, Yolanda Willis, Mr. Labov, and some of the working-class regional speakers discussed in the following chapters) may be seen as more successful (more purposeful, more fulfilled) than others in Wallace's fiction.

The US society is set up so that upper-class white people never have to acknowledge or interact with people from any other categories. Wallace's narrators are limited in their interactions to those who share the same small demographic; as Thompson[22] points out, they "rarely if ever move beyond the confines of their own narrow cultural sphere." It is only through assimilatory pressure that some others come into Wallace's world—and in so doing, they erase their previous other identity. Thus, although there are kids of various ethnic and regional backgrounds at *Jest*'s Enfield Tennis Academy, the "jock" and "nerd" identities embodied simultaneously there are so strong, they appear to erase the possibility of any projection of ethnicity, national, or regional origin.

---

[22] Thompson, *Global Wallace*, 14.

Tennis is and traditionally has been a white-dominated sport (requiring expensive specialized facilities, and therefore not as commonly accessible to poorer communities). By having an elite sports academy also be extremely challenging academically—with students doing at least college-level work in all their classes—Wallace played with both the "jock" and the "nerd" stereotypes. It may be surprising to some readers that one can be both a "mindless" athlete (a "machine") and a brilliant scholar—but it is not at all surprising that both scholarship and tennis are associated with whiteness. In her ethnographic study of a California high school, Bucholtz[23] notes that "nerdiness was ideologically viewed as an extreme version of whiteness, one in which African American culture and language did not play even a covert role." Sadly, she feels the need to add an endnote explaining that "as a result of this ideology, youth of color who engaged in nerdy practices were often understood by other students to be aligned with whiteness or "acting white," although they did not view themselves in this way" (253). The double bind is apparent for regional speakers as well, who may also feel pressure to maintain "nonstandard" usages as a mark of identity, even as they feel insecure about those ways of speaking. Niedzielski and Preston[24] document in various different communities "folk sensitivity to the use of status-related speech which may be taken as 'showing off' or 'putting on airs.'"

It is not surprising that regional voices typically occupy the associated regional space—but in a mobile United States, this is not necessarily the case. Can people still be "Southern" if they *sound* Southern, even if they're living in Boston? Can they be authentically "Midwestern" if they don't *sound* Midwestern, even if they live in rural Illinois? As with ethnicity, Wallace sometimes encoded regional identity in direct dialogue; more often, with regional dialects, he had characters or the narrator comment on someone's dialect. Just as his African Americans code-switch, his regional characters turn up or down their dialect features based on the situation, especially based on whether they're speaking within group or across group lines.

Salient Absences

Gender and Sexuality

The social categorizations in Figure 1 are purportedly gender neutral, but Wallace's characters are not: he tended to default to a male identity the same

---

[23] Bucholtz, *White Kids*, 161–2.
[24] Niedzielski and Preston, *Folk Linguistics*, 147.

way he defaulted to white and American identities. In looking at the quilt of voices Wallace created as symbolic of the larger system, his default maleness makes as much sense as his default whiteness. Obviously, there are men and women within each social category at every level, but Wallace overwhelmingly privileged male perspectives. Hayes-Brady[25] points out that Wallace's "notably few" female characters "are, almost uniformly, engaged in struggles to tell their own stories, either because they have difficulty with language or because someone else is trying to tell their story for them." (Thus, although Lane Dean's girlfriend Sheri is the one faced with the difficult decision of whether or not to bear their child, abandoning her own professional ambitions, her story is filtered entirely through Lane's perspective.) The girls at ETA and the women IRS agents show that it is also possible for women to avail themselves of this same upward-mobility loop in claiming jock or nerd identities, even if their stories are not showcased as often.

Sociolinguistic reality is itself strongly gendered: not only have male voices been privileged in public discourse but quantitative/variationist research has also consistently shown men using higher levels of stigmatized variables in their speech than women in the same region and social class.[26] The ideal respondent of traditional dialectologists is the "N.O.R.M.," the Nonmobile Older Rural Male,[27] as women are believed to be more subjected to and, therefore, more sensitive to social pressures and judgments, and, therefore, less forthcoming with stigmatized speech. When asked to describe their own speech, men will not just admit greater levels of nonstandardness than women will (which might just reflect the greater pressure put on women to conform to social expectations), but men will claim greater levels of nonstandardness than they are demonstrated to use. That is, they boast of breaking the "rules" more than they actually do break them. Trudgill[28] attributes this to "covert prestige"—the solidarity rewards that men give other men for behaving in a way that society overtly says is "bad."

The large body of research into the intersection of language and gender has (until very recently) almost entirely assumed a binary system of gender (as well as a corresponding binary system of biological sex),[29] and for its

---

[25] Hayes-Brady, "'Personally I'm Neutral on the Menstruation Point,'" 65.
[26] Jenny Cheshire, "Sex and Gender in Variationist Research," in *The Handbook of Language Variation and Change*, ed. J. K. Chambers, Peter Trudgill, and Natalie Schilling-Estes (Malden, MA: Blackwell, 2004), 423–43, esp. 426.
[27] Jack K. Chambers and Peter Trudgill, *Dialectology* (Cambridge University Press, 1998), 29.
[28] Peter Trudgill, "Sex, Covert Prestige and Linguistic Change in the Urban British English of Norwich," *Language in Society* 1, no. 2 (1972): 179–95.
[29] Cheshire, "Sex and Gender in Variationist Research," 244.

first several decades also largely ignored questions of sexual identity.[30] Wallace was no more advanced in his understanding of those issues than the academics of his time. Despite a few sympathetic portraits of homosexual relationships—David and René in "Lyndon," Julie and Faye in "Little Expressionless Animals"—Wallace defaulted to heterosexual identities as much as he did to stereotypically male ones. Although *Jest*'s Hugh Steeply seems to be discovering many new things about himself as he maintains his cover as a female journalist, this is not explicitly presented as a coming out story or a discovery of trans identity. When endnote 31 of *Jest* reveals that Schtitt refers to deLint as his "*Lebensgefährtin*," (which according to the endnote "means technically 'soulmate' or 'spouse'" (994), though the literal translation is "life companion"), the idea of the two men being lovers is immediately and emphatically refuted: "But isn't meant at all sexually w/r/t deLint, we can rest assured"). The projection of traditional heterosexual (if not toxic) masculinity in Wallace's own narrative voice will be explored more in Chapter 9.

Age

Wallace's characters tend to have a default age as well, ranging only from adolescent to young adult, leaving salient gaps in this category of identity also. Younger children, the middle-aged, and the elderly are more like "figurants" (nonspeaking background roles in films), seldom speaking for themselves, despite a couple of notable exceptions. Wallace's adolescents, such as Hal and his ETA cohort in *Jest*, but also Lenore and LaVache in *Broom*, Julie and Faye in "Little Expressionless Animals," tend to be freakishly intelligent, but this doesn't always help them to be emotionally mature. As one of the main questions explored throughout Wallace's work is "the establishment of the self among selves,"[31] it makes sense that he would be most interested in adolescents and young adults who would still be struggling with those questions head-on. Younger children may not yet be faced with such existential awareness, and older people have presumably survived as a result of having already established who they are in relation to others. Edilyn in "My Appearance" and Solomon Silverfish are middle-aged—but both have to grapple with some of these same questions. Edilyn, despite having a grown daughter and an established career, is just now coming into her own, just now figuring out who she is and who she wants to be. Solomon Silverfish figured

---

[30] Scott F. Kiesling, *Language, Gender, and Sexuality: An Introduction* (Abingdon and New York: Routledge, 2019).
[31] Hayes-Brady, *The Unspeakable Failures of David Foster Wallace*, 93.

out the answers to those questions long before Wallace's story begins, but has to convince others of his authenticity. Mr. Labov and Mrs. Tagus are elderly, their characters long since established—which is precisely why they are not the central characters of "Say Never," even though the story begins and ends with Mr. Labov. The existential crisis there belongs to Lenny, who is in his mid-thirties.

Unvisited US Regions

Wallace did not attempt to represent every US region, including enough to create an impression of kaleidoscopic heteroglossia, but actually reduced the linguistic landscape to a few exemplars he could explore as archetypes, resulting in some surprising gaps in his representations. Perhaps because regional identity is a much less fraught topic in the contemporary United States, nobody has suggested that these gaps reflect prejudice on Wallace's part.

Although he visits Maine, the title essay of *Consider the Lobster* does not represent the dialect of anybody he spoke with there, although he does include one local lexical item in a footnote: "Midcoasters' native term for a lobster is, in fact, 'bug,' as in 'Come around on Sunday and we'll cook up some bugs'" (*CTL* 237). Likewise, there are no representations of New York City dialects, even when Wallace visited the city for "Democracy and Commerce at the U.S. Open." The most prominent mention of a "New York accent" in Wallace's work comes when Wallace misidentifies a group of speakers as New Yorkers. A long footnote to the title essay of *A Supposedly Fun Thing I'll Never Do Again* (281) refers to the "thick and unmistakable NYC accents" of his tablemates on a weeklong Caribbean cruise, although they "swore up and down that they'd all been born and raised in south Florida." Wallace adds parenthetically that "it did turn out that all [their] own parents had been New Yorkers, which when you think about it is compelling evidence of the durability of a good thick NYC accent." This anecdote is similar to the one in the same essay in which he was ashamed to catch himself thinking that he could identify people as Jewish by the way they look, but in this case (as with the anecdote in "Democracy and Commerce at the U.S. Open," when he misidentifies someone's heritage as Italian), there is no sense of shame. On the contrary, Wallace would seem to be praising his own "good ear," arguing that his tablemates really *do* sound like they're from New York. There is explicit acknowledgment here that a regional-*sounding* accent does not necessarily correspond to the expected region, that it may be performing a different identity altogether.

As noted previously, whiteness is not associated with virtue or intelligence in Wallace's work; it is not inherently positive or negative; it is simply an absence of ethnicity, which can lead to a loss of community, making it harder for people to connect with others. Anyone who thinks the regional dialect speakers in Wallace represent some ideal of the "real" American has missed the point. Working class regional speakers are certainly "real," as are the black Americans who can't assimilate, the Jewish Americans who have chosen not to assimilate, and all the others who exist in a more liminal state. They seem authentic to readers who are not familiar with their dialect, but who accept on faith that Wallace is presenting a realistic portrayal. And it is clear that these "audible" differences keep these "othered" communities as separate and as stigmatized as visible (racial) differences do. The next level of distinction is socioeconomic and geographical. In Wallace's work, Americans are damned if they do, damned if they don't (to echo Lakoff's[32] claim for US women). If they maintain a sense of ethnic or regional identity, they are subject to all kinds of racism and classism, persistent and harmful social and economic inequality. If they are white enough to be allowed to blend into the melting pot, they are pressured into doing so; and if they go along with this, losing their ethnic and regional markers of identity, they are then plagued by loneliness, loss of community, and imposter syndrome. This is what it means to be American—and the fact that Wallace's works are dominated by well-off white protagonists such as Lenore Beadsman and Hal Incandenza and "Dave Wallace" is as much symptomatic of the problem as are the very brief forays into the minds and mouths of Wallace's more marginal and marginalized characters.

Wallace's protagonists seem oblivious to the assimilatory pressures that swirl around them but do not affect them. They have inherited all the privilege of their default whiteness and upper-class status, yet feel empty and alone. Wallace told his NPR interviewer that the impetus for *Jest* was his awareness that he and his friends were "grotesquely overeducated and privileged our whole lives," but were still "extraordinarily sad."[33] Wallace's protagonists try to reject the traps of narcissism and solipsism, but cannot find the community that would allow them to overcome these. This is mirrored linguistically by allowing a single voice speaking the most privileged dialect to dominate, unable to connect with (or sometimes even hear) speakers of other more stigmatized dialects.

Wallace avoided vast swaths of the country—his writing never ventured West of the Rockies, never went into the "deep South," never spent any time in the Upper Midwest (what dialectologists would call North Central dialect

---

[32] Robin Lakoff, *Language and Woman's Place* (New York: Harper & Row/Colophon, 1975), 6.
[33] Gross, "*Fresh Air* Interview with David Foster Wallace."

areas). His brief forays into the "Inland North" territory (setting *Broom* in the suburbs of Cleveland, and his two stories about Jews in the Chicago/Skokie area) mostly avoided the representation of regional dialect, except for the character of Mikey Tagus, who assimilates to the default working-class white regional identity. Mikey, as well as *Broom*'s Texan Andy Lang (and the "real-life" Texans in "Lyndon"), show that a performative regional identity *can* contribute to a sense of community, although this is not very common in Wallace's work. In the same way that ethnic dialects symbolically express internal resistance to assimilation or societal segregation preventing assimilation, regional dialects further illustrate social divisions and what an individual can (and cannot) do to overcome them.

The Underspecification of Identity

The identity of Wallace characters is often underspecified, perhaps deliberately to frustrate readers, to make them realize that the desire to know certain identity characteristics ultimately says more about a reader's own character than it does about the character on the page. Why should it matter whether a given addict in *Infinite Jest* is male or female, black or white, Irish or Jewish, from a particular region—should readers therefore care more or less about the character's pain?

Speakers can't *not* have accents, but characters in stories can; "standard" words written in "standard" grammar need not reveal anything specific about the character. The primacy of face-to-face communication (which is how everybody acquires their native language) trains most people (except the visually impaired and/or neuro-atypical) to interpret visual cues about ethnicity and gender and other identity characteristics, often before interlocutors say a word; sometimes, these judgments need to be adjusted as more is learned about the interlocutors, including the way they speak. Those who overhear an unseen speaker will still automatically, if unconsciously, form impressions of the speaker's identity, based solely on the speaker's phonology: pitch, tone (e.g., "creaky" phonation or vocal fry), intonation, timing, and rule-governed dialect-specific articulations. Wallace's penchant for thrusting readers into a conversation that is already underway, of letting readers "eavesdrop" on a character who is not already known and recognizable, is especially disorienting when the speech does not trigger easy identification of some of the basic identity categories. Readers may find themselves wondering "Who is this?" (What is this person's ethnic identity? Where's this person from? Who is this person in terms of gender, or sexuality, or age?)

Wallace seemed to take pleasure in thwarting readers' ability to practice their accustomed unconscious categorizations, sometimes making them "deal with" characters for hundreds of pages before they can "figure out" the social categories they belong to. Johnette Foltz, for instance, a staffer of Ennet House in *Jest*, is seen on multiple occasions, but is given direct dialogue only once; her ethnicity is never specified. (Physically, she is described only as having a partially removed tattoo and a nose pin.) It is only because the racist residents of Ennet House are able to refer to her without mentioning her race that readers can eventually infer that she is white. Perhaps Wallace was trying to make the point that caring too much about these distinctions can distract people from everyone's basic shared humanity. The more readers get frustrated at not being able to make such easy identifications, the more they should ask themselves why it matters.

In his review of Garner's *A Dictionary of American Usage* (the pretext for, though not the bulk of, A&AU), Wallace realizes that despite the use of "the 1-S pronoun" throughout the work, Wallace has "no idea whether Bryan A. Garner was black or white, gay or straight, Democrat or Dittohead" (*CTL* 119). Somehow, Garner had kept him engrossed without "any sort of verbal style at all." It is this feat, as much as Garner's judgments on particular items of usage, that makes Wallace repeatedly deem Garner a genius. Wallace couldn't fail to appreciate someone who could use language effectively to connect to other people exclusively through an assumed shared love of that language—exactly the goal Wallace had adopted for himself. (Characteristically, Wallace ignored the one element of identity of which he was certainly aware, and which both men shared: their maleness and associated male verbal styles.)

"Everything is Green" (*GWCH* 229–30) is another linguistic Rorschach test for readers. No external description of the narrator, Mitch, is available, although his working-class status (emphasized by the fact that he lives in a trailer park) is revealed through multiple linguistic markers. He uses nonstandard past tense verb forms ("I have gave you," "what I seen"), singular *is* in plural existential constructions ("there is things I know," "in me there is needs," "there is too many needs"), multiple negation ("the whisper is not to me no more"), *got* for *have* in both main verb and auxiliary uses, and the pseudo-reflexive construction "got him some kids." None of these features is diagnostic with respect to regionality. Without any more localized phonological or lexical clues, this could be working-class sociolect in almost any region. It would be an interesting experiment to see if readers make assumptions about Mitch's regional identity (and whether such assumptions are affected by the readers' own identities). Interestingly, the speech of Mitch's younger lover (as presented by Mitch) does not contain any of the same working-class features, which in addition to the repeated age difference between them may be intended to show that the relationship is doomed—although it could simply reflect the realities of "covert prestige" for nonstandard men, as discussed earlier.

Wallace understood that relevant dialect differences are not simple binary distinctions of "standard" versus "nonstandard." Some ethnicities are more accepted into the "melting pot," and there is similarly a hierarchy of prejudices attached to different regional dialects, from highly stigmatized Southern dialects to the rural Midwestern to the East Coast. In "The Suffering Channel," when Skip Atwater believes that the rural Midwestern Amber Moltke is "deferring to him because he lived and worked in New York City, the cultural heart of the nation," he is "absurdly gratified" (*Oblivion* 276). He himself clearly does defer to people with more NYC cred, insecure in his own (ex-)Midwestern identity. As it turns out, he is quite incorrect about Amber, who is considerably more secure linguistically than he is. As Skip puts it, "the whole geographical deference issue could get very complicated and abstract" (*Oblivion* 276). When he does realize that she "might be patronizing him a bit, playing up to a certain stereotype of provincial naiveté," this is neither surprising nor disqualifying, as he recognizes the performativity of regional identity: "He did this himself in certain situations" (*Oblivion* 276).

In representing regional dialect, Wallace grapples with many of the same questions already discussed with respect to ethnic dialects: What kind of group identity can be claimed without any apparent birthright? Who feels pressure to "assimilate" to a local variety to claim in-group membership, or to a supposed "standard" variety to claim authority or status? How does the use of a marked variety vary across social classes, across social and geographical settings? How may a dialect emerge unconsciously in moments of heightened emotion, and how may it be deployed more deliberately to show authenticity and to convey social messages such as affiliation or *dis*affiliation—and how can listeners (or readers) tell the difference? Ironically, Wallace's white rural regional speakers have more in common with his ethnic characters than either group would perhaps imagine or acknowledge.

6

Texan Pride and Southern Shame

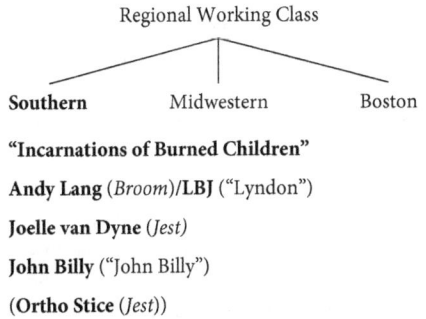

"Incarnations of Burned Children"
Andy Lang (*Broom*)/LBJ ("Lyndon")
Joelle van Dyne (*Jest*)
John Billy ("John Billy")
(**Ortho Stice** (*Jest*))

Figure 5 Wallace's Southerners.

Wallace did not spend much time in the South (in his life or in his art), but his differential treatment of characters Joelle van Dyne (*Jest*), Andy Lang (*Broom*), and John Billy (in the story of the same name) reveals a good deal about Wallace's view of the performative nature of regional identity. These characters' lived experience, the reactions their dialects inspire from others, and the linguistic choices the characters subsequently make are all presented as understandable and natural. Joelle's attempt to completely lose her stigmatized Southern accent is the diametric opposite of the way that Lang uses his Texan-ness as a form of social capital; in neither case, however, do they have complete control over the way that their use of language projects their identities. The "Texan" dialect portraits are especially interesting in that they are the only cases in which Wallace represented regional dialects for characters born into comfortable circumstances.

There is a long tradition of literary representations of Southern dialects. Skaggs[1] compared Southern dialect representations in the work of Joel Chandler Harris, claiming that he was the only Southern writer of his time beside Mark Twain "who could make subtle social distinctions between two characters by using two different dialects." Such portraits, however, were

---

[1] Skaggs, *The Folk of Southern Fiction*, 211.

often mocking, as discussed in the Chapter 1. William Faulkner said in a lecture that he would not portray "the false heartiness of 'slang and our "hard" colloquialisms,' since that was to ape the poverty of the inarticulate."[2] Mair[3] points out that in Steinbeck's *Grapes of Wrath*, the dialect of the Okies "connotes honesty and human worth, not poverty, backwardness, and lack of education," although this may still allow the reader to feel "doubly smug," as discussed in Chapter 1.

Flannery O'Connor was the Southern author apparently most important to Wallace; he kept her books on his shelf, annotated with his characteristic marginalia, brought her up (unasked) in multiple interviews,[4] and assigned her stories to his students. Her influence on his fiction has been traced by Thompson.[5] It is all the more interesting, then, that Wallace's Southerners do not sound like O'Connor's. According to Rubin,[6] O'Connor "draws upon one of the oldest devices of southern humor: the contrast of the literary language of culture and the vernacular language of uneducated speech." Wallace turns the joke around on the reader, not laughing at the "vernacular" speakers, but at readers' expectations of them. As with the depictions of AAE, readers are confronted with their own (in at least some cases unconscious) prejudices, not just to make them squirm, but to force some recognition of how ridiculous and unfair these prejudices are, how they interfere with the human connection we crave and should be capable of.

Bailey and Tillery[7] recognize that Southern American English is "the regional dialect that is most negatively evaluated" across the country, perhaps a lasting echo of the Civil War that still resonates today. Perceptual dialectology studies have shown that the connection between salience and harsh judgment is not coincidental: "Areas perceived as least correct have greatest distinctiveness."[8] In Fought's[9] perceptual dialectology study of California college students, students labeled Southern areas "country sounding" as well

---

[2] Louis D. Rubin, Jr., *A Gallery of Southerners* (Baton Rouge: Louisiana State University Press, 1982), 22.
[3] Mair, "Literary Sociolinguistics," 11.
[4] Lipsky, *Although of Course You End Up Becoming Yourself*, 81; McCaffery, "An Expanded Interview with David Foster Wallace," 50; and Miller, "The Salon Interview: David Foster Wallace," 62.
[5] Thompson, *Global Wallace*.
[6] Rubin, *A Gallery of Southerners*, 116.
[7] Guy Bailey and Jan Tillery, "The Lone Star State of Speech (Texas)," in *American Voices: How Dialects Differ from Coast to Coast*, ed. Walt Wolfram and Ben Ward (Malden, MA: Blackwell, 2006), 11, 36–41.
[8] Niedzielski and Preston, *Folk Linguistics*, 57.
[9] Carmen Fought, "California Students' Perceptions of, You Know, Regions and Dialects?" in *Handbook of Perceptual Dialectology*, vol. 2, ed. Dennis Preston and Daniel Long (Amsterdam: John Benjamins, 2002), 113–34, esp. 128.

as "redneck, rancher, hillbilly, crude, unsophisticated, terrible, and lazy." While stereotypes of the upper-class Southern belle and Southern gentleman are still occasionally invoked, associated with gentility and courtliness, the more common stereotype is of poverty, ignorance, and belligerence, a tradition that McIlwaine[10] demonstrates goes back in American literature to the eighteenth century. McWhiney[11] cites the observation of a British woman traveling through the south in the nineteenth century that "however violent may be the discussion, the courtesy of the 'sir' is never omitted." In an experimental study, Kinzler and DeJesus[12] found that linguistic prejudices are already fully formed by ages nine to ten, with children in both Illinois and Tennessee evaluating the "Northern-accented" Illinoisans as sounding "smarter" and "in charge," and the Southern-accented Tennesseans as sounding "nicer." It may seem somewhat paradoxical that Southern speech is associated both with "ignorance and belligerence" and with "exaggerated courtesy" or "being nice," but as Johnstone[13] points out, "the presence of the kinds of elaborate deferential politeness we have seen indicates the need for them."

Outsiders may understand a speaker despite a stigmatized accent (and in the case of Wallace's fiction, the phonology of the dialect may not be represented on the page at all), but they may find unfamiliar lexical items completely opaque in meaning, even with some context clues. Carver[14] notes that the "relative insularity" of the South led to the preservation of a high number of relic terms (words that come from older dialects of English but are no longer used in the same form in other dialects of modern English) and "an unusually high number of regionalized terms."

The notion of a uniform Southern dialect is recognized by dialectologists as a "convenient fiction"; it is, rather "a quilt-work of dialects,"[15] not surprising for such a large geographical region. Pederson[16] names eighteen different

---

[10] Shields McIlwaine, *The Southern Poor-White from Lubberland to Tobacco Road* (Norman: University of Oklahoma Press, 1939).
[11] Grady McWhiney, *Cracker Culture: Celtic Ways in the Old South* (Tuscaloosa: University of Alabama Press, 1988), 163.
[12] Katherine D. Kinzler and Jasmine M. DeJesus, "Northern = Smart and Southern = Nice: The Development of Accent Attitudes in the U.S.," *Quarterly Journal of Experimental Psychology* 66, no. 6 (2013): 1146-58, esp. 1146. doi: 10.1080/17470218.2012.731695
[13] Barbara Johnstone, "Features and Uses of Southern Style," in *English in the Southern United States*, ed. Stephen J. Nagle and Sara L. Sanders (Cambridge: Cambridge University Press, 2006), 189-207, esp. 196.
[14] Craig Carver, *American Regional Dialects* (Ann Arbor: University of Michigan Press, 1987), 94.
[15] Ibid., 93.
[16] Lee Pederson, "Dialects," in *The Cambridge History of the English Language, vol. 6: English in North America*, ed. John Algeo (Cambridge: Cambridge University Press, 2001), 253-90.

Southern varieties. Wallace was aware of this in the abstract, though he was undoubtedly fuzzy on the distinctions. The only reference to a generic "Southern accent" in Wallace's work is when Mario Incandenza (who is characterized as innocent of spirit, but not particularly intelligent) is "trying to fake" one in *Jest* (122). The acknowledged linguistic diversity in the region may make an author's job a bit easier, if (like Wallace) the intention is to use dialect more symbolically than realistically: A vague "Southernness" can be evoked by using of one or more of the features common across Southern dialects. Schneider[17] provides several options: "The pronoun *y'all*, the use of double modals like *might could* . . . the use of perfective *done*, counterfactual *like to*" (indicating that an event could have, but did not actually, occur). Bailey and Tillery[18] also include the near future intentional *fixin' to*.

Ironically, although most people believe they know it when they hear it and it is the most salient and stereotyped feature of Southern speech in the United States, "neither laypeople nor linguists have a clear, unified notion" of what constitutes a "Southern drawl."[19] Carver[20] observes that "the so-called Southern drawl and the much parodied 'y'all' are features on most of our 'mental' dialect maps." Vowel systems are also literally moving targets, changing more quickly over time than consonants. For decades, linguists have been tracking the "Northern Cities Chain Shift," a series of six different vowel changes (each change triggering the next in the chain) that has affected the large cities of the Inland North around the Great Lakes, from Chicago to upstate New York. There is an even more complicated but entirely distinct series of changes known as the "Southern Vowel Shift," and large parts of the country are participating in neither set of changes.[21] All the different pronunciations that result from these changes would be very difficult to capture using the English alphabet, which has only five vowel letters with which to encode dozens of different dialectal variant vowel pronunciations. Next to the Southern vowel shift, the most salient part of a "Southern" accent (to more Northern ears) is its traditional "r-lessness," although Davies[22]

---

[17] Edgar Schneider, "Shakespeare in the Coves and Hollows? Toward a History of Southern English," in *English in the Southern United States*, ed. Stephen J. Nagle and Sara L. Sanders (Cambridge: Cambridge University Press, 2006), 17–35, 29.
[18] Bailey and Tillery, "The Lone Star State of Speech (Texas)."
[19] Rachael Meghan Allbritten, *Sounding Southern: Phonetic Features and Dialect Perceptions*. PhD Dissertation, Georgetown University, 2011, iii.
[20] Carver, *American Regional Dialects*, 93.
[21] William Labov, *Principles of Linguistic Change: Internal Factors* (Oxford: Blackwell, 1994).
[22] Catherine Evans Davies, "'We Digress': Kathryn Tucker Windham and Southern Storytelling Style," *Storytelling, Self, Society* 4, no. 3 (2008): 167–84, esp. 179.

points out that "as younger Southern speakers adopt r-fulness, this accent is fading into Southern history."

The "Porousness" of Regional Borders

Although no geographical setting is specified for "Incarnations of Burned Children,"[23] and the speech of the narrator does not directly encode Southern phonology, Wallace apparently wrote it with some variety of Southern dialect in mind. His letter to a translator dated June 20, 2001, urges her to "keep in mind that the story's narrated in something like the rural 'voice' of a semiliterate Southern US male," and explains *twangy* as "an adjective that both connotes the 'twangy' guitars Country music uses and the 'twang' of a Southern accent—most Country musicians are Southern and their accent has a 'twang'" (HRC Wallace Papers, container 31.8).

The story, the letter says, "while short, seems to me almost impossible to translate, mostly because of the very large number of non-standard and very English-specific punctuation and syntax devices." It is "the non-standard English stuff that (in my opinion) gives the story its power," Wallace added. The non-standardness of the (default white) rural narrator is much more subtle than his attempt at AAE in Clenette's internal monologue, although the frequent repetition of very simple vocabulary and names is reminiscent. The story is one long paragraph, with a couple of very short sentences ("If you've never wept and want to, have a child") mixed in with extremely long sentences that trap the reader as witness to a seemingly inescapable and increasingly horrible sequence of events that inflicts excruciating pain and suffering on a baby. That the narrator is both wise and poetic (e.g., "its self's soul so much vapor aloft") is in no way seen as incongruous with Wallace's characterization of him as "semiliterate."

Wallace often gave real geographical reference points but generally preferred fictional settings and hometowns, playing with regional boundaries, stressing the allegiance of characters (other than his Texans) to particular towns, not States or larger abstract regions. Thus, for example, *Jest*'s Ortho Stice hails from Partridge, Kansas, a fact that is repeated over a half dozen times. The real Partridge is not "a part of southwest Kansas that might as well be Oklahoma" (100), nor is it "just outside Liberal KS on the Oklahoma border" (628); it is much closer to Wichita, in the center of the state. My

---

[23] "Incarnations of Burned Children," *Esquire* (April 20, 2009). https://www.esquire.com/entertainment/books/a500/incarnations-burned-children-david-foster-wallace-0900/.

guess is that Wallace couldn't resist being "just outside Liberal," and was playing with the "porousness of borders" with respect to regions. It's possible that the name is an homage to lexicographer Eric Partridge, whose famous *Usage and Abusage* (1942) Wallace praised in A&AU for its "mordant pith" (*CTL* 80). That Wallace may have been playing with the name of the town is made more likely by the obvious playfulness in the naming of the character: *Ortho* meaning *straight* or *upright*, and *Stice* evoking *interstice*, a small place in-between. (Note that *Ortho* is the character's given name, as his nickname is "(The) Dark(ness).")

In the minds of most Americans, Kansas is quintessentially (flatly) Midwestern, "a reservoir of middle-class, Midwestern rural values," and "one of the more typical parts of the region."[24] Yet the description of Stice's accent as "flat and twangy" (189) necessarily evokes Southernness. He also pronounces *tired* "tard" (99, 100), uses adverbial *real* ("It's real short-sighted" 104), and "drops the G" in "studyin'" (101). "The Darkness" is a liminal character, both quintessentially Midwestern, yet Southern at the same time, just as the young people of ETA can be both jock and nerd. The social categories that we impose on ourselves and others are not fixed and immutable; some people are trapped in between, and some people may manage to transcend them.

Joelle van Dyne

Joelle van Dyne is the only Wallace character who intentionally loses a native accent. Earlier typescript drafts of *Infinite Jest* had Joelle's hometown as "Meyer, Arkansas," with Joelle being asked (by her boyfriend's mother) "to describe rural Arkansas"—with the correction "Kentucky" handwritten in the margin (HRC Wallace Papers, container 16.7). Another early draft fragment (container 16.6) shows some inconsistency about her origin, with her father described as "Mr. van Dyne of Shiny Prize Kentucky," but with Joelle saying to Gately, "In Arkansas? Meyer, where I'm from, originally?" In this latter draft, Joelle uses *y'all* and the verb *scudge*, but neither of these lexical items makes it into the final draft. Wallace didn't have to change much about the way Joelle speaks, despite his decision to change her home state, since what stands out about her speech is her avoidance of markers of Southernness.

---

[24] Leo E. Oliva, "Kansas: A Hard Land in the Heartland," in *Heart Land: Comparative Histories of the Midwestern States*, ed. James H. Madison (Bloomington: Indiana University Press, 1988), 248–75, esp. 253.

On the radio as "Madame Psychosis," Joelle has "the accent of someone who's spent time either losing a southern lilt or cultivating one," in the opinion of Hal (who is always interested in and extraordinarily sensitive to language). He adds that "it's not flat and twangy like Stice's, and it's not a drawl like the people at Gainesville's academy" (189). Joelle's pre-suicide-attempt confessional monologue ("I want to tell you everything") includes the boast that "I now have no accent except under stress" (234). The narrator, however, contradicts this claim, observing that she has "the elisions and apical lapses of a mid-Southern accent" (299), and later further specifying "a strange and it turns out Kentuckian lapse in the pronunciation of all apicals except *s*" (366). ("Apicals" are sounds articulated with the tip of the tongue, including /t,d,n,l,s,z/. Wallace does not explain this to readers, not even deeming it worthy of an endnote, although it is hardly part of the popular language-related terminology wielded by nonlinguists.) Gately also finds her accent "just barely Southern" (366), "slightly Southern" (368).

Ironically, although Joelle has apparently gone to some effort to lose the accent, the hint that remains (unbeknownst to her) is generally approved of and found attractive. Joelle is described by her former boyfriend Orin as the "Prettiest Girl of All Time," so it is possible that people meeting her in person would be so overwhelmed by her physical attractiveness (despite her appearing only veiled later in the novel) that they would find her attractive regardless, but as the radio personality Madame Psychosis, her voice can be judged on its own merits. Although Joelle is proud of *not* having a southern accent, her self-consciousness about this may keep her silenced her to some degree. She is able to speak fluently and comfortably as Madame Psychosis, but not as Joelle van Dyne. Hayes-Brady[25] attributes Wallace's "silencing" of women to a "lack of engagement with female characters . . . palpable throughout his work," but it seems entirely plausible that Joelle's linguistic insecurity is the culprit of her silencing, much as she has consciously chosen to hide her face.

Later in the novel, after Gately has been wounded, Joelle has a clearly symbolic dream, in which she finds herself physically unable to speak as Gately performs a dental exam on her, and assures her that her teeth (which she fears destroyed by cocaine) can be saved. In the dream, Gately is "unhurt and mid-South-accented" (724). Despite the unpleasantness and discomfort many people associate with dental exams, Joelle is clearly comforting herself that Gately himself "can be saved," that he will help her in *her* recovery, and that the meaningful connection they have already

---

[25] Hayes-Brady, *The Unspeakable Failures of David Foster Wallace*, 167.

begun to forge will grow, which her unconscious frames as him speaking with her native dialect. Speech convergence is in fact one of the ways we show solidarity and affiliation, even love, although it would be surprising for someone to switch regional dialects quite so dramatically. Gately, who has never left the Boston area, cannot realistically adopt a Southern dialect; the dream may illustrate her fantasy that he could accept *her* speaking in her native dialect, accept her in all her identities. Consciously, she believes she can change her identity by changing the way she speaks; unconsciously, she recognizes that she has not achieved the desired change, that there are some boundaries on such performative identity construction, that she is—at least temporarily, like a dental patient—unable to speak freely. Gately's reciprocal dream of Joelle pictures the two of them about to have sex "in a Southern motel . . . in the U.S. South" (846), again illustrating both that she has not really lost her accent, and that Gately does, indeed, find the accent attractive. She "whispers" to him in the dream, rather than speaking aloud, "promising him a P.M. of near-terminal pleasures" (847). She must actually have said "P.M.," too, as the dream has her finally removing her veil to reveal the face of former British prime minister Winston Churchill. (This is a good candidate for an instance in which Wallace simply could not resist a pun.)

Although Joelle teases Gately about his accent, he never mocks hers. This asymmetry may be due to their mutual awareness of class issues—Gately's Boston-blue-collar dialect being unmistakably working class, while Joelle's effaced accent could pass for an upper-class Southerner—but it may also be a subtle reminder of her linguistic insecurity and therefore also proof of his sensitivity toward and protectiveness of her.

"Texan": Andy Lang and LBJ

Despite popular stereotype (and "evidence" from TV and film), there isn't actually a distinct Texas dialect. As Bailey and Tillery[26] note, "The uniqueness of TXE [Texas English] is probably more an artefact of the presence of Texas in the popular imagination than a reflection of linguistic circumstances." Only a few features of Texas speech are unique to the state; they cite specifically local lexical items and the use of /ar/ for /or/ in *horse, for*, and so on. Johnstone[27] notes that "Anglo-Texans tend to think of themselves primarily as Texans and Americans, and as Southerners only incidentally." But the state of which they

---

[26] Bailey, and Tillery. "The Lone Star State of Speech (Texas)."
[27] Johnstone, "Features and Uses of Southern Style," 200.

are so proud is not at all uniform, linguistically, even among just the Anglo-Texans. Atwood[28] shows that a major dialect boundary runs longitudinally through the state, dividing East Texas from West Texas; nor is there uniformity within each half, even ignoring the differences associated with the ethnic segregation in the state, with North Texas dominated by Anglo-Americans and South Texas by Mexican-Americans.

Wallace's general lack of familiarity with Texas and the South did not discourage him from taking a stab at what he thought might sound like a realistic central, Anglo "Texas" dialect in his first novel. Wallace also mimicked the speech of President Lyndon Baines Johnson in "Lyndon" (*GWCH*), but there he had an historical Texan figure and actual idiolectal patterns to use as a target. It may be that he already had that model in mind when writing *Broom*; the main difference between Wallace's portrayals of Andy Lang and President Johnson is that Wallace attributed a great deal more profanity and general vulgarity to the latter. Wallace did not meet Texan poet Mary Karr (with whom he became obsessed) until several years after his literary representations of Texan speech had been published; his familiarity with her speech patterns, and whatever feelings he may have had about her, could have no influence on these, although it has been suggested that Joelle's character is based on her[29] and that his desire to impress her was a driving force behind the creation of *Jest*.[30]

Andy Lang, Wallace's first extended dialect portrait, was born into wealth in "Nugget Bluff, Texas," another fictional town. He does not feel any pressure to change the way he speaks; on the contrary, he is able to leverage his dialect to support his privilege, proudly identifying as "the Texan" when he goes to a private East Coast college. When he is first introduced, it is not clear if he has a regional dialect or is just slurring his words because he is drunk. Lenore (who is from Ohio) notes that "Lang's [voice] is soft and smooth and nice, although he does seem to fall in and out of some sort of accent, at times" (15). The "although" is telling: in her view, at least, "an accent" would work against a voice being "nice." Andy's nickname at college is "Wang-Dang," a ridiculous rhyme, but also a constant reminder of his maleness, evoking crudeness but also a modicum of polite restraint (as "dang" is a mild, minced oath, and "wang" is a fairly gentle euphemism for a penis).

---

[28] E. Bagby Atwood, *The Regional Vocabulary of Texas* (Austin: The University of Texas Press, 1962).

[29] Max, *Every Love Story Is a Ghost Story*, 177.

[30] Megan Garber, "David Foster Wallace and the Dangerous Romance of Male Genius," *The Atlantic Monthly* (May 9, 2018). https://www.theatlantic.com/entertainment/archive/2018/05/the-world-still-spins-around-male-genius/559925/.

Wallace signals Lang's "Texan-ness" so frequently that it is by far the most important feature of this character. Not only does the narrator refer to him in passing as "the Texan" (259), and a character (who is a stranger to Lang) call him "Tex" (512), but practically every word that comes out of Lang's mouth is also intended to remind us. Nonstandard spelling is consistently used to show monophthongization of aɪ̂ (*high* as "hah" [14], *might* as "maht" [16], "requahred" [19], "fahv" [19], etc.) in a way that Wallace seldom indulges in again with other dialect portrayals—capturing one of the two phonological traits that most Southern US dialects have in common.[31] The other is the "pen"/"pin" merger (neutralizing the difference between lax vowels ɛ/ɪ before nasals), which Wallace does not capture, although he does include a few other "folksy" pronunciations such as *naw* (259) and *figger* for "figure" (19). There is also orthographical encoding of deletion of unstressed syllables—*spiritchul* (14), *unfortchnit* (18) *'nitiation* (19), *more'n* that (306), *'fore* (472)—and substitution of alveolar nasal for velar not just in -*ing* suffixes (*sayin'* [478], *goin'* [491], *makin'* [510], *hopin'* [515]), but also in the compound indefinite noun *somethin'* (508). These casual pronunciations are fairly common in all US dialects, but Hall-Lew and Stephens[32] observe that "features that index informality in general may simultaneously index layered meanings of both Southernness and rurality." Encoding such informal features visually allows Wallace to enhance the perception of Lang's speech as nonstandard, despite also giving him the chance to show some variation within the character's speech—for example, occasional velar pronunciation of the suffix -*ing* as in *getting* (477, 491).

Lang's phonology is matched by his nonstandard morphology and syntax. He frequently uses adverbial *real, good, awful,* and *easy* (*real sorry* [15, 455], *real nice* [257], *didn't get along too good* [261], *I know her pretty good* [262] *take them awful seriously* [451], *like a chainsaw, that could cut you up as easy as some tree* [451]) , and nonstandard superlatives (*doublest chin I ever did see* (345), *beautifulest* [267, 293]). Several other nonstandard features—unmarked third-person singular negative auxiliary *don't* (*she don't remember me* [295]), use of *ain't* (*ain't she?* [295]), nonstandard wh-question formation (*whyn't you*) . . . (515), and coordinate subject *me* (*Sometimes me and Daddy just take a while to see eye to eye* [437])—appear only once each in his dialogue, but work with the more frequently used features to cumulative effect.

---

[31] Bailey and Tillery, "Sounds of the South," 13.
[32] Lauren Hall-Lew and Nola Stephens, "Country Talk," *Journal of English Linguistics* 40, no. 3 (2012): 256–80, esp. 266.

Lang's frequent use of the phrase *little lady* is certainly intended to register as sexist (he also calls Lenore *sugar doll* [500]), but he also refers (as a grown man) to his *Daddy* (throughout), and calls a minister *padre* (315, 346). There is some exaggerated politeness, as when he calls Lenore's father *Sir* and refers to her as *Miss Lenore* (515), and calls two young women *Ma'am* (15, 312). He says he would *be obliged* (15, 18), and euphemizes swearing in some instances, as in *shoot* (436) and the use of *dung beetle* as insult (439). In other contexts, he is happy to curse more openly, as in *Sheeit* (257, 262), *Shit on fire* (304, 346, 449), and *Christ on a Kawasaki* (305).

Naturally, there are also words and phrases that are also intended to signal down-home/folksy/ Texan identity: *Yes indeedy* (296), *just a tinch* (297), *can't say as . . .* (305), *hold up . . . whoa there* (458). He frequently ends clauses with *and all*, calls a male stranger *bud* (508, 512), uses the verb *to git* (*You better just git!* (511), *Let's just git. . . . Let's git* [439, 513]). His expressions of surprise are *I will be dipped and fried and completely goddamned* (262) and *I will be slapped, pinched, and rolled* (267).

Of the nonstandard grammatical features that Bailey and Tillery[33] claim "remain robust" in Southern dialects, generally, Lang uses only *y'all*. Double modals, *fixin' to*, perfective *done*, and counterfactual *like to* do not appear. Presumably, Wallace was simply unfamiliar with these and, even from the start of his writing career, saw the use of dialect as symbolic rather than mimetic. In this, his first extended portrayal of nonstandard dialect (and one of the very few to use altered spellings to encode nonstandard phonology) the dialect demonstrates and reinforces the speaker's pride and privilege and is called out explicitly in the novel as a self-conscious performance. After they've finally succumbed (somewhat) to a mutual attraction, Lenore asks Lang, "What happened to the way you talk all of a sudden? Why aren't you saying stuff like, 'Well, strap me to the hind end of a sow and sell me to Oscar Meyer?'" (464). Lang laughs at Lenore's imitation of his speech, and acknowledges in his most extended *standard* utterance, "I guess maybe we all talk differently with different people. The good old boy stuff is what I grew up on, and then at school I was from Texas and so everybody expected this sort of talking, and so it kind of became my thing, at school" (465). (Note here not just the *absence* of supposedly Texan lexical items and exaggerated politeness, but the use of the velar pronunciation of the *-ing* suffix and the derivational adverbial *-ly* suffix.)

Lang's "Texan" is inauthentic, not just because Wallace didn't know enough about central Texas speech to mimic the dialect realistically, but because

---

[33] Bailey and Tillery, "The Lone Star State of Speech (Texas)."

Lang, a member of the mobile upper class, is self-consciously exaggerating regional features to perform the voice of the white working class. At the same time, readers can believe his explanation, since readers also quickly come to "expect this sort of talking." Thus, his motivations appear pure: he is trying to perform the identity that others want from him, trying to please his audience. His ability to drop the act with Lenore is a sign of their new intimacy, as is the fact that she notices the change before any reader could. (There is no apparent change in his way of speaking until Lenore points out her perception of it.)

John Billy

Wallace's only extended first-person narrator with a regional dialect is in the story "John Billy," one of Wallace's favorites in the GWCH collection.[34] The story is labeled a "faux mythic narrative" by Thompson,[35] and is seen as "inflating lyric voices found in the literature of the American South, from William Faulkner to Cormac McCarthy."[36] Boswell[37] judges it "a serious attempt . . . to explore the role of myth and the metaphysics of identity" (86).

Wallace's friend Gale Walden recounted how on their road trip to Tucson,

> Wallace listened to the southwestern accents. . . . "He started to talk out 'John Billy' at rest stops," Walden remembers. "He was trying to get the cadences of the dialogue down." . . . That the story was not easy to read mattered not at all to Wallace; all he cared about was the sentences.[38]

As noted in Chapter 1, Walden also reminisces that "John Billy" was inspired by William Gass's *Omensetter's Luck*. In that novel, Gass employs free indirect discourse with three different narrators, and also avoids respelling to indicate phonology. Gass's fictional 1890s rural Ohio town is clearly supposed to be Appalachian, and readers can infer that Wallace's fictional "Minogue, Oklahoma" is set in the Ozark dialect area (on the Eastern side of Oklahoma, near the Osage Reservation, to which the story obliquely refers). Similarities

---

[34] Max, *Every Love Story Is a Ghost Story*, 131.
[35] Thompson, *Global Wallace*, 208.
[36] Ellerhoff, "Proteus Bound," 120.
[37] Boswell, *Understanding David Foster Wallace*, 85.
[38] Max, *Every Love Story Is a Ghost Story*, 74.

between Appalachian English and Ozark English are well known.[39] But if Wallace was inspired by Gass, he certainly was not mimicking him; the dialect in "John Billy" is like the dialect of *Omensetter's Luck* on steroids. Gass's novel has many fewer dialect markers, and those that are incorporated (notably adverbial *real*, preference for past tense *was* for all person/number combinations of subject, items that are marked but not highly stigmatized) occur with far less frequency. Situating this story in the Ozarks allows Wallace some fuzziness with respect to regions (and the dialects and stereotypes one might associate with them). The Ozarks are usually deemed "Southern" (the "Upper South" rather than the "Lower South" in Schneider's[40] terms), although the largest part of the mountain range is in Southern Missouri, which is considered by some (including by many of my Missouri students) as "Midwestern."

Wallace undoubtedly greatly enjoyed refining the distinct idiosyncratic voice he created for the story, but he was also aware of and responding to a tradition of Southern storytelling, which Davies[41] claims to be characterized by digression: "Associations of thought are encouraged." Boswell[42] also points out the parodying of John Barth's stylistic tic, in *Lost in the Funhouse*, of using "etc." over and over again.

The eponymous narrator in "John Billy," who claims a white identity by distinguishing himself from both the "neighboring reservation's Native Americans" (125) and a "nigra" on the visiting team (126), has an enormous and erudite lexicon and a very strong regional dialect. Nor is this combination seen as extraordinary in the context of the story: one of his friends, Glory Joy, likewise juxtaposes lofty vocabulary such as *recalcitrant* with the regularized reflexive pronoun *hisself*, and another, T-Rex, casually specifies "macrocosmic speculation" as the intended direct object of "We done some together" (143). The point is not that this is an "authentic" Oklahoman performance, but that there is no reason that highly intelligent and educated people shouldn't continue to use the dialect that best encodes their personal identity and feels most comfortable to them. If the juxtaposition of "highbrow" words with "lowbrow" grammar and vulgarity strikes readers as incongruous or funny at first, challenging their stereotypes, the consistency of the presentation over twenty-six pages should undermine that response.

---

[39] Donna Christian, Walt Wolfram, and Nanjo Dube, "Variation and Change in Geographically Isolated Communities: Appalachian English and Ozark English," National Science Foundation Report, 1984. https://files.eric.ed.gov/fulltext/ED246682.pdf
[40] Schneider, "Shakespeare in the Coves and Hollows?" 20.
[41] Davies, "We Digress," 175.
[42] Boswell, *Understanding David Foster Wallace*, 87.

O'Connor featured "narration from outside and above, in which an educated, sophisticated storyteller writes about simple vernacular characters for the edification of readers who are not simple rustics but likewise persons of education and sophistication";[43] Wallace, on the other hand, lets the vernacular speaker speak for himself, to prove that *he* is a person of education and sophistication. Boswell[44] says that this story "employs the full range of Wallace's linguistic virtuosity," referring specifically to the title character's "more than a little syntactical inventiveness," but also notes that "the gag here is that neither Glory Joy nor John Billy would be aware of such terms as 'mythopoeic'" (87). In part, I disagree, this is only *part* of the gag, which works on several levels (and like many of Wallace's jokes is simultaneously deep and dark). The sad underlying truth is that people are routinely discouraged from higher education because of their dialect; Wallace understood that there is no reason other than social pressure that these linguistic features should not co-exist. So the rest of the joke is on the reader who *assumes* that the local population of Minogue, Oklahoma wouldn't know such terms. As with other dialect portrayals, Wallace triggers readers' sense of superiority and negative judgment only to pull the carpet out from under them.

The opening line of the story contains multiple prescriptive "errors," pretty much guaranteeing a strong knee-jerk reaction from SNOOTs: "Was me supposed to tell Simple Ranger how Chuck Nunn Junior done wronged the man that wronged him and fleen to parts unguessed." The same narrative framing device ("Was X (did Y)") is used seventeen times throughout the story, seeming quite familiar by the end. *Ain't* is used several times, but more noticeable is the frequent use of auxiliary and copular *was* with plural subjects, for example, "We was on exhibit to animals" (142), or "after they was busted" (143)). Wallace winks a bit at readers with "things was dark and singular" (145)—because *things* is plural, though the agreement is, indeed, singular.

Ozark English does have a preference for past tense *was* with all person/number combinations of subject, as illustrated in Christian, Wolfram, and Dube,[45] although again, there is no evidence that Wallace did any linguistic research for this story. John Billy's dialect also includes verb aspect markers such as completive *done* + *V-ed* (in addition to the example given earlier, *done nodded* [140], *done gone* [144], *done gave* [144]) and inchoative *commence to*

---

[43] Louis D. Rubin, Jr., *A Gallery of Southerners* (Baton Rouge: Louisiana State University Press, 1982), 128.
[44] Boswell, *Understanding David Foster Wallace*, 85.
[45] Christian, Wolfram and Dube, "Variation and Change in Geographically Isolated Communities," 198.

(+ infinitive) or *got to* (+ verbal noun), showing the beginning of an action ("Upright citizens commenced to lift too," [139], "T-Rex commenced to hand up jars" [146], "She'd got to caressing" [132]), past tense *come* ("She come back over, toting menace" [134], "when Chuck Nunn Jr. come three days past" [139]), other nonstandard (often regularized) verb conjugations (simple past *seen* [137] or past perfect *'d swore* [134], *'d growed* [144]). In addition to the regularized reflexive pronoun (*hisself*), John Billy uses *ever* as determiner ("ever time" [132], "ever month" [140]), and frequently has the indefinite article *a* followed by vowel (with no use of *an*, as in "a analogy" [125], "a ambulance" [130], "a eternity" [134], etc.). He also frequently uses the preposition-final locative Wallace repeatedly claimed as part of his own Midwestern dialect (the "where X is at" construction, also found in this story as "where X lives at"). Multiple negation occurs with and without *ain't* ("never got seen no more" [136], "ain't no" + noun [144, 145]), and use of preposition *out* without *of* to indicate movement, as in "how Nunn's eyes got busted out his head" (130), "hanging right out his head" (130), and so on. A relative pronoun is omitted when subject of the relative clause ("was the first saw the rich orange of the jelly jars" [137]). There are nonstandard comparative forms "peculiarer" (133), and "hostiler" (137). There is a single use of the *a*-prefix, which is a commonly known feature of both Appalachian and Ozark English, but is here rather humorously attached to a verb borrowed from Yiddish to describe sexual intercourse: "Chuck Junior, who was, remember, a-shtuppin' the little lady" (126). (This relates back to the discussion in Chapter 4 of Yiddish borrowings as a common cultural resource, available to all; the usage could not be more "nativized" than it is here.)

Taken in isolation, any one of these stigmatized features would stand out from a standard text, triggering negative judgments. In this story, however, they are so commonly used that the reader quickly becomes accustomed to the dialect; in that context, it is the lofty, learned vocabulary that pops out as unexpected. Readers are not expecting someone who speaks this way to have access to words such as *vicissitudes* (121), *limpid* and *Euclidean* (125), *diarrhetic* (132), or to Latin phrases such as ex officio (124). Not only is the narrator comfortable with such language but he is also able to use it creatively: there are frequent neologisms—mainly verbs created via functional shift from other parts of speech, such as *angstified* (125), *emergencying* (129), *smithered* (131), *vameesed* (134), *proned* (137), *incredulized* (142). He even puns on the Latin phrase prima facie ("at first impression") by using "prime face" (130) to describe how Chuck Junior's face had healed after his car accident. His "prime face" was just a first impression; he continues to suffer the effects long after, as the narrator makes clear. On the other hand, there is one instance of faux German in *vengeancelüst* (139), and John Billy spells the Latinate derivational suffix *-esque* as *-esk* (138).

Along with Latin and the Yiddish borrowings, the narrator uses words from Greek, German, French, Arabic, and Chinese in his list of "Nunn's putative virtuous qualities" (140). Wallace wrote in the Arabic and Chinese by hand on his typescript manuscript of the story (HRC Wallace Papers, container 28.7). John Billy uses metalinguistic terms playfully (if not entirely correctly): he compares "the noun T-Rex Minogue" to "the near-gerunds confrontation, reparation, possibly even reciprocation (i.e. detonation)" (127). Like gerunds, these nouns are derived from verbs—and the narrator brings our attention to this, to stress these as actions Nunn might soon be taking. Not only does John Billy use language in these creative and self-aware ways, but he points out that his friend Glory Joy does the same. "Focus in on that verb *lose*, S.R.," John Billy tells Simple Ranger, "The lady means it special" (132).

Readers start out feeling superior to this nonstandard speaker, are soon amazed that he knows such terminology, find themselves honestly amused (not condescendingly) by his playfulness with descriptions and words themselves, and eventually realize that they are struggling to keep up with this "simple" story, that it's much more complicated than they had initially realized. Readers are *meant* to wonder whether John Billy is "for real," and the punch line to the joke is that, like a stage magician, Wallace has misdirected readers' attention; they were asking the right question about the wrong character. The narrator is 100 percent "for real" in the context of the story; it is "Simple Ranger" (the ostensible audience for John Billy's story) who turns out to not be who John Billy (and by proxy, readers) thought he was. He is, in fact, not "simple" at all, although his performance does indeed "range." (There are no native American Indians in Wallace's work—one of the gaps in his simplification of ethnicity, as discussed in Chapter 3.) Part of the shock of the revelation in "John Billy" (similar to the effect of the Scooby Doo gang peeling the mask off the villain at the end of the episode) is that if identity is so easily assumed, then the narrator must be *choosing* (in almost every utterance) to be both "hick" and deep thinker, both regional and global. Readers who think themselves superior to John Billy may believe that he grew up in "waist-deep shit," but he argues that that experience is universal, not exclusive to Minogue, Oklahoma, the South, or just rural locations in general: "The waist-deep shit *we all grew up in*" (143, emphasis added).

For T. Rex, who took Chuck Nunn, Jr., to the window and forced him to look out, where you're from is your destiny. It's not coincidental that T. Rex's surname is also the name of the town. "Fore I die . . . I need to know where y'all think you live," T. Rex challenges his friends (145). "I need to know where y'all think you *live at*" (146) he repeats, adding emphasis to the regional construction, and then again a third time: "Tell me where y'all think you live at" (146). He may be "king" of his small town, but he is also a dinosaur, doomed to extinction, literally on the verge of death. Chuck Nunn, Jr., whose abbreviated name "C. Nunn" (136), Boswell[46] points out, is a pun for "see none," cannot see what T. Rex wants to show him, because his eyes have literally fallen out; another example of Wallace's trademark of "literalizing difficult questions and working them out in a living context."[47]

John Billy has his own answer to T. Rex's repeated question, which he does not give before T-Rex dies: "A point in time, which is where we lived at" (146). The landscape disappears, melts away, as the survivors get drunk, "levitating" around "the seated form of Minogue Oklahoma's expired T. Rex Minogue" (146). This story is not just about identity, but about mortality, a memento mori; not just about Chuck Nunn, Jr., or John Billy, but about the readers, too. "Was me supposed to tell Simple Ranger" (the opening line of the opening section) turns into the opening line of the closing section: "Was me supposed to tell you" (146). John Billy challenges readers directly to "go on and ask me" (147). Like Simple Ranger, the reader may be anybody. It is not John Billy who embodies "chaotic unboundedness," as Hayes-Brady[48] argues—it is the unknown readers. Wallace has been criticized for imagining readers much like himself, but what is the alternative? How does one tell a coherent story—the *same* story—to radically different audiences?

Wallace deliberately blurred distinctions between regions, problematizing the "convenient fictions," not just of the South, but also of the Midwest, as the next chapter will detail. He understood that dialects are not all alike (nor should be), but that our gross stereotypes about regions and their associated dialects are easily falsified. Wallace's dialect portrayals show awareness of and sensitivity to the additional stigma that rural and impoverished speakers everywhere bear for their dialects, although these dialects are in no way inferior to the dialects of upper-class speakers in those or other regions; the message that these speakers also deserve our empathy and respect is implicit, but so often repeated as to be unmistakable.

---

[46] Boswell, *Understanding David Foster Wallace*, 88.
[47] Hayes-Brady, *The Unspeakable Failures of David Foster Wallace*, 12.
[48] Ibid., 112.

7

Midwestern and Rural

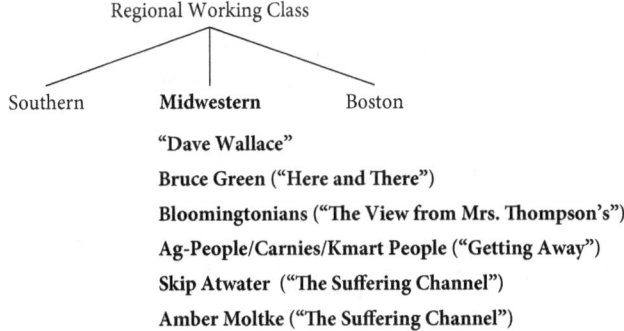

Figure 6 Wallace's Midwesterners.

In "Host," Wallace challenges readers "to try seeing things from the perspective of, say, a God-fearing, hard-working rural-Midwestern military vet" (*CTL* 288–9). An arrow, from the word "directly" (which Wallace puts in the mouth of this hypothetical construct), leads to a box with a parenthetical side note: "(In the real Midwest, this word is pronounced with a long *i*)" (289). Neither the accent nor the conservative point of view is mocked; nor is there any implication that a person who speaks this way must have this attitude; the implication is simply that readers can't really imagine this person, can't really understand his point of view, unless they *hear* the words coming out of his mouth.

The very concept of a "Middle West" is an early twentieth-century construct, whose borders continue to be disputed (or perhaps continue to evolve). The Midwest is "generally considered the most American and the most amorphous of regions."[1] Several critics have explored Wallace's relationship with the Midwest, but almost none have included consideration

---

[1] Andrew R. L. Cayton and Susan E. Gray, eds. *The American Midwest: Essays on Regional History* (Bloomington and Indianapolis: Indiana University Press, 2001), 1.

of dialect features, specifically. Although Wallace-the-author and "Wallace"-the-narrator and several alter ego protagonists acknowledge their history with/in and appreciation for the Midwest, they very sparingly incorporate linguistic features of Midwestern dialects. Joffe[2] discusses how (particularly after 9/11), Wallace "homes in on the white working-class Midwest, rendering this population with extraordinary complexity and richness." She offers a thorough exposition of the rhetorical strategies with which Wallace positions male Midwesterners as a symbol for all Americans in both TPK and "The View from Mrs. Thompson's." Daalder[3] refers to the latter essay, along with "Derivative Sport in Tornado Alley" and "Getting Away from Already Being Pretty Much Away from It All" as Wallace's "autogeographies" or "geographic metafiction," saying that they offer "a clear sense of place, but one that can only be known from its geographic intertexts" (221)—that is, myths and symbols of the region.

As the dialect map in Chapter 5 illustrates, major dialect boundaries separate the "Upper Midwest" (including northern Wisconsin, Michigan's Upper Peninsula, Minnesota, northern Iowa, and most of the Dakotas) from the "Inland North" (including NE Illinois, Michigan, the northern edges of Indiana and Ohio) from the "Midland." Of course, the real boundaries of each are quite fuzzy, as is the distinction between North and South Midland, and the dividing line between South Midland and "Southern."

It is a common myth that the Midwestern United States is "home to 'General American,' a bland, deregionalized variety of English spoken by everyone in the region."[4] In fact, the geographical region currently called the "Midwest" does not entirely fall within a single dialect area (or vice versa). There is a definite mismatch between the idealized geographical "Midwest" and the dialect areas defined by linguists, as well as the stereotypes associated with each. Do rural identities all over the United States have more in common with each other than they do with nearby urban areas in their own region? Are the stereotyped images of "redneck" or "hillbilly" even associated with region? According to Ferrence,[5] "People expect rural Americans to

---

[2] Joffe, "In the Shadows," 143.
[3] Jurrit Daalder, "Wallace's Geographical Metafiction," in *The Cambridge Companion to David Foster Wallace*, ed. Ralph Clare (Cambridge: Cambridge University Press, 2018), 220–34.
[4] Timothy C. Frazer, "An Introduction to Midwest English," in *American Voices: How Dialects Differ from Coast to Coast*, ed. Walt Wolfram and Ben Ward (Malden, MA: Blackwell, 2006), 101–5, esp. 102.
[5] Matthew J. Ferrence, *All-American Redneck: Variations on an Icon, from James Fenimore Cooper to the Dixie Chicks* (Knoxville: The University of Tennessee Press, 2014), 162.

be Redneck" regardless of their geographical region, although Fox[6] points out that "redneck identity is ambivalent," and "relational," "an appealingly rebellious yet conservative political ideology for American's modern white working class."

Wallace did not include the Upper Midwest (also known as the North Central dialect area) in his "travelogue" of the country; none of his major characters hail from there, and he never attempted to represent the dialects found there, although I imagine he would have had a lot of fun with some of the Scandinavian influences. Many immigrants to the Upper Midwest sought "the freedom not to become American, but to retain European ways and values."[7] As such, these ethnic pockets might have fit into Wallace's examination of ethnicity and assimilation, but they would not further the exploration of the default white working class that his regional dialect portraits typically index.

Most of Wallace's portrayals of Midwestern speech are specifically varieties of "South Midland," a dialect area that is often caricatured "as rustic, poorly-educated, and the like."[8] Wallace's depictions of rural, working-class speakers in Southern Indiana and Southern Illinois would more likely signal Southern identity to readers than trigger associations with the "rural nostalgia" Americans seem to feel for "formerly white, Anglo-Saxon, and Scandinavian origin communities" built around family farms.[9] "Nostalgia for the Midwest," Daalder[10] agrees, "runs deep in the American grain: for generations, the country's heartland has been the home of all Americans, even those who have never lived there but miss it all the same."

It is the "North Midland" that is recognized in folklore as "the seat of the fictional home of Standard American English (where national radio and television announcers and newspersons are supposed to come from)" according to Niedzielski and Preston,[11] who point out that it is "an area little caricatured," and "an area of high linguistic security." As Gordon[12] points out, "Even Midwesterners think they speak without an accent." Perceptual dialectology studies have repeatedly shown that speakers all over the country

---

[6] Aaron A. Fox, *Real Country: Music and Language in Working-Class Culture* (Durham, NC and London: Duke University Press, 2004), 25.
[7] Cayton and Gray, *The American Midwest*, 2.
[8] Niedzielski and Preston, *Folk Linguistics*, 28.
[9] Katherine Fennelly, "Prejudice Toward Immigrants in the Midwest," in *New Faces in New Places: The Changing Geography of American Immigration*, ed. Douglas S. Massey (New York: Russell Sage Foundation, 2008), 151–78, esp. 152.
[10] Daalder, "Wallace's Geographical Metafiction," 220.
[11] Niedzielski and Preston, *Folk Linguistics*, 17.
[12] Matthew J. Gordon, "Straight Talking from the Heartland (Midwest)," in *American Voices: How Dialects Differ from Coast to Coast*, ed. Walt Wolfram and Ben Ward (Malden, MA: Blackwell, 2006), 106–11, esp. 107.

rate "Midwestern" dialects highly on scales of correctness and pleasantness (categories that clearly correlate in the popular imagination).

Daalder[13] associates Wallace's Midwestern fiction with two classics he dubs the "ur-texts" of the Midwest (222): Sherwood Anderson's *Winesburg, Ohio* (whose author Wallace lauds in TPK) and Sinclair Lewis's *Main Street*, although Daalder does not detail any real connections between Lewis and Wallace, other than Wallace's explicit labeling of the opening paragraph of "A View from Mrs. Thompson's" as synecdoche (as "main street" has come to symbolize all of small-town America). Daalder also points to an essay by Michael Martone, "The Flatness," which appears to have particularly resonated with Wallace, noting Wallace's marginal note "Not object but medium" by the following underlined sentences: "I grew up in a landscape not often painted or photographed. The place is more like the materials of the art itself—the stretched canvas and paper."[14] Another version of the essay was included in Wallace's teaching materials, and on this copy, he wrote: "Q: Is there a point? Or is this just an excuse for some cool descriptions? Q: Does it need to have a point? Q: Who is this for? Non-natives, or natives (to appreciate the beauty of their own land), or both?" (HRC Wallace Papers, container 32.8).

In the *Harvard Book Review*, Wallace called Martone's *Fort Wayne is Seventh on Hitler's List* (1990)[15] "way better than good" (13), citing particularly its "study of the Midwest in all its self-conscious averageness, a place that understands itself as always origin and never end," and its "full and accurate evocation of Indiana as place." Wallace acknowledged that "the reviewer, who's from rural Illinois, might be prejudiced by sentiment." All the stories in *Fort Wayne* are monologues, and Wallace noted that "Martone's voices are superb." Notably, however, Martone does not incorporate many nonstandard dialect features into those voices, with most differentiated only by personality, except for the final story, which is written from the point of view of the bank robber John Dillinger (who uses *ain't*, some double negation, and the non-interrogative discourse marker *why*).

According to Martone,[16] he and Wallace "were to each other, each other's footnotes." Their "casual . . . informal, trivial" relationship began when Martone asked "a passel of Midwestern writers" to contribute to a book of

---

[13] Daalder, "Wallace's Geographical Metafiction."
[14] Michael Martone, ed. *A Place of Sense: Essays in Search of the Midwest* (Iowa City: Iowa Humanities Board, 1988), 33.
[15] Michael Martone, *Fort Wayne Is Seventh on Hitler's List: Indiana Stories* (Bloomington: Indiana University Press, 1990); "Review of *Fort Wayne Is Seventh on Hitler's List: Indiana Stories* by Michael Martone," *Harvard Book Review* 15/16 (Winter–Spring, 1990): 12–13. https://www.jstor.org/stable/27545484.
[16] Michael Martone, "Footnotes & Endnotes," *Sonora Review* 55 (2009): 51–8, esp. 53.

essays called *Townships*; Wallace's response was "Derivative Sport in Tornado Alley." It was Martone's thesis that "only in the Midwest did the grid of the township take hold as a telling geographic feature," and Wallace took this one step further, "subdividing the squares within squares down to the boxes within boxes of the tennis court."[17] Martone notes that Wallace's text featured all sorts of "goofy graphic geometry" at a time when writers were just "beginning to understand that our Macintoshs were not typewriters . . . that a writer now had also at his fingertips this material edge, the book-ness of the book, as an aesthetic strategy."[18]

Wallace would later contribute "Another Pioneer" to a special issue Martone edited of the *Colorado Review* entitled "Trying Fiction," pun intended—both attempting to do new things, and difficult, a perfect fit for Wallace. After Wallace included the description of *Jest*'s Hugh Steeply's television-addicted father becoming obsessed with and writing letters to the fictional Dr. Frank Burns of M*A*S*H, Martone claimed in a footnote in his fictional travel guide *The Blue Guide to Indiana* (2001)[19] that Dr. Frank Burns had both delivered him as a baby and attended his (still living) mother's death. A footnote to a letter Wallace wrote to Martone asks "Really? Dr. Frank Burns?"[20]

According to Hering,[21] "In Wallace's fiction the Midwest is rarely, if ever, afforded the chance to exist as an unmediated environment." The "mediation" comes via Wallace's portrayals of institutional spaces—but most Americans, regardless of region, spend the majority of their lives navigating various institutional spaces, schools, businesses, churches, and the like. Wallace was not a nature writer; his treatment of the Midwest is no more "mediated" than his exploration of the Boston area in *Infinite Jest*, and his ambivalence over his regional identity was no greater than his ambivalence and self-consciousness over every other aspect of life. Hering is more on point with his observation that Wallace's treatment of the Midwest evolved over the years: "In 1997 Wallace is somewhat archly asking *What Is Peoria For?* but in the post-2005 *Pale King* material his description of the Midwest has become more attuned to economic and social problems in the region."[22] What remains unchanged is Wallace's blurring of the boundaries of the region, and his rejection of the conflation of "region" and "dialect." How one speaks is, to a large extent, a

---

[17] Ibid., 54.
[18] Ibid.
[19] Michael Martone, *The Blue Guide to Indiana* (Tuscaloosa: University of Alabama Press, 2001).
[20] Martone, "Footnotes & Endnotes," 52.
[21] Hering, *David Foster Wallace*, 41.
[22] Ibid., 148.

reflection of who one is (or aspires to be)—but who one is does not have to be determined or dominated by a regional identity, if such an identity even exists, beyond allegiance to a more specific place.

When Wallace characters sound "Midwestern," they use not only Wallace's own North Midland speech patterns but also the more stigmatized South Midland variants. Habick[23] details the dialect of Farmer City, Illinois (an actual location, not a metaphor, only twenty miles from Champaign-Urbana), perhaps the best linguistic description of what Wallace would have seen as "the hard-earned Rural Midwestern of most of my peers" (*CTL* 99). Habick's study contrasts the speech of "rednecks" and "burnouts" at the Farmer City high school (each group named by the other, the former more conservative and the latter made up of marijuana smokers). He describes the local dialect as "predominantly Northern," but "with strong Southern influence" (107). The most common shared Southern feature in Farmer City is /uw/ fronting, in which the vowel of *coop, soup* has moved toward the front of the vowel tract. (I have seen this reflected in writing, for instance, *kewl* for *cool*.) Wallace can be heard performing this in the word "shoot," in his recorded reading of "The View from Mrs. Thompson's," in the line "Well shoot, boy, get over here," in which he also flattens the diphthong in "boy," with the distance between the starting and ending tongue positions notably reduced, compared to his usual articulation. He is quoting a hypothetical neighbor in this sentence, not speaking in his own voice, thus positioning himself as distinct and separate from the "good people" of Bloomington. Joffe[24] points out that "despite his easy belonging among the white Midwestern community, he positions himself as a marginal, marginalised figure."

North Midlanders may like to think they have the "default" American speech, a non-accent, but there are certainly features that non-Midwesterners can identify as dialectal. Hurt[25] recounts a stranger who overhead his conversation with a friend in a hotel lobby telling them "You talk funny.... You have a flat 'a.'" Morphosyntactically, "elliptical verbal constructions with verbs of desire," are common (e.g., *the baby wants fed, the car needs washing, I want off*).[26] Positive *anymore* (as in "we go to the movies a lot anymore") began

---

[23] Timothy Habick, "Farmer City, Illinois: Sound Systems Shifting South," in *"Heartland English": Variation and Transition in the American Midwest*, ed. Timothy C. Frazier (Tuscaloosa: University of Alabama Press, 1993), 97–124.
[24] Joffe, "*In the Shadows*," 108.
[25] R. Douglas Hurt, "Midwestern Distinctiveness," in *The American Midwest: Essays on Regional History*, ed. Andrew R. L. Cayton and Susan E. Gray (Bloomington and Indianapolis: Indiana University Press, 2001), 160–79, esp. 161.
[26] Frazer, "An Introduction to Midwest English," 103.

in the Midlands, but according to Murray[27] "continues to spread outward." Midland speakers commonly substitute the alveolar stop (d) for the fricative (z) before nasals (as in *wudn't*, *idn't*), prefer the alveolar pronunciation of *-ing* suffixes, use *ain't* with multiple negation, and use deictic *them* as determiner (as in "leave them kids alone").

South Midland commonly features perfective *done* and shares other features with AAE, as detailed by Riney.[28] *Pin/pen* are merged, but also *feel/fill* and *pool/pull*.[29] Whereas in the South, āi is generally monophthongized, in the South Midland, it is merely "flattened" somewhat,[30] with less distance between the tongue's starting position and ending position than would be found in, say, an East Coast dialect. Wallace's Midwestern speakers display very few of these features, despite his ongoing collection of "Midwesternisms" in research notebooks (which will be discussed later in this chapter). A&AU strongly defends the "Rural Midwestern construction '*Where's it at?*'" saying that its "apparent redundancy" is "offset by its metrical logic." Wallace's command of the linguistic terminology ("What the *at* really does is license the contraction of *is* after the interrogative adverb") and of the terminology describing traditional poetic meter ("a strong anapest" vs. "a clunky monosyllabic foot + trochee" (*CTL* 99) lends a sense of objective analysis and authority to what might otherwise be seen as merely a quirky individual preference.

Midwesternism in Wallace's Own Speech

An idealized, bland "accentless" speech is not what Wallace was referring to when he claimed a fondness for rural Midwestern English. As a childhood SNOOT born in Ithaca, New York, but quickly transplanted to Champaign-Urbana, Illinois, Wallace internalized more of "the SWE of my hyper-educated parents" (*CTL* 99) than any stigmatized features of working-class rural classmates, but would certainly have had ample opportunity to observe these. In an interview with Paul Quinn,[31] Wallace's sister Amy said that the

---

[27] Thomas E. Murray, "Positive *anymore* in the Midwest," in *"Heartland English": Variation and Transition in the American Midwest*, ed. Timothy C. Frazier (Tuscaloosa: University of Alabama Press, 1993), 173–86, esp. 175.
[28] Timothy J. Riney, "Linguistic Controversies, VBE Structures, and Midwest Attitudes." In *"Heartland English": Variation and Transition in the American Midwest*, ed. Timothy C. Frazier (Tuscaloosa: University of Alabama Press, 1993), 81–93, 84.
[29] Frazier, "An Introduction to Midwest English," 102.
[30] Ibid.
[31] Quinn, "'Location's Location': Placing David Foster Wallace."

Midwestern kids they grew up with "treated us as if we were East-Coasters," while the people on the East Coast treated her brother "like a hayseed," causing Wallace to realize "he was from a place no one else was. *Somewhere in the middle, I think that was David's Midwest, the neither here nor there*" (95, emphasis original). Cohen[32] echoed this, saying that he "was and was not from Illinois," that it was "a home to which he was in some ways alien"— hence his need for a "Native Companion" to guide him through the State Fair in "Getting Away From Already Being Pretty Much Away From It All."

Hering[33] calls Wallace "a putatively Midwestern but effectively transregional writer" (60), finding a "performative Midwestern persona" (76) only in his nonfiction (76), and positing that this "'performative regionalism'" is an outgrowth of his "deep ambivalence over his own sense of regional identity."[34] If he was ambivalent, he was not alone: Cayton and Gray's[35] collection of essays on Midwestern history explains that Midwesterners have never been consciously regional (in comparison to Southerners, Westerners, and New Englanders), and questions whether regional identity is even a valid way to approach Midwestern history. Nonetheless, persistent stereotypes about "Midwestern" character pervade popular culture. Booth Tarkington, for instance, observed over a century ago that Midwesterners are "pleasant," "easy-going, yet not happy-go-lucky," and "hospitable without exertion,"[36] stereotypes that endure even today. Hurt[37] summarizes Midwestern character as "friendly," but "disciplined." He notes that "most people still identify the Midwest with rural America, to which they attribute traditional American values such as self-reliance, democracy, and moral decency" (175). Linguistic stereotypes, as Gordon[38] points out, "have less to do with the actual speech of a region than with popular perceptions of the region's people." For the Midwest, this means that the dialect will be seen as "average, boring or nondescript"[39] as the people who supposedly speak this way.

A&AU presents evidence that Wallace code-switched when talking to rural Midwesterners (although it doesn't use that term) out of "a naked desire to fit in": "I tend to use constructions like 'Where's it at?' for 'Where is it?' and sometimes 'He don't' instead of 'He doesn't'" (*CTL* 99). Code-switching

---

[32] Cohen, "The Whiteness of David Foster Wallace," 235.
[33] Hering, *David Foster Wallace*.
[34] Ibid., 41.
[35] Cayton and Gray, *The American Midwest*.
[36] Booth Tarkington, "The Middle West," *Harper's Monthly Magazine* 106 (1902): 75–83, esp. 76.
[37] Hurt, "Midwestern Distinctiveness," 161.
[38] Gordon, "Straight Talking from the Heartland (Midwest)," 11.
[39] Ibid.

is not necessarily a sign of ambivalence or inauthenticity; it may reflect an unconscious indexing of one aspect of identity over another in a given situation, although it can also be consciously and strategically deployed to signal a particular aspect of one's identity within a particular interaction when it becomes relevant, to converge with or diverge from another's speech.[40] Well-known "Midwestern Expatriate" writer (or "ExMid," as he coined it) Calvin Trillin[41] argues that "continuing to think of oneself as a Midwesterner despite all geographical evidence to the contrary is not necessarily an 'act' or a 'number,' and thinking that it is, I keep telling my wife, is merely a manifestation of her fancy Eastern ways. (She says phrases like 'fancy Eastern ways' are part of my Kansas City act.)"

In most of the public readings that are available commercially or online, Wallace adheres more to prescriptive standard pronunciations than to regional Midwestern ones. In his most "standard" public performances, there are only intermittent (and perhaps inadvertent) Midwestern pronunciations, such as articulating an /l/ in "folk" (which is not recognized as standard pronunciation by the *American Heritage Dictionary*, on whose usage panel he served). Wallace's casual speech with interlocutors was predictably less "correct." Lipsky[42] refers to Wallace's "universal sportsman's accent: the disappearing Gs, 'wudn't,' 'dudn't,' and 'idn't' and 'sumpin.'" The dialogue in that book, memorializing their five-day road trip at the end of Wallace's publicity tour for *Infinite Jest*, was recorded and transcribed. Lipsky quotes Wallace alternating between adverbial *really* and *real* (the latter often used when intensifying adjectives), for example, "I'm real embarrassed" (215), "That stuff's rhetorically real interesting" (215), and "makin' real sure" (218). He also uses adverbial *near* ("I wasn't near as smart as I thought I was" (214)). These features can be clearly heard in the audio,[43] and are faithfully captured by Jason Segel's performance of Wallace in *The End of the Tour* (2015), based on Lipsky's book.

On the air with Terry Gross for National Public Radio's *Fresh Air*,[44] Wallace maintained "standard" (i.e., prescriptive) pronunciations for almost the entire seventeen-minute interview, even when clearly speaking spontaneously, quickly, and passionately, except once toward the end, when he said "sumpin"

---

[40] Robert Le Page and Andrée Tabouret-Keller, "*Acts of Identity*": *Creole-Based Approaches to Language and Ethnicity* (Cambridge: Cambridge University Press, 1985).
[41] Calvin Trillin, "The Midwest Is What's Left Over," *The New York Times*, September 9, 1974, 35.
[42] Lipsky, *Although of Course You End Up Becoming Yourself*, iv.
[43] Ryan Walsh and Jordyn Bonds, *The David Foster Wallace Audio Project*, n.d. http://www.dfwaudioproject.org/.
[44] Gross, "*Fresh Air* Interview with David Foster Wallace."

(although I might represent it as *sump'm*, phonetically [sʌ̃ʔm]). Quite a few of his sentences begin with *Boy, Oh boy,* or *Well,* although I do not read these as Midwestern per se—these seem to echo a more innocent *era*, a 1950s fantasy of white America, like the TV show "Leave it to Beaver" (which could have taken place in any suburb of the United States). I disagree with Dettmar,[45] who reads the voice in Wallace's earliest known story ("The Planet Trillaphon as It Stands in Relation to the Bad Thing," originally published in an undergraduate journal and now collected in the *David Foster Wallace Reader* [5-19]) as Midwestern, mostly on the basis of such "faux-yokel Midwestern interjections that pepper the character's speech,"[46] although he also finds "Midwestern, too, the narrator's reticence: 'I really don't wish to go into a gigantic amount of detail' (following which, he goes into a gigantic amount of detail)."[47]

Minced oaths and "wholesome" expressions of surprise or emotion are not confined to any region, and the first-person narrator of the story says specifically that he lives in New Hampshire. I include this mischaracterization to show how much of literary dialectology is in the eye of the beholder, how much people assume that if there is "no accent," the speaker must be Midwestern, and also how much of an autobiographical lens readers can unwittingly bring to a text. Knowing that Wallace was from the Midwest, they anticipate a Midwestern voice in his fiction.

Wallace did not remain an ExMid, returning to Bloomington to teach at Illinois State University for a decade of his adult life. He repeatedly returns to the region in his writing as well—in "Westward the Course of Empire Takes Its Way," "Getting Away From Already Pretty Much Being Away From It All," "The View from Mrs. Thompson's," "The Suffering Channel," TPK, and in passing elsewhere.

The "Dave Wallace" narrator falsely claims (in both "Derivative Sport" and TPK) to be from Philo, Illinois, and Coughlan[48] accepts Wallace's father's interpretation that this was because "Wallace wanted a home in 'Love.'" It would also appear to be an unabashed declaration of his love *for* Illinois, a formulation akin to the bumper sticker slogan "I ♡ NY." His appreciation for this region was apparently sincere, if somewhat sheepish. Wallace took a bit of a potshot at his own attempts to allegorize the region in "Derivative Sport," when discussing his move to Massachusetts to attend

---

[45] Kevin J. H. Dettmar, "Afterword," in *The David Foster Wallace Reader*, ed. Bonnie Nadell et al. (New York: Back Bay Books/Little, Brown and Company, 2015), 20-1.
[46] Ibid., 20.
[47] Ibid.
[48] Coughlan, "Sappy Or No, It's True," 174.

college: "Alienation-from-Midwest-as-fertility-grid might be a little on the overmetaphysical side, not to mention self-pitying" (ASFTINDA 14). He only designated the region as "the Heartland" once, perhaps thinking this too obvious a metaphor; the exception occurs when he imagines that the "swanky East Coast magazine" that commissioned his coverage of the Illinois State Fair will find it "rural and heartlandish" (83).

GWCH is "much more directly focused on the Midwest as a problematized cultural territory," according to Hering,[49] but there is little to no use of a "Midwestern" dialect in that volume. Bruce in "Here and There" describes himself as "a hulking pigeon-toed, blond, pale, red-lipped Midwestern boy" (GWCH 153) who graduated from an elite college in Massachusetts before returning to his home town of Bloomington. He now wants to be a writer, "the first really great poet of technology" (155). Although details are tweaked such as hair color, college (MIT, rather than Amherst), major (engineering, rather than English and Philosophy), and home state (Bloomington, Indiana, rather than Illinois), Wallace could hardly deny Bruce as an alter ego; in a letter to Jonathan Franzen, he calls the story "sentimental pseudo-autobiographical crap."[50] Indeed, Bruce's voice is familiar as Wallace's "Dave Wallace" persona, engaging here in an extended bit of "fiction therapy." Neither one has the characteristics that Wallace attributes to his "Midwestern" (i.e., South Midland) speakers; the "Dave Wallace" persona and alter egos will therefore not be further discussed in this chapter, although I shall return to them in the penultimate chapter, in an exploration of the "default" dialect with which Wallace's dialect representations are implicitly but unavoidably contrasted.

Cleveland, Ohio

Wallace's set his first novel in Cleveland—which at the time he had never visited[51] and might as well have picked out of a hat to represent the Midwest. There are no noticeable dialect markers in the speech of the main character, Lenore Beadsman, or her family members, who are supposed to be native to the region, but are notably upper class. (Her father is CEO of a corporation that has kept the family in wealth for generations.) In reality, Cleveland has been at the forefront of a fairly significant sequence of vowel shifts (known

---

[49] Hering, *David Foster Wallace*, 55.
[50] Max, *Every Love Story Is a Ghost Story*, 131.
[51] Helen Dudar, "A Whiz Kid and His Wacky First Novel," in *Conversations with David Foster Wallace*, ed. Stephen J. Burn (Jackson: University of Mississippi Press, 2012), 8–10, esp. 10.

collectively as the Northern Cities Vowel Shift), which would be tricky to capture orthographically. (For instance, the initial change resulted in the low vowel in words like "bad" rising dramatically and developing an off-glide, to sound more like the second vowel in "idea." This was followed by the low back vowel in "pot" moving forward to occupy the space in the vocal tract formerly held by the vowel of "bad.")

Wallace said in an interview that Lenore's speech was mostly patterned after his own, and that "one of the weaknesses in this book is that a lot of the characters seem to have the same voice."[52] Lenore's mockery of Andy Lang's "Texan" dialect was mentioned in the previous chapter, but the only apparent "regional linguistic clash" (229) between Lenore and her New Yorker lover Rick Vigorous is that he refers to "hamburg pizzas" and she says "hamburger" (229). (Vigorous does not reflect New York usage on this—at least not in the 1960s–1980s when I lived there.)

Lenore's great grandmother (also named Lenore Beadsman) studied under Wittgenstein, is "obsessed with words," and "believes she is in possession of some words of tremendous power"(82). Others have already detailed at great length Wittgenstein's philosophy of language at work in this novel (especially Ramal[53] and Hayes-Brady[54]), so I'm not going to re-tread that ground, other than to point out that Wittgenstein doesn't even mention dialects or sociolinguistic variation in either his *Tractatus Logico-Philosophicus*[55] or his *Philosophical Investigations*,[56] which may explain why these critics likewise ignored these issues in Wallace's work. As explored in earlier chapters, the novel represents Walinda's ethnic dialect and Lang's regional one, so it is not simply that Wallace was so focused on his "poststructural gag" that he didn't consider dialect issues. Rather, Lenore's lack of evident regional dialect not only underlines her wealth and privilege, it also contributes to her fear that she is "nothing but a linguistic construct." While Lenore is the central character, there is nothing memorable about her voice, compared to her grandmother (who remains missing for most of the novel, but is eminently quotable), compared to Andy and Walinda, whose performances are simultaneously

---

[52] Ibid., 13.
[53] Randy Ramal, "Beyond Philosophy: David Foster Wallace on Philosophy, Wittgenstein, and the Dangers of Theorizing," in *Gesturing Toward Reality: David Foster Wallace and Philosophy*, ed. Robert K. Bolger and Scott Korb (New York: Bloomsbury, 2014), 177–98.
[54] Hayes-Brady, *The Unspeakable Failures of David Foster Wallace*.
[55] Ludwig Wittgenstein, *Tractatus Logico-Philosophicus* (New York: Routledge, 2013 [1921]).
[56] Ludwig Wittgenstein, *Philosophical Investigations* (Malden, MA: Wiley-Blackwell, 2009 [1953]).

"real," yet constructed to accommodate their audience, compared even (or perhaps especially) to the talking parrot.

Bloomington and Central Illinois (Ag-People, Carnies, Kmart People)

"The View From Mrs. Thompson's" (originally published in *Rolling Stone* as "9/11: The View from the Midwest") includes several comments about language, showing how important Wallace believed language to be, even or perhaps especially at the most terrible of times, how it can bring people together yet simultaneously reinforce social divisions. The opening passage, as mentioned earlier, is labeled "SYNECDOCHE" (caps sic, *CTL* 128):

> In true Midwest fashion, Bloomingtonians aren't unfriendly but do tend to be reserved. A stranger will smile warmly at you, but there normally won't be any of that strangerly chitchat in waiting areas or checkout lines. But now there's something to talk about that outweighs all reserve, like we were somehow all standing right there and just saw the same traffic accident.

The "prototypical working-class Bloomington" people (134) with whom Wallace watches the news unfold "are not stupid, or ignorant" (139). The implication that he needs to assert this is a sad commentary on US attitudes toward the working class, generally, and it is characteristic that his evidence for the assertion is entirely linguistic: "Mrs. Thompson can read both Latin and Spanish, and Ms. Voigtlander is a certified speech therapist who once explained to me that the strange gulping sound that makes Tom Brokaw so distracting to listen to is an actual speech impediment called a 'glottal L'" (139). A footnote explaining that "*Pace* some people's impression, the native accent isn't Southern simply rural, whereas corporate transplants have no accent at all (in Mrs. Bracero's phrase, State Farm people 'sound like the folks on TV')" (133). There is a single instance of multiple negation (also in a footnote), but no other direct representations of regional dialect markers which would detract from the image of language as a unifying force, bringing all Americans together.

"Westward the Course of Empire Takes Its Way" is set in Central Illinois, but focalized by visitors from "the East Chesapeake Tradeschool Writing Program" (which Boswell 2014 identifies as a fictional version of the Johns Hopkins Writing Program, based on the pervasive Barth references, as discussed in Chapter 4). As both outsiders and as people especially interested in language, the visitors might be expected to comment directly on the local dialect, yet they remain fairly oblivious to any differences: The only nonstandard usage represented is "Hibbego," used three times (238, 299, 342), which Wallace seems to have invented himself, though the speaker explicitly labels it Midwestern: "as we say in the nation's flat green gut" (238). It is possible that the speaker, DeHaven, is doing some performative Midwesternism of his own, to pre-empt anticipated mockery from the visitors. The only metalinguistic commentary the visitors make is eighty pages into the story, when "for the first time Mark can hear a Midwestern twang in DeHaven's sullen voice" (315). "Twang" is generally associated with the South, as Wallace himself told the translator of "Incarnations," and it is significant that Mark only hears it when DeHaven more explicitly claims a Midwestern identity, distancing himself from the visitors, whom he deems "Yuffies," defined as "Young Urban Foppish Farts"—that is, "Yuppies without the taste for quality that's maybe a Yuppie's one redeeming quality." According to DeHaven, this term "is what we call them out here" (315).

Wallace's essay about the Illinois State Fair ("Getting Away," published three years earlier as "Ticket to the Fair" in *Harper's*) contains a particularly unflattering paragraph about "Kmart People" that Ribbat[57] views as exemplifying "a distinct kind of disgust with everyday Americans."

> Kmart People tend to be overweight, polyestered, grim-faced, toting glazed unhappy children. Toupees are the movingly obvious shiny square-cut kind, and the women's makeup is garish and often asymmetrically applied, giving many of the female faces a kind of demented look. They are sharp-voiced and snap at their families. They're the type you see slapping their kids in supermarket checkouts. . . . I'm sorry, but this is all true. I went to high school with Kmart People. I know them. (*ASFTINDA* 120–1)

This paragraph certainly does not claim that all Midwesterners are "Kmart People," but the harshness and the inherent classism are nonetheless jarring. Cohen labels Wallace's attitude in this article as "distaste for the Kmart people and the carnies, . . . condescension for the rural ag-people," but also "self-mockery."[58] When Ann Fadiman assigned that essay to her creative writing

---

[57] Christoph Ribbat, "Seething Static: Notes on Wallace and Journalism," in *Consider David Foster Wallace: Critical Essays*, ed. David Hering (Los Angeles and Austin: Sideshow Group Press, 2010), 187–98, esp. 194.
[58] Cohen, "The Whiteness of David Foster Wallace," 235.

class at Yale, a student asked Wallace how a writer can "find a balance between mocking one's target and mocking oneself." In his reply, Wallace acknowledged "stuff about clinically fat people engaged in peripatetic eating that made them look bovine," but also recalled

> a certain tenderness for the Midwesterners there (of whom I was, by origin and upbringing, one) and an attempt to explain, for the mainly cosmopolitan readers of *Harper's*, some of the effects rurality, physical distance, lack of stimulation, etc. have on people. Still, I must also admit that I got some pissed-off letters indeed from Midwesterners, along with some aggrieved press mentions in the Midwest.[59]

Wallace was joined on his trip to the Fair by a "Native Companion" from his hometown who "likes to put on a parodic hick accent whenever I utter a term like 'peripatetic,'" giving as examples of this: "She's '*storvin*,' she says, 'to *daith*'" (ASFTINDA 102). He later admitted that "it's not really her voice, it's somebody else's voice."[60] There was no particular need for an article about a Fair to focus so extensively on language, but Wallace couldn't seem to help himself, making both lexical and phonological observations: "Midwesterners say tomāto" (103); "Illinois farmers call their farms 'operations,' rarely 'farms' and never 'spreads'" (106). "There's a Midwestern term, 'drape,' for the kind of girl who hangs on to her boyfriend in public like he's a tree in a hurricane" (133). It's not surprising that Wallace would notice and mention particular usages—he did that throughout his career, in almost every work, wherever it was situated—but how would he know what Illinois farmers *never* say? This isn't just a bid to appear authoritative; it contributes to the fictionalization of the narrative persona, who could not logically be omniscient.

Wallace took some pains with his representation of the speech of the local "ag-people" and the itinerant (but presumably still Midwestern) carnies. On a copy-editing draft, he marked "Stet syntax" twice (on both the left and right margins) of one quote, and wrote it in large letters vertically down the page for the duration of the speech of the "old withered guy in an Illinois Poultry Association cap" to make sure the nonstandard speech survived copy editing (HRC Wallace Papers, container 1.5). Specifically, the carnies make comments like "Git on over and git some if she's a mind to" (98), "Ain't no sweat off my balls" (98), "Ever last thing" (102), and "the fuck you talking bout" (135). The "old withered" Ag-person calls the carnies "*Traish . . . . Lowlifes.*" He is

---

[59] Ann Fadiman, "Afterword," in *The David Foster Wallace Reader*, ed. Bonnie Nadell et al. (New York: Back Bay Books/Little, Brown and Company, 2015), 759–62, esp. 761.
[60] Lipsky, *Although of Course You End Up Becoming Yourself*, 243.

uninterested in any part of the fair, other than the livestock competitions: "Swindle you nekked, them games. Traish. Me I ever year we drive up, why, I carry my wallet like this here." When Wallace ask if his kids would want to "ride the rides, eat, . . . mingle a little," he replies "*Hail* no. . . . Shows're over Tuesday, why, we go on home" (110). He says the "rest of all this here's for city people" (which Wallace glosses for readers: "He means Springfield, Decatur, Champaign"), who buy "soovners" (110). Wallace thinks he's referring to his kids when he says, "Ain't no folks they know down there," and "we all stayin' up to the *motel*" (111).

The Fair, Wallace explains, is "rural IL's moment of maximum community," but "Us's entail Thems," and "carnies make an excellent Them" (110). It is hard to imagine that Wallace was not thinking about the "Us" of supposedly sophisticated *Harper's* readers (who would presumably *not* think of natives of Decatur as "real city people") and the "Them" (supposed hicks) portrayed in the story as he wrote this. The "old withered" guy may hate carnies, but he seems almost as dismissive of the "city people." The joke here is that Wallace depicts both "Ag-people" and "carnies" with similar South Midland features, including *git* for *get*, multiple negation with ain't, *ever* and *them* used as determiners; without him explaining who is who to "Us," readers would be unable to distinguish any of "Them."

Southern Indiana

Wallace's most extended fictional portrait of rural Midwestern speech is Amber Moltke of Mount Carmel, Indiana, in "The Suffering Channel" (*Oblivion*). Amber's speech is contrasted with that of Skip Atwater (native but longtime expatriate of the region) and the de-regionalized speech of the staffers at *Style* magazine (which is headquartered in New York City, although most of the staffers do not appear to be native New Yorkers).

Skip arrives to interview Amber's husband, Brint, who has bowel movements that emerge, fully formed, as detailed, recognizable statues, veritable works of art. Ribbat,[61] Quinn,[62] and Hering[63] all see Skip as a transparent alter ego for Wallace, and there are plenty of apparent similarities to support this: he is white heterosexual male writer, a native Midwestern transplant to the East Coast, excruciatingly self-conscious at all times, and

---

[61] Ribbat, "Seething Static: Notes on Wallace and Journalism."
[62] Quinn, "'Location's Location': Placing David Foster Wallace."
[63] Hering, *David Foster Wallace*.

especially awkward with women, who seeks to interpret the Midwest in his writing. Hering finds significance in Skip's real name, Virgil, emphasizing "his role as guide to a disturbing topographic space";[64] the nickname also seems significant in more than one sense: He has attempted to "skip" out of the Midwest, and has missed some things. If one is inclined to read autobiographically, though, it is also possible that Wallace saw himself as much in Brint Moltke, producing works of art in private, experiencing tremendous anxiety about revealing these works to the world, afraid that his work is shit, trapped by his peculiar talents and his need to please others.

Mount Carmel is a real town of under a hundred people in Southern Indiana, close to the Kentucky border. It is closer still to Ohio (only a half hour from Cincinnati), but the linguistic influence is from the South, as Niedzielski and Preston[65] point out. The speech of Southern Indiana is considered "caricaturistic South Midland ['hillbilly'] speech."[66] "Hoosiers have their own peculiar way of speaking," Hurt[67] notes, "half-Southern and yet not Southern." This is therefore an area of notable linguistic insecurity. Skip resembles the "redneck academic" narrator of Chappell's (1996) *Look Back All the Green Valley*, Jess Kirkman, who "finds himself conflicted, distanced from his geographical home and similarly distanced from his regional identity. He is resident and tourist at the same time."[68]

For page after page of the story, "seated together in the standard Midwest attitude of besotted amiability" (247), the Moltkes hardly speak at all, but this doesn't seem to be due to linguistic insecurity, at least not on Amber's part. When she finally gets going, she is completely unselfconscious about her dialect. Indeed, she finds it "peculiar" that Skip does not sound *more* regional, commenting that "sometimes I can hear it and then other times not. . . . [Y]ou said up to home you were from back here, and sometimes I can hear it and then other times you sound more . . . all business, and I can't hear it in you at all" (277). Skip doesn't hear any regionality in his own voice (which Wallace represents as entirely standard on the page); he is as unaware of any "slippage" in dialect as he is that his preference for "navy blazer and catalogue slacks ensembles" is "the number one thing that betrayed his Midwest origins" (239) to his *Style* co-workers.

Skip wonders if Amber is "playing up to a certain stereotype of provincial naivete" (276), as his own linguistic insecurity makes him

---

[64] Ibid., 76.
[65] Niedzielski and Preston, *Folk Linguistics*, 66.
[66] Ibid., 45.
[67] Hurt, "Midwestern Distinctiveness," 161.
[68] Ferrence, *All-American Redneck*, 150.

think that her dialect is inconsistent with her knowledge of legal terms like "conferral" and "serial right," and especially the Latin phrase "*sic vos non vobis*, which latter Skip did not even know" (255). (It is a quote from the Roman poet Vergil, meaning "for you, but not yours.") Here, as in "John Billy," Wallace seems to insist that it is the linguistic prejudice that is absurd, not the regional speaker. Amber is Midwestern *and* smart, feminine *and* powerful; there is no contradiction. She not only overwhelms the reporter, she also speaks for her husband: "He'll do it," she says three times (278–9) without consulting him. "He will because he'll do it for me, Skip. Because I say" (279).

Brint hardly ever speaks for himself. When Skip asks him how he produces the statues, Brint is silent until Amber physically hits him, at which point he offers only "I'm not sure" (252). He shares his "first person account of how his strange and ambivalent gift had first come to light" (255) only after more extended coercion: Amber takes her husband into another room "where they took inaudible counsel together" (255). Skip's transcript of the brief account is shown, but it does not contain a single sentence without the reporter's own interjected explanations and interpretations, and his conclusion that the anecdote was "more or less pointless, but could foreseeably be edited out or massaged" (256). The only words Brint offers (apparently) voluntarily in the story are not spoken aloud; he excretes them and leaves them in a bucket outside the reporter's hotel door, "ornate and calligraphic, quotation marks sic": "HELP ME" (314)—a plea that is entirely disregarded, perhaps because he cannot speak the words aloud, emphasizing again the performative nature of spoken language. Things do indeed happen "because I say."

Hayes-Brady[69] discusses Wallace's "apparent reluctance or inability to write strong female characters," which contributes to "the silence and silencing of the female voice"[70] in his work, but Amber Moltke ranks among Wallace's strongest characters, using every resource available to her (her body, her speech, her husband, Skip, *Style*) to achieve the celebrity she wants, without much concern for what happens to the men she manipulates. (Skip gets off easy with a knee injury and wounded self-pride; her husband is sure to have a much more tortured existence.) She'll fit in with the celebrities Atwater has known, "not, in his experience, very friendly or considerate people . . . not actually functioning as real people at all, but as something more like symbols of themselves" (285).

---

[69] Hayes-Brady, *The Unspeakable Failures of David Foster Wallace*, 19.
[70] Ibid., 7.

The only South Midland linguistic features Amber shares with the "ag-people" and "carnies" at the Illinois State Fair are the sentence-initial "Why" and *ain't*, although unlike them, she does not use multiple negation. Nor does she sound like the more Ozarkian Oklahoman John Billy—both use nonstandard past tense conjugations of "to be," but where John Billy uses plural *was*, Amber uses singular *were*: "It surely weren't like that at my house growing up, I can tell you" (268). Both Amber and John Billy have nonstandard preposition usage, but not the same ones. (In addition to the "up to home" already cited, Amber says her husband's parents "whipped on him with electric cords and burnt on him"). She uses Wallace's preferred "Where X is at" construction once ("David Letterman on the TV talks about Ball State all the time, that he was at" [278]). Her reference to people as "bodies" ("I don't bet there's a body in town that. . . .") registers as a folksy part of her dialect, but in a story that is very preoccupied with the functioning of actual human bodies, this usage also has deeper resonance. (Cf. Derdeyn's[71] observation that in a bit of "Wittgensteinian language game/name play," Wallace gave the narrator of "Lyndon" the surname Boyd, an anagram for *body*.)

Language is not just used symbolically in this story to show identity and affiliation (and how these can slip and shift); Wallace crafted a specific way of speaking that works with the themes of this particular story, as he did with "John Billy." Amber is particularly fond of structures with *all*, repeatedly using *and all, is all, what all, you all, them all*, together with use of *all* as adverb in *all through, all right, all business, at all*, and several uses of *whole*. She overwhelms Atwater, not just physically with her body, but linguistically as well. "Her voice was a dulcet alto with something almost hypnotic in the timbre" (283). To be fair, she takes advantage of him before he can take advantage of her; together, they conspire to manipulate her husband.

The power of language is not one of the main points of this story, but for Wallace, language is inextricably intertwined with both identity and art, and is the key to human interaction. It is important for Amber not just to have a voice in this story, but to have one that dominates, that represents not just a stereotype of a manipulative woman (although she definitely is one), and not just a stereotype of the Midwest (although she is described at one point as "less a person than a vista, a quarter ton of sheer Midwest pulchritude" [250]). In order for the story to work, readers have to not just understand Amber, but empathize with her. If she is a monster (which she is), so is Skip (if less honest with himself about it), and so is every reader who would seek the empty prize of fame.

---

[71] Derdeyn, "Love the Jackalope," 763.

Hering[72] sees in this story "a simulacra of all the cultural tropes of the 'Midwest' generated within the American coastal media," later specifying these tropes as "obesity, corn, vast space, sincerity" (75). In his view, the "authentic, non-mediated Midwest" has been replaced with "a culturally encoded 'Midwest.'"[73] Of course, a "non-mediated literary representation" is an oxymoron; there are only different degrees to which the representation itself mediates, and the methods it uses to do so. Wallace took liberties with Amber's South Midland dialect not to express any sense of inauthenticity—on the contrary, she is recognized as sincere, if wrongheaded—but to underline her agency and ambition as much as her regionality. Her desire for fame is monstrous (as she is willing to exploit her husband's suffering to gain it), and the irony is that such fame will ultimately be unfulfilling.

Amber is driven by her memory of once "getting to stand near" a daytime television star, which made her realize that her own "deepest and most life informing wish" (287) was to have the same effect on others. Amber did not achieve any meaningful connection with the star, even temporarily, and achieving the fame she seeks would be equally isolating for her. She does not desire connection with others, but for them to "get quiet when her and Brint came in, and to feel people's eyes, the weight of their gaze" (283). Skip recognizes the sincerity of her desire, if not the futility of it. For him, the anecdote of her brush with fame and the ambition it inspired is "a completely perfect representative statement of what it was like to be one of the people to and for whom he wished his work in *Style* to try to speak" (287); it provides "objective dignification of his work" (288). Her ultimate desire is not just to be one voice among many; it is not enough for her to be heard—others need to "get quiet"; similarly, Skip wants to "speak for" the common people. He is able to empathize with her, because he is no different: he exploits people for his own ends, to achieve equally futile goals.

This story is focused on consumer culture, how global patterns of consumption affect everyone locally, seducing people with the shiny false prize of isolating fame rather than soul-nourishing human relationships or the uplifting pursuit of art. It's notable that Brint, who has an inexplicable ability to turn the most ordinary, universal, and disgusting of acts into art has no desire for fame. More of the story revolves around the offices and staffers of *Style* magazine than around the Moltkes; yet it is the scenes in Mount Carmel that are memorable, that feel real and important, because readers are given the chance to get to know and understand Amber and Skip. Most of the *Style* staffers have titles rather than names, and when they are named, both first and

---

[72] Hering, *David Foster Wallace*, 73.
[73] Ibid., 75.

last names are used, which isn't just to distinguish interns Laurel Manderley and Laurel Rodde, since Ellen Bactrian is also always fully named. The full-naming serves only to create a sense of social distance: they're never on a first-name basis with each other, which also prevents readers from feeling any sense of intimacy with them. It's not even clear whether the chief executives of *Style* and the cable "Suffering Channel," Mrs. Anger and R. Vaughn Corliss, even have first names. All the staffers at *Style* (largely women who went to "Seven Sisters" schools) sound alike, adding to the sense of impersonality. Konstantinou[74] criticizes Wallace's "inability to represent a genuine cosmopolitanism" in this story, but that would seem to be part of the point. Wallace's *readers* are likely more cosmopolitan—they would be expected to have more in common, at least aspirationally, with New York sophisticates than with Amber Moltke—but Wallace's carefully crafted portrait of Amber, including her distinctive use of language, makes them sympathize with her despite themselves (much as Skip is attracted to her in spite of himself).

The story is set in June 2001, and the address of *Style* magazine is 1 World Trade Center, forcing readers to evaluate everything in this story in light of the 9/11/2001 attack on America "by which *Style* would enter history two months hence" (245). It was the *Style* magazines and "Suffering Channels" of the world that were under direct attack, not the Amber Moltkes, but Wallace understood that this was a false distinction. The greed and exploitation of the corporations cannot exist without the existential emptiness of people who yearn for a different identity; they are flip sides of the same coin. Some Americans, like Skip, may cut themselves off from a sense of community by rejecting their regional identity, but are never fully able to fit in anywhere else. Others, like Amber, accept their regional identity, but are still lured into empty pursuits (fame and/or money) that cannot make them happy. Wallace's America has an inexhaustible supply of Amber Moltkes and Skip Atwaters, and not just in the Midwest. The "South Midland" dialect's simultaneous evocation of Southernness and Midwesternness was a perfect choice to illustrate that it is not just the Midwest that is spiritually empty—it transcends regionality.

Midwesternisms

McGurl[75] sees Wallace's final unfinished novel, TPK, set in Peoria, as "belated midwestern regionalism," and "a strategic embrace of rooted provinciality,"

---

[74] Konstantinou, "The World of David Foster Wallace," 77.
[75] McGurl, "The Institution of Nothing," 28.

arguing that Wallace "never fully cut loose from its defiantly 'normal' cultural moorings." TPK does characterize what Burn[76] calls "the empty, flat land of the Midwest," as "a vista with nothing really particular to hold the eye" (123), but it does not include any salient or extended portrayals of Midwestern dialects, with the exception of the very little bit of rural eastern Missouri dialect that Toni Ware overhears and unconsciously echoes when passing through, as discussed in Chapter 5, which also argued that the assimilation of IRS agents into the corporate identity cost them whatever local previous identities they might have had.

Wallace made numerous notes on "Midwesternisms" in the "evidence notebook" that he kept during the time that he wrote TPK, but it is unlikely that he intended them for that particular work, as comparison between his handwritten drafts of other works with the final published versions shows little evidence that he ever significantly changed the way characters spoke in subsequent revisions. On the contrary, he appears to have *started* with voices and built stories around them. Wallace's collection of "Midwesternisms" was ongoing: the Harry Ransom Center collection includes both this notebook of 300 pages (container 43.1) and a different (black, wide-ruled, 70-sheet, one-subject) notebook devoted entirely to "Midwesternisms" (container 31.12). It is not practical to catalog these completely, let alone discuss all of them, (although he did quite often repeat some observations on multiple different pages, sometimes with different illustrative example sentences), but this chapter will conclude with some general observations and examples for those who do not have the luxury of visiting the Ransom Center themselves.

Phonologically, Wallace showed awareness of specific pronunciations, including "theater like it had a y in it—theayter, theyater," "Hundred as 'hunnerd,'" "Picture as 'pitcher,'" "Excetera, expecially," and "Rural MW— Eenihilated. 'I got enihilated.'" "Pronouncing the h in 'vehicle'" would also undoubtedly involve shifting the primary stress to the second syllable (as would also occur in the newly tri-syllabic *theyater*), though Wallace does not make this explicit. Some of the pronunciations would no doubt be highly stigmatized, as for example "wash as 'warsh,'" yet despite his awareness of such associated stigma, Wallace also had a note characterizing the "MW accent": it "makes you think of freckles and creased jeans."

Wallace's observations included just two morphological features: infixation of *you know* ("In-ya know-consistent"), and suffixation of -s ("Alls," "Alls I have is twenty," "Alls I'm saying is . . . ," "Alls I want is . . . ," "Anyways,"

---

[76] Stephen J. Burn, "Toward a General Theory of Vision in Wallace's Fiction," *English Studies* 95, no. 1 (2014): 85–93, esp. 87. DOI: 10.1080/0013838X.2013.857758.

"Nowadays," "Somewhere along the lines," "Many a times." (The *Oxford English Dictionary* does list an -s suffix, distinct from the plural, genitive, and third-person singular present tense agreement markers, that evolved from the Old English genitive to form adverbs like "anyways" in Middle English. The Midwestern usage observed by Wallace therefore has a rather long pedigree.)

In terms of syntax, Wallace noted the use of "except for w /complete sentence 'Except for I could also see him standing there,'" and the doubled conjunction "but yet." He noted the use of positive *anymore* (without the downward entailing environment that would license its use in other dialects): "I used to do it all the time, but anymore I only do it once, twice a week."

The bulk of Wallace's attention was devoted to the lexicon—particular words and phrases: "That irks my feelings," "It just got all scrassled up in my head," "Whatnot," "and whatnot," "'set' for 'sit,'" "Howmuchever," "Off of," "'Run off' for 'made to leave' 'She run him off,'" "breasts = 'ninnies' (Rural slang.)," "'lay' for 'lie,'" "Referring to a vacuum cleaner as a 'sweeper,'" "Ref to 'laundry' as 'wash,'" "'Humorous' for 'funny.' 'He's just so humorous,'" "'Moreso' for 'more.' 'The moreso I do it, the happier I get,'" "'I intend on . . . ,' 'I intend to working as hard as I can, see,'" "'Big of a' 'It's not that big of a deal,'" "'work ethics'—'He's got good work ethics,'" "'A little inkling' 'I started to get a little inkling of what all this is about.'" One of the few entries in the notebooks that I can track to Wallace's publications is "'Visit' for 'talk.' 'You two can sit and visit.'" In the *Harper's* article "9/11: The View from the Midwest" (but edited out of the version collected in *CTL*), there is a footnote that "the native term for a conversation is *visit*."

Wallace explicitly labeled some items in these notebooks as "Solecisms," including "Itty-tiny," "'Involved' for 'evolved.' 'And it involved into a bad situation.'" "'Take 'er easy' instead of 'take it easy.'" "Expand/Expound—'Let me expound on this point a little bit,'" "I had a circumstance happen," "MW Solecism: 'I've never really enforced my point of view on anybody,' "I don't want to suscum to temptation." "'Indefaggotable' for 'indefatigable.'"

He also noted the use of "among" (as opposed to "between") to refer to two people, specifically: "You two settle this among yourselves."

Other observations relate more to discourse conventions, spanning more than one category of grammar, for instance the following entry, which appears to start with an observation of pronunciation, but then extends into response tokens and turn-initiations: "Ahkay. (for OK) 'Aaaahkay,' when dubious. 'Okeydoke then.' 'And along the same vein, I want to say also . . .'"

Also of interest are putatively Midwestern swear words and insults: "Midwest mobile home curse: 'You scagmaggot.' 'Fucking scagmaggot.' 'Turdslurper,'" "'Shitchess' for 'Shit yes.' 'Fuck you with a table leg.' 'Shitsucker'

'Megafop'—pretentious artiste," "To get really mad at X, go off on X—'to eat his ass.'" "His wife really ate his ass about it."

There are also a couple of nonlinguistic observations, including "Rural IN + MO—men with big belt buckles and down vests; men who spit in mid-sentence," and "A kind of grace among ~~hard-working~~ Midwest people: they are WASPS who do not know they're Wasps."

It is impossible to read these notebooks without wondering how Wallace would have used these words and snippets of dialogue, without regretting the novels Wallace did not live to write, the Midwestern characters whose voices we will not get to hear.

8

Boston and Urban

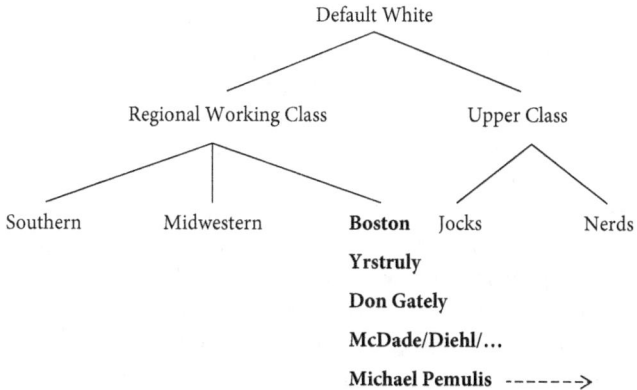

Figure 7 Wallace's Bostonians.

Infinite Jest spends roughly a thousand pages in the Boston area, featuring Wallace's only real attempt to capture a white urban dialect. In addition to portraying dialect features directly in the speech of the working-class Bostonians, both narrator and characters themselves comment explicitly on various dialect performances. Wallace gained familiarity with Boston dialects when he was an undergraduate at Amherst College (which is two hours away from Boston, but Wallace biographer Max[1] shows he spent at least one week with friends there). He later spent a couple of years in the Boston area, which appear to have been deeply unhappy ones, despite an early letter to his agent that claimed "Boston is *fun*."[2] During this time, he enrolled in and then quickly abandoned a Harvard graduate program in philosophy, taught as an adjunct at Emerson college, had stays in psychiatric hospitals and halfway houses, had an extremely unhealthy relationship with Mary Karr which became abusive when he refused to believe she wanted

---

[1] Max, *Every Love Story Is a Ghost Story*, 37.
[2] Ibid., 123.

to end it—and began writing the "big thing" that would eventually become *Infinite Jest*.

Interestingly, despite the fine gradations of the Boston dialects represented in the novel, *Jest* contains only a passing reference to a "cultured Cambridge stutter," the sort of speech Hartley[3] associates with "Harvard University professors, Boston Brahmins, and . . . U.S. presidential candidate Senator John Kerry." It is explicitly stated that Madame Psychosis's broadcast accent has no trace of this (189), and the speech of one caller to her radio show who does have a "cultured stutter" (192) is not directly represented.

Carver[4] identifies Boston as "a cultural hearth," one of the "five original coastal centers from which most of the American dialects developed" (the others being Philadelphia, tidewater Virginia, Charleston, and New Orleans), which may explain why Hartley's[5] perceptual dialectology of the area finds that native Bostonians are as liable to label their dialect region "New England," "Northeast," or even "East Coast" as they are to specify "Boston" (400). Wolfram and Schilling-Estes[6] explain that Boston is one of the centers from which the merger of low back/central vowel /ɒ/ with low back vowel /ɔ/ (the so-called *cot/caught merger*) has spread; they note that this area is not undergoing the "sweeping rotations" of the Northern Cities Vowel Shift. Laferriere[7] compares the speech of Irish, Italian, and Jewish Bostonians, finding that "the standing of one's ethnic group in a community may be more of a determinant of social class and self-image than one's income and education" (603). Boston remains one of the most racially "hypersegregated" cities in the United States today.[8]

Boston's famed r-lessness continues to be socially diagnostic in Boston[9] and occurs only in the coda of a syllable; not only is /r/ maintained in the onset (before a vowel sound) within a word, but Boston speakers sometimes *insert* an /r/ at the end of a vowel-final word if the following word also begins

---

[3] Laura Hartley, "The Consequences of Conflicting Stereotypes: Bostonian Perceptions of U.S. Dialects," *American Speech* 80, no. 4 (2005): 388–405, esp. 388. https://digitalcommons.georgefox.edu/lang_fac/16.
[4] Carver, *American Regional Dialects*, 7.
[5] Hartley, "The Consequences of Conflicting Stereotypes."
[6] Wolfram and Schilling-Estes, *American English*, 151.
[7] Laferriere, "Ethnicity in Phonological Variation and Change."
[8] Douglas S. Massey and Jonathan Tannen, "A Research Note on Trends in Black Hypersegregation," *Demography* 52, no. 3 (2015): 1025–34.
[9] Naomi Nagy and Patricia Irwin, "Boston (r): Neighbo(r)s Nea(r) and Fa(r)," *Language Variation and Change* 22, no. 2 (2010): 241–78; Joshua Levy, "The Social Stratification of (r) in Boston," *Toronto Working Papers in Linguistics* 33, no. 1 (2010): 1–12; and Rebecca Day Babcock, "Folk-Linguistic Attitudes in Eastern Massachusetts," *Open Journal of Modern Linguistics* 4, no. 3 (2014): 415.

with a vowel, as in "the idear of it!"[10] (Bostonian /r/ insertion is a productive phonological pattern, as opposed to the "intrusive-r" pronunciation of "wash" as "warsh," which affects only that single morpheme in the Midwest). Levy[11] found that r-lessness in Boston was more common among men, lower socioeconomic classes, and "employees in neighborhoods that claim strong local identity" (associating masculinity with nonstandardness, as with the Labovian concept of "covert prestige"). Although usage varied quantitatively, r-lessness was found among all groups. Fitzpatrick[12] describes Boston dialect as "one of the most widely recognized throughout the United States," including in his description not just the "dropped r's, lowered and broadened vowels," but also "distinctive vocabulary" such as "*That's wicked pissa!*, i.e., very good."

Hartley[13] finds that Bostonians "have internalized two common but conflicting American stereotypes of Boston residents—the educated elite and working class descendants of immigrants" (388), sometimes relying on the former stereotype to deem the local dialect "correct," but sometimes on the latter, leading to an unusual combination of linguistic security and insecurity. Fitzpatrick[14] agrees that "the divide between the immigrant-descended working class and the descendants of the original Puritan settlers . . . is manifested linguistically even in the present day." *Infinite Jest* captures this dichotomy perfectly with the Incandenza family and Kate Gompert representing the educated elite (despite Avril and Jim Incandenza being transplants themselves and despite all of these characters having no noticeable regional dialect features associated with their speech), and Don Gately (as well as a host of other characters) representing the working class. When the transplanted Southerner Joelle van Dyne thinks back on her first dinner with the Incandenza family, she recalls that "everybody Please-and-Thank-You'd in a way that was sheer Yankee WASP" (745); when interacting with the working-class Don Gately, however, she not only notices but mocks his r-lessness, albeit affectionately: "*Harrd. Harrrrrd. Sound it out*" (563).

Kate Gompert, whose hospital chart lists her address in Newton, MA (a predominantly white and white-collar area, with some of the most expensive real estate in the country), and her occupation as "data-clerical in a Wellesley

---

[10] Jim Fitzpatrick, "Beantown Babble (Boston, MA)," in *American Voices: How Dialects Differ from Coast to Coast*, ed. Walt Wolfram and Ben Ward (Malden, MA: Blackwell, 2006), 63–9, esp. 66.
[11] Levy, "The Social Stratification of (r) in Boston."
[12] Fitzpatrick, "Beantown Babble (Boston, MA)," 64.
[13] Hartley, "The Consequences of Conflicting Stereotypes."
[14] Fitzpatrick, "Beantown Babble (Boston, MA)," 65.

Hills real estate office" (69), is clearly part of the "educated elite"; her inner thoughts and direct speech are captured more than any other female character in the novel, with no Boston dialect markers included. The sad Pamela Hoffman-Jeep, who is described by Gately as "upscale" (924) but whose extreme alcoholism has caused her to fall in with a disreputable crowd, likewise maintains unmarked speech, except that the narrator notes in endnote 374 that she pronounces *chivalrous* "with the hard-*ch* sound distinctive of North Shore pronun. of words like *Chicago* and *champagne*" (1078). The adjective "upscale" is used over forty times in the novel by a variety of focalizers and with a variety of referents, a clear indication of the permeating class-based anxiety. Johnette Foltz uses the term to describe Hal, when he comes to Ennet House seeking information about twelve-step programs, noting that he's "like Ewell and Day and snotty . . . Ken E. that knew how to long divide and say *whom* but didn't even know how to look up shit in the Yellow Pages" (786).

Freudenthal[15] argues that "readers want to let Wallace off the hook for the clichéd contradictions of working-class identity defining Gately . . . because he's so dang likeable." Although it is clear (from Joelle's playful "correction") that Gately does not pronounce postvocalic /r/, neither his inner monologue nor his direct speech in the novel reflect this, other than his representing "Norm" from the sitcom "Cheers!" as "Nom" in his thoughts (834, 836, 883). Hoberek[16] cites examples of "fragments of speech clearly reflective of Gately and his Boston underclass milieu" such as "He took zero in the way of shit" (55) and compares these to the "fascination with the white ethnic southern New England accent" found in Boston crime novels and films. The narrator makes this explicit in endnote 372: "Surely *skeet* and *vig*, meaning debt and bookmaker's automatic percentage (usually 10% subtracted from winnings or added to skeet) are not just metro Boston terms" (1078). The lexical items provide constant reminders of identity without necessarily triggering the same negative judgments that representing the r-lessness of the dialect undoubtedly would.

Warren[17] discusses the pervasive use in *Infinite Jest* of what he calls "jargony argot," showing how "local" terminology that "starts out as a way of modeling community within the novel becomes a tactic for organizing community outside of the novel." As example of this, he cites the recurrence of "Storrow (Drive)" the local highway referred to by the student engineer at Madame

---

[15] Freudenthal, "Anti-Interiority," 191.
[16] Andrew Hoberek, "The Novel after David Foster Wallace," in *A Companion to David Foster Wallace Studies*, ed. Marshall Boswell and Stephen J. Burn (New York: Palgrave Macmillan, 2013), 211–38, esp. 221.
[17] Andrew Warren, "Narrative Modeling and Community Organizing in *The Pale King* and *Infinite Jest*," *Studies in the Novel* 44, no. 4 (2012): 389–408, esp. 397.

Psychosis's radio station (184), by Joelle van Dyne (234), Orin (289), Gately (478), Mario (769), and Rodney Tine, Sr. (877), with endnote 202 (1034) explaining Gately's use of the road's more local name "the Storrow 500." (Warren notes that Wallace does not just use local geographical and cultural referents in this way, but also more abstract concepts, like the "squeak" sound effect that recurs across "just about every register in the novel."[18]) This device works well on a lexical level, where meanings are easily acquired and words freely borrowed. The initial use of such local references signals shared group identity between and among characters, but their unfamiliarity to readers emphasizes readers' distance from the social milieu depicted; as repeated references become increasingly familiar, readers may begin to feel like part of the in-group. It is not clear that repeated exposure to nonstandard phonology and syntax has the same effect. If Wallace had encoded Gately's phonology directly, it would have clearly signaled his affiliation with the other working-class Bostonians so represented—but it likely would have continued to represent and emphasize his distance from most readers.

R-lessness is strongly associated with AAE as well as different regional dialects, and Wallace may have wanted to avoid any ambiguity with respect to the ethnicity of his characters. The only time Wallace has a little fun with the visual encoding of Boston phonology is in a few short lines uttered by the security guard who arrives on the scene after Gately has been shot. "Secyotty! Hold it right thaah. . . . I'm *oddering* desis until who's in chahge that I can repot the si*chation*. . . . I'm oddering the whole sitchation halt it *right* thaah whey*aah*" (618–9). The guard is presumably white, since Gately does not mention otherwise, although he does recognize him as "one of the ex-football E.M. Security guys . . . the drunk" (618), "his name's Sidney or Stanley" (619), who "always asks Gately how it's hanging" (619). If, nonetheless, readers misidentify the guard's ethnicity, this shouldn't make any difference to their reading of that scene.

Ennet House residents Wade McDade and Gavin Diehl visit Gately in the hospital and apologize that they can't make legal depositions on his behalf "like they'd be ready to do in a fucking *hatbeat*" if it weren't "tittymount to like judicio-penal suicide" (893), but although the free indirect discourse makes it difficult to attribute the precise words and pronunciations, these seem to belong to McDade and/or Diehl rather than to Gately himself, as they also say that "the G-Man" (a name Gately never uses for himself) is "wicked missed back at the House" (894). Very little information is ever given about these two, other than that Diehl and Gately had done some time together

[18] Ibid.

in prison, but they are clearly working-class Bostonians, as is the despicable Randy Lenz. Despite playing a rather pivotal role in the action of the novel, Lenz only has two lines of direct dialogue; neither represents r-lessness visually, although Bruce Green notices that "the way Lenz pronounces *brother* involves one *r*" (578). The narrator also comments in an endnote that a word used by Lenz, *mitts*, is the "Charlestown/ Southie street term for meters" (1037). "Southie" itself is not explained, as it is fairly transparent Boston slang, for South Boston, the working-class neighborhood depicted in the film *Good Will Hunting*, which came out the year after *Jest* was published.

Yrstruly

The only first-person representation of a "Boston blue collar" dialect is "yrstruly" (128–35). Some readers misidentify this character as African American, due to the "bad" English (according to Cohen,[19] and according to my experience teaching the novel last year), but this performance is completely distinct from the AAE dialect representations discussed in Chapter 3. The second sentence of the monologue begins with a bit of nonstandard grammar and vocabulary that should trigger recognition of a white working-class background: "The AM" (i.e., a.m., the morning [singular]) "were wicked bright." Although Wallace did not understand AAE verb patterns, he never put a singular *were* in the mouth of a black speaker, and he reserved the intensifier *wicked* for white Bostonians as well, along with *map* for *face*.

Alexander[20] considers yrstruly "gender indeterminate," although he fits all the linguistic stereotypes of toxic masculinity, and every critic who has attempted to associate him with a recovering addict at Ennet House has pointed toward a male addict. In his truly extraordinary attempt to capture all the relationships between the different characters in *Infinite Jest* in a single diagram, Sam Potts[21] equates yrstruly with Emil Minty, perhaps because yrstruly repeatedly refers to "nigers [sic]," and it is revealed that the white punk/skinhead Minty has "an amateur swastika" tattoo that says "FUCK NIGERS" (207). Wollitz[22] presents additional evidence for this identification,

---

[19] Cohen, "The Whiteness of David Foster Wallace," 237.
[20] Alexander, "David Foster Wallace and Repressive Taboos," 1.
[21] Potts, Sam. n.d. http://sampottsinc.com/ij/IJ_Diagram.pdf.
[22] Michael Gibson Wollitz, "Figurant Society: Post-Postmodernity and David Foster Wallace's *Infinite Jest*," 2009, 68–9. MA Thesis, Georgetown University. https://repository.library.georgetown.edu/bitstream/handle/10822/552982/WollitzMichaelGibson.pdf?sequence=1.

but if this was the intended association, then Wallace was quite sloppy with the representation of Minty's language: Minty only has two lines of direct dialogue in the novel, but one of them features multiple negation ("He can't go in no E.R. with a gunshot" [617]), whereas yrstruly talks nonstop for eight pages without ever using multiple negation, despite opportunities to do so, as in "He doesnt' notice anything" (134), and "I didnt' say anything" (135). Staes[23] believes that yrstruly might be Randy Lenz, because the narrator appears to once refer to Lenz as "yrstruly" (562), but although Lenz expresses himself crudely at times, he knows how to use an apostrophe ("I ain't got time for this shit" (271), for instance), and he "thinks of himself as a kind of hiply sexy artist-intellectual" (279), which doesn't fit yrstruly at all. In all likelihood, yrstruly is a different addict whose experience intersected with some of the more major characters—perhaps one who didn't survive long enough to make it to Ennet House. (He is perhaps also former military or the child of someone in the military, as he uses the term "rickytick" several times to mean "right away," a usage not shared by anyone else in the novel. I was unable to find any scholarly study of this term, but the online Urban Dictionary[24] identifies it as associated with US military, particularly the Marine Corps.) In any case, he clearly appears to represent a lower-class white Boston dialect, which Letzler[25] (without sound linguistic basis) deems "semi-decipherable English."

Yrstruly's performance is significant because it contains Wallace's only extended use of "eye dialect"—misspellings that trigger strong awareness of incorrectness (and therefore perceptions of ignorance and lack of education), despite encoding perfectly *standard* pronunciation. Pervasive use of abbreviations, words strung together with nonalphabetic symbols and/or without spaces in between them (2B for "to be," $, *hiclass*, *nite*, *gosofar*, *XMas*, *aprox*, *outwego*, *sortof*, *kindof*, etc.), no doubt seemed much stranger to readers in 1996 than these conventions do now, due to pervasive abbreviation and use of nonalphabetic symbols in text messages and social media postings. The effect of these is greatly amplified by nonstandard placement of the apostrophe (which always appears word-finally in the monologue) and alterations that cannot be interpreted as intentional abbreviation, such as Enfield and Central *Squar*, an *arguement*, *wurse/wurst*, *materil*, *realy*, *pryor*, *avrege*, *decesed*, *dumsters*, *cryng*, and so on. The only misspelling that seems

---

[23] Staes, "Rewriting the Author."
[24] "Ricky tick." *Urban Dictionary*. http://www.urbandictionary.com
[25] David Letzler, *The Cruft of Fiction: Mega-Novels and the Science of Paying Attention* (Lincoln: University of Nebraska Press, 2017), 90.

motivated by dialect phonology is the repeated use of *pernt* for *point* (with an intrusive /r/, again associated with the white population).

Some solecisms were no doubt intended to evoke particular associations, such as *conversession* (129, 130, 132, 133), which seems to imply elements of planning and duration rather than brief spontaneous exchanges. *Elemonade* for *eliminate* (129, 134, 135) may trigger incongruous images of people drinking *lemonade* as they plan a murder, and perhaps planning it in an overly *elementary* way. It is implausible that yrstruly, desperately trying to score drugs, is being intentionally playful with words—he is very focused and serious in these scenes; he is not having fun. It is equally unlikely that Wallace could resist some intentional wordplay or would fail to appreciate that yrstruly's unintentional portmanteau *cusually* (133, 134) is a perfect metalinguistic commentary on how *usually* this character is *casual*. *Conceited* for *conceded* (134) seems almost Freudian.

As with Clenette, readers have to work to decode the nonstandard writing and to get past their own knee-jerk negative reactions to these. Wallace keeps these sections short, presumably recognizing this level of difficulty, but he doesn't let readers off the hook entirely. The extra effort required to understand what Clenette and yrstruly are saying may give readers some social distance from the painful events recounted, emphasizing just how different the reader is from the person thinking these thoughts. This social distance, in turn, makes the horrifying events recounted easier to digest. On the other hand, the decoding effort also slows readers down, forcing them to spend more time with these characters than they might otherwise wish to, prolonging the discomfort they feel. I believe that Wallace was attempting a repeat of the same lesson, and making the further point that this is not ethnicity or gender specific: that initial negative reactions based only on dialect are shameful; that superficialities of language differences distract us and cause us to blame the victim; that all these characters deserve our empathy. Two brief pages from Clenette could not achieve a lasting effect on readers, however much they engage in that section and however deeply they feel its gut-wrenching conclusion. With repeated exposure to the same lesson, involving different characters, black and white, male and female, addicted and sober, very young to fully adult, these points might eventually sink in. This is just good pedagogy, as Professor Wallace surely knew.

Jocks and Nerds

Michael Pemulis, discussed in Chapter 4 as part of a family illustrating assimilation into nonethnic default whiteness, also shows that social mobility is possible for those of working-class background who can excel as an athlete and/or an intellectual; as both of these, he is able to aspire to the upper class. Pemulis's immigrant father worked "on the Southie docks" (683), and readers are reminded multiple times that the family lived in Allston: he is "Allston's Michael Pemulis" (322), and in case readers are not aware of the meaning of this, an endnote describes it specifically as "blue-collar Allston" (1035).

Although Pemulis maintains the stereotypical Boston area use of "wicked" as an intensifier, he is not represented as r-less in the text, and his use of language is otherwise perfectly standard, if not pedantic enough for his friend Hal (the lexical prodigy). That these very minor linguistic differences nonetheless continue to reflect real differences in socioeconomic status is made explicit during the Eschaton game (an enactment of geopolitical warfare, played with tennis balls), when Hal admits to himself that he may be "a secret snob about collar-color issues and Pemulis" (335). Hal acknowledges that his friend is "a born tech-science wienie," but emphasizes at the same time that Hal's "most valiant efforts barely get Pemulis through Mrs. I's triad of required Grammars" (154). Hal continues to comment on Pemulis's language throughout. When Pemulis refers to a "psychosensual distorter," Hal interjects, "Think you mean psycho*sensory*, unless I don't know the whole story here" (211). When Pemulis talks about avoiding entrapment, endnote 55 clarifies that Hal "personally thinks the term that'd apply here would be *suborned*, not *entrapped*" (996). Endnote 123 begins, "Pemulis here, dictating to Inc, who can just sit there making a steeple out of his fingers and pressing it to his lip and not take notes and wait and like inscribe [*sic*] it anytime in the next week and get it verbatim, the smug turd" (1023). This *is* Hal's transcription, of course, and the "[*sic*]" is Hal's commentary that Pemulis has again used the wrong word. Readers are clearly meant to admire Hal's precision with language but are also likely to agree with Pemulis's judgment of Hal's unattractive smugness, the sting of which indictment is lessened somewhat by Hal's apparent good-natured willingness to own up to it by including it in the transcription.

Social categories like "jock" and "nerd" are, in theory, orthogonal to questions of age, ethnicity, social class, and gender—but in practice, there are often constraints that preclude full participation in athletics and academics, traditionally excluding members of marginalized groups from claiming these identities. Whereas the Detroit students studied by Eckert[26] position themselves as "jocks" versus "burnouts," and Habick's[27] Farmer City students

---

[26] Eckert, *Linguistic Variation as Social Practice*.
[27] Habick, "Farmer City, Illinois: Sound Systems Shifting South."

claim "redneck" and "burnout" identities, Bucholtz's white California high school students label themselves "nerds," "hip-hop fans," and "preppies." (Cf. Kirkham[28] and Drummond[29] for similar studies on UK youth.) In all these cases, young people do not prioritize categories they were born into but align themselves with categories they themselves help to construct. Although these group memberships may not be as enduring, they are no less real or important for the adolescents who inhabit them. Each of these groups differentiates itself not just by label or superficial in-group slang lexical items, but by (presumably less conscious) quantitative differences in pronunciations.

Bucholtz's nerds use "a highly and sometimes exaggeratedly formal version of Standard English . . . distinguished phonetically by careful articulation and especially resistance to processes characteristic of colloquial speech, like consonant cluster simplification and the reduction of unstressed vowels."[30] They exhibit "an extraordinarily playful attitude toward language," with "a high degree of metalinguistic awareness, and they took pleasure in manipulating linguistic forms for humorous effect" (157), particularly delighting in puns. This sounds very much like a description of Hal and his ETA friends—and of Wallace. McGurl[31] argues that being "a weenie-American—or geek American, or nerd American, in this context the subtle differences between these terms is not important—is the technomodernist's version of having a cultural identity, a paradoxically nonethnic ethnicity, or technicity." That is, the erasure of ethnicity discussed in Chapters 3 and 4 gives rise to a need to create new ways of belonging.

Nugent[32] discusses "the relationship between nerdiness and ethnicity"—specifically, that Americans are more willing to associate whites and Asians with nerdiness, and to associate whites and African Americans with athleticism (73). As a result, whites may claim any social identity they choose, whereas Asians (and presumably unassimilated Europeans and Jews) face resistance in being accepted as athletes, and African Americans (and presumably Latinx) face resistance in claiming scholarly identities. Because the nerd identity is claimed predominantly through hyperstandard language, anyone whose speech codes as nonstandard (whether ethnic or regional/lower class) appears to disavow their claim to nerdiness; likewise,

---

[28] Sam Kirkham, "Intersectionality and the Social Meanings of Variation: Class, Ethnicity, and Social Practice," *Language in Society* 44, no. 5 (2015): 629–52. https://doi.org/10.1017/S0047404515000585.

[29] Drummond, *Researching Urban Youth Language and Identity*.

[30] Bucholtz, *White Kids*, 151.

[31] McGurl, "The Institution of Nothing," 44.

[32] Benjamin Nugent, *American Nerd: The Story of My People* (New York: Scribner, 2008), 9.

any working-class person or person of color who stakes a linguistic claim to nerdiness seems to reject their ethnic, regional, and class identity. This leads to a dangerous cycle, when considering how much of one's identity may be formed in response to the perception of and treatment by others, and how a lack of representation and role models within a category can lead to future exclusions.

Hal Incandenza, like his creator, serves as an archetype for both the "jock" and "nerd" identities, showing the false dichotomy of these now familiar social constructs, so often viewed as incompatibly opposed. In "Derivative Sport," Wallace describes how at Amherst "I found my identity shifting from jock to math-wienie" (*ASFTINDA* 14). Success within these categories (i.e., excelling at sports or scholarship) depends largely not on natural ability alone but a strong sense of discipline. The training regimen and curriculum at ETA both on and off the court emphasizes that there is no dichotomy between body and the mind, despite popular stereotype—indeed, there is a strong mind-body connection. Those fortunate and disciplined enough to achieve excellence as jocks or nerds receive clear social rewards, gaining them entry to the upper class, if they were not fortunate enough to be born into it. A "burnout" identity, on the other hand, requires no such discipline and receives no such reward; on the contrary, with the obvious threat of addiction, the adoption of such an identity presents particular peril. It is important that Hal, despite his penchant for "getting covertly high" (49), very much does not want to publicly identify as a "burnout." His getting "outed" as such—potentially through the mandated drug testing, or when John Wayne ("without question the best male player" (260) at ETA) reveals everyone's secrets over the campus public address system—threatens his claims to the identities that are most important to him. The threat is much more real for his working-class friend, Michael Pemulis, who was not born into wealth: success at the academy is Pemulis's only chance at joining the upper class. He may have the "street smarts" to make money on his own— to continue his lucrative career as designer and peddler of drugs ("Mrs. Pemulis raised no dewy-eyed fools" [156])—but that will not gain him status.

The taxonomy of identity that I have identified within Wallace's work makes it relatively simple to consider different aspects of identity separately: How are foreigners distinguished from Americans? How are African Americans treated differently from other US ethnicities? Why is only the white working class shown speaking regional dialects? What other social identities can people claim to raise themselves out of the working class? This approach has, I hope, illustrated the social hierarchies and assimilatory pressures that Wallace's work makes evident (moving left-to-right in Figure 1), although it has mostly ignored other important dimensions of identity including age, gender, sexuality, and (dis)ability. It is more difficult to try to put all these pieces back together, to consider how all the different pieces of a given person's identity intersect and contribute to a coherent "self" whose performances range and vary based on context. The next chapter nonetheless attempts to grapple with such complexity, taking a more complete look at Wallace's most important character: himself.

9

"Dave Wallace" and His Readers

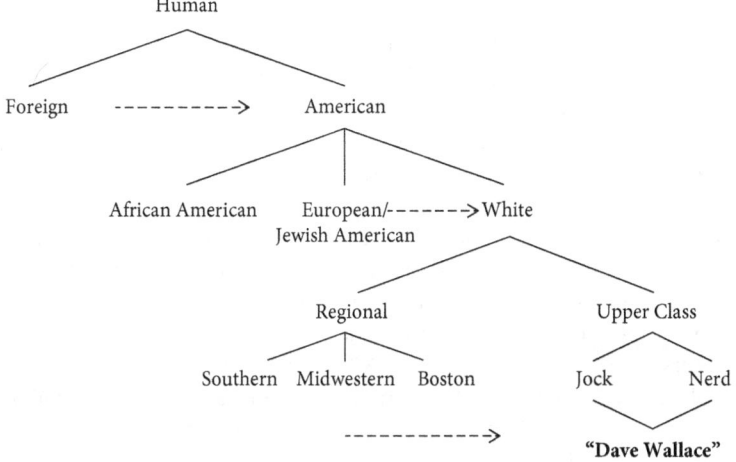

Figure 8 The Isolation of the "Dave Wallace" Idiolect.

> When I say or write something, there are actually a whole lot of different things I am communicating. The propositional content (i.e., the verbal information I'm trying to convey) is only one part of it. Another part is stuff about me, the communicator. Everyone knows this. (CTL 96)

"An author, like everyone else, speaks some variety, or dialect, of a language, not 'the language' itself," Ives[1] observes. Whether this voice is a conscious linguistic construct or whether it is truly the voice of the author himself (as the "David Wallace" narrator insisted in TPK, all the while adding easily falsifiable fictional details such as the wrong age and birthplace) is not important. The narrator can be (re)constructed separately from the bottom-up, in each

---

[1] Ives, "A Theory of Literary Dialect," 152.

text, as one encounters him. But for people who read across Wallace's work, there is surely some top-down mental work going on—a shock of familiarity triggered by a recognition of the author-cum-narrator-cum-character that allows readers to apply what they have already learned about him in other texts. In this chapter, I argue that although Wallace's use of *other* dialects was not mimetic, his projection of his own voice (through various characters and narrators) was self-consciously so, and that he used this to build what Boswell[2] refers to as "an amiable, self-effacing relationship with his readers," encouraging them to continue to be part of an ongoing conversation with him. Wallace's students discovered that "his goals were traditional. The story should connect reader and writer."[3] The fandom Wallace inspired is evidence that he succeeded in connecting with many.

"Dave Wallace" is emphatically *not* foreign (i.e., American), *not* ethnic ("resoundingly and in all ways white" (CTL 102)), *not usually* regional in his speech (i.e., upper class), a former jock and perpetual nerd. The nerdiness is the only positive identity he publicly enacted (although he sometimes also *claimed* a Midwestern regional identity). This constellation of characteristics also constitutes the identity that the author claimed publicly, in many interviews that also formed part of the ongoing conversation with readers. Miley[4] summarizes Wallace's "persona and image as a writer and public Figure" in three words: "footnotes, bandannas, and sincerity," but his characteristic uses of language go far beyond digressive footnotes and play a much larger role in the construction of his persona than an easily changed (or omitted) bandanna.

Because Wallace occupied the right-most place on Figure 8—the "default" settings of an American, in not just his own worldview, but in popular imagination built upon media representations—he could easily have created a disembodied, personality-less omniscient narrator. He chose instead to draw readers' attention to distinctive idiolect features, creating a narrative persona that readers could connect with across texts, a personality that readers could get to know, one they might by turns admire, feel sorry for, find infuriating, one who has no social filter (telling us things we'd rather he didn't), but also withholds answers to our burning questions, distracting us with wit and style. The speech acts he regularly accomplished, the conversational turn-taking and repair mechanisms he unexpectedly incorporated into his

[2] Boswell, *Understanding David Foster Wallace*, 180–1.
[3] Max, *Every Love Story Is a Ghost Story*, 188.
[4] Mike Miley,. " . . . And Starring David Foster Wallace as Himself: Performance and Persona in *The Pale King*," *Critique: Studies in Contemporary Fiction*, 57, no. 2 (2016): 191–207, esp. 194. DOI: 10.1080/00111619.2015.1028611.

writing, and his characteristic linguistic politeness strategies help to lessen the distance between narrator and reader, leading even those who do not share all or any of his social categorizations to nonetheless accept him as a guide to the chaotic world presented—or even as a friend (explaining the passionate fandom of his readers).

From a lesser author, the dominance of a single voice across works might appear to be the result of a deficit, an inability to inhabit different points of view and identities at any length or depth; however, that explanation is unsatisfying for Wallace, given his prodigious skills and imagination. Another possible explanation is implicit racism, sexism, classism, and so forth—that Wallace was simply uninterested in (if not hostile to) identities other than his own. This account, however, is belied by the systematic way he sought to distinguish all the "not-me" identities from his own throughout his career, and the sympathetic treatment given to most of the "not-me" characters (often more sympathetic than the portrayals of Wallace's alter egos). The pervasiveness of Wallace's distinctive voice must therefore be seen as a deliberate choice, serving both thematic and philosophical goals—specifically, to reconnect with readers at each opportunity, to provide them with that sense of being in an ongoing conversation with "the living human holding the pencil" (TPK 66).

Early in his career, Wallace took Barth's *Lost in the Funhouse* narrator's writerly advice to avoid using first-person narration if one identifies closely with one's narrator. (Sheridan[5] describes how Wallace noted "this is me" in the margin by that particular passage.) In *Broom* and early stories, he mostly hid behind alter ego focalizing characters. His creative nonfiction essay writing freed him up considerably to inject an admittedly fictionalized but quite realistic "Dave Wallace" narrative persona, and by TPK, he was not just using first-person narration, but adamantly insisting that this was not "some abstract narrative persona," but "the real author . . . a real person, David Wallace" (66). The name of this narrator varies (from unnamed to "Dave" to "Dave Wallace" to "David Wallace")—but I do not make much of this; people typically do use different versions of their names, and do not necessarily specify who is speaking when leaving messages for friends. Konstantinou,[6]

---

[5] Mark Sheridan, "Interpret You, INTERPRET-ME? Or, Fictional Pasts and Fictional Futures: The Predecessors and Contemporaries of David Foster Wallace," in *Critical Insights: David Foster Wallace*, ed. Philip Coleman (New York: Grey House Publishing/Salem Press, 2015), 78–93, esp. 81.
[6] Lee Konstantinou, "Unfinished Form," *Los Angeles Review of Books* (July 6, 2011). https ://lareviewofbooks.org/article/unfinished-form/#.

Staes,[7] Boswell,[8] and Miley[9] have all debated the extent to which the "David Wallace" persona is fictional, but they have paid little attention to consistency of the language and conversational strategies used to construct it across works. Miley notes "the degree to which [Wallace] continually attempts to shatter layers of performance and fakery in his writing, to step out from behind the curtain, as it were, and speak directly to the reader without the mediation of performance" (195). He was, of course, deliberately *performing* the "Dave Wallace" identity, projecting the image he wanted others to see—as everybody does, if somewhat less consciously.

A psychoanalytic approach (which, given Wallace's scathing portraits of psychotherapy in multiple works, he would probably hate) might argue that Wallace became increasingly unable to hide behind his writing, that he "burst free" of the confines of traditional omniscient narration. In *Jest*, where the narrator is mostly revealed in endnotes (and in the existence of such endnotes), the narrator clearly wants readers to recognize how smart and funny and human he is, but has a conflicting and even more powerful desire to have readers focus on anything (and everything) other than him. Wallace told one interviewer that "I'm an exhibitionist who wants to hide, but is unsuccessful at hiding; therefore, somehow, I succeed,"[10] and another that writing is "kind of like exhibitionism in private."[11] *Jest*'s narrator puts it best: "People are virtually unlimited in their need to give themselves away, on various levels. Some just prefer to do it in secret" (53).

Less psychologically inclined critics might interpret all this simply as Wallace starting with safer, traditional modes of omniscient narration before moving on to more postmodern experiments. Boswell[12] traces the development of the narrator across Wallace's fiction, including some of the non-Dave-named (though sometimes *originally* Dave-named) characters/ focalizers, such as LaVache Beadsman in *Broom*, Mark Nechtr in "Westward," and Hal Incandenza in *Jest*. Oddly, Boswell relegates discussion of LaVache's sister Lenore to a footnote, even though she is the main character, and Boswell acknowledges that Wallace explained *Broom* as a "coded autobio"

---

[7] Staes, "Rewriting the Author."
[8] Marshall Boswell, "Author Here: The Legal Fiction of David Foster Wallace's The Pale King," *English Studies* 95, no. 1 (2014): 25–39.
[9] Miley, ". . . .And Starring David Foster Wallace as Himself."
[10] McCaffery, "An Expanded Interview with David Foster Wallace," 43.
[11] Anne Marie Donahue, "David Foster Wallace Winces at the Suggestion That His Book Is Sloppy in Any Sense," in *Conversations with David Foster Wallace*, ed. Stephen J. Burn (Jackson: University of Mississippi Press, 2012), 70–2, esp. 71.
[12] Boswell, "Author Here."

with a "sex-change."[13] Lenore "is David Foster Wallace in disguise" (Joffe forthcoming).[14] *Jest's* Kate Gompert also does not seem like a big stretch for Wallace, despite her sex. Natalini[15] argues that Don Gately can also be seen as a stand in, although this is belied by clear differences not just in class, education, upbringing, and temperament, but above all by his use of language.

We don't expect friends to sound exactly the same in every situation or circumstance, easily recognizing the core of their personality across moods and registers; so, too, readers recognize the same "voice" across Wallace's work. Hayes-Brady[16] describes Wallace's use of voice as "the most striking element of his writing, the one gushed over or excoriated by critics, the one remembered and imitated by readers (and critics)." Aubry[17] finds the narrative voice so intrusive that it "disrupts the reader's ability to empathize with the plight of the characters," adding that "there is truly only one character in [*Infinite Jest*], and it is the narrator."

Just as language itself "is a system of interdependent terms in which the value of each term results solely from the simultaneous presence of the others,"[18] all the dialects in Wallace's work may be evaluated and understood in contrast to the others, part of a greater semiotic framework. It is all the more important therefore to study Wallace's own recognizable "voice" in the context of its privileged place in the linguistic landscape, the voice of "normality."

Literature as Literal Conversation

Wallace frequently discussed writing as "an act of communication between one human being and another" (something he says we "know in our gut") (*ASFTINDA* 144). He elaborated that "this process is a relationship between the writer's consciousness and her [the reader's] own, and that in order for it to be anything like a full human relationship, she's going to have to put

---

[13] McCaffery, "An Expanded Interview with David Foster Wallace," 41.
[14] Daniela Franca Joffe, "No Man's Land: David Foster Wallace and Feminist America," *The Journal of David Foster Wallace Studies* 1, no. 1 (forthcoming): 1–. https://s3.amazonaws.com/academia.edu.documents/56681900/Joffe_JDFWS_copyedited.pdf.
[15] Roberto Natalini, "David Foster Wallace and the Mathematics of Infinity," in *A Companion to David Foster Wallace Studies*, ed. Marshall Boswell and Stephen J. Burn (New York: Palgrave Macmillan, 2013), 43–57.
[16] Hayes-Brady, *The Unspeakable Failures of David Foster Wallace*, 165.
[17] Aubry, "*Infinite Jest* and the Recovery of Feeling," 116.
[18] Ferdinand de Saussure, *Course in General Linguistics* (New York: McGraw-Hill, 1966), 114.

in her share of the linguistic work." That literature communicates is self-evident, and the metaphor of literature as conversation may be as old as literature itself. Plato imagined dialogues between Socrates and his students to stand in for conversations between himself and his readers, and Sartre breathed new life into the literature-as-conversation metaphor in the 1940s, giving as the answer to his own question of "Why write?"[19] that authors initiate "conversation" with the reader, seeking to have their consciousness recognized, and that readers likewise read to satisfy their own desire for recognition, seeing aspects of themselves reflected in the work. But as a credentialed SNOOT, steeped in the philosophy of language, Wallace understood the difference between *communication* and *conversation*; when he said that "a piece of fiction is a conversation,"[20] or that he wanted his writing to be "like a late-night conversation with really good friends, when the bullshit stops and the masks come off,"[21] I suspect that he meant it quite literally.

The main problem with taking seriously the idea of literature as literal (not metaphorical) conversation is that, by definition, conversation involves multiple turns-at-talk from multiple speakers, the pattern of which is not decided in advance, each turn shaped by the context of previous turns and shaping the context of future turns.[22] This may work metaphorically for any one of Wallace's pieces, as he typically allows different speakers to speak, and (in his fiction, at least) different consciousnesses to share their perspectives— as detailed throughout this monograph—but it works more literally when considering Wallace's writing as an ongoing conversation with readers that goes across his career. Readers have only one possible *actual* speech act within that conversation: the de facto invitation to Wallace to continue (performed each time they pick up one of his texts), but Wallace anticipates and ventriloquizes imagined speech acts for readers in such subtle ways that readers feel like they're actively taking part.

For instance, readers of *Jest* who had read Wallace's earlier work would recognize Hal as a Wallace alter ego, but an unsuspecting reader who is jolted by the shifts in focalization may be looking for what Wallace's editor Michael Pietsch, called "an 'I' who may be the one trying to put everything together"

---

[19] Jean-Paul Sartre, "Why Write?" in *Critical Theory Since Plato*, ed. Adams Hazard, Rev. ed. (Fort Worth: Harcourt Brace Jovanovich, C1992 [1948]), 983–92.
[20] Miller, "The Salon Interview: David Foster Wallace," 62.
[21] Donahue, "David Foster Wallace Winces at the Suggestion That His Book Is Sloppy in Any Sense," 71.
[22] Emanuel Schegloff, Gail Jefferson, and Harvey Sacks, "A Simplest Systematics for the Organization of Turn-Taking for Conversation," *Language* 50, no. 4 (1974): 696–735.

(quoted in Max[23]). Staes claims that "readerly attempts to empathize with the novel's global narrative are ultimately centered around an absence in the text" (421), but there *is* a narrator there, albeit one who plays peekaboo with readers. He begins to address the reader directly, although it is possible to interpret the repeated use of the second-person pronoun as generic rather than addressee-oriented, as in "where you're dreading whatever you think of" (42), and "you can tell where the sun is without looking" (43). When the narrator offers a "by the way" (endnote 2, 983, introduced on page 46), it begins to become clear that this is an extended conversation between narrator and reader. Soon thereafter, a specific detail is selected "to give you an idea" (47). The next section begins with the presentational structure "Here's Hal . . . " and exhorts the reader, "let's face it" (49). Endnote 7 (introduced on page 52) has a likewise conversational interjection: "and—yes—alcohol" (983), which only makes sense if the narrator is anticipating a response from the reader, and here is where Wallace proves himself to be a genius at fostering a sense of connection with his readers, who will feel "heard" no matter what their opinion actually is, as the interjection works equally well for anticipated agreement or for anticipated disagreement, including all potential readers in the conversation. (That is, the "yes" can be interpreted as "yes, I know you're way ahead of me here, and I'm finally getting to it" or as "I know you disagree with me, but yes, I maintain that this is really true.")

As Boswell[24] points out for BIHM, the reader "assumes the position of someone who literally cannot get a word in edgewise"—a position also frequently occupied by Wallace's characters, not just the interviewer in BIHM, who is never heard at all. In the first stretch of the conversation between Marathe and Steeply (87–95), the men are frequently interrupted mid-utterance, and there are more than twice as many words devoted to narration than both men speak combined (2,453 to their combined 956, not counting an interrupting chunk of narration about feral hamsters). Most readers cannot identify directly with undercover operatives or wheelchair assassins, but they *can* imagine having a conversation with Wallace's narrator *about* these. Marathe and Steeply are not-very-believable people, transparently symbols for more abstract political philosophies—there is more of a real "personality" with which readers can identify in the ostensibly less personal narration.

Readers should more easily be able to identify with Hal, as Martínez[25] points out, as the opening passage "is likely to activate readers' 'socially

---

[23] Max, *Every Love Story Is a Ghost Story*, 182.
[24] Boswell, *Understanding David Foster Wallace*, 189.
[25] Martínez, *Storyworld Possible Selves*, 25.

isolated' individual possible self," while other readers "may be schematic in . . . the 'sportive self'" or may have a "past self . . . as a 'university applicant.'" Martínez outlines "linguistic footprints marking the presence of these hybrid mental constructs [i.e., storyworld possible selves] in the construal of narrative storyworlds,"[26] but does not explicitly consider the role of dialect representations in that process. Wallace acknowledged the "paradox" of "allowing the reader to sort of escape self by achieving some sort of identification with another human psyche—the writer's or some character's, etc.—and you're *also* trying to antagonize the reader's intuition that she is a self, that she is alone and going to die alone."[27] Wallace's lack of concern for realistic dialect portrayals may limit readers' ability to project themselves onto the characters, but the multiplicity of dialect portrayals creates a universe in which any reader could be one of the crowd. Readers may identify with the "Dave Wallace" narrator directly—but if not, they can still feel like he is speaking *to* them with empathy and respect.

The narrator of *Jest* is never named, and no biographical details are given, although some can be gleaned (for instance, he has local insider information about Boston neighborhoods and slang). He is extraordinarily well informed in both arcane realms of scholarship and the seamy underbelly of society. His knowledge of drugs and halfway houses might tend to raise doubts about his reliability, which in turn motivates the demonstration of wide-ranging scholarly knowledge, to show that the narrator is quite credible, on this topic at least. The establishment of narrative reliability is especially important, as readers are asked to believe some frankly incredible things, even within the parameters of *Jest's* strange near-future society (e.g., when the wraith of the late James Incandenza communicates with Gately in the hospital). The extent to which these details mirror facts about the author is remarkable and contributes to the reader's sense of actually engaging in conversation with the author. As impressive as his demonstration of knowledge is, coupled with his compulsion to monopolize the conversation, the narrator will probably come across as a show-off, so it is all the more important that he treats readers with respect for their own intelligence and demonstrates indirectly, via his explicit warnings, that he cares about them.

Another extended example (also from the endnotes of *Jest*) shows some of the same techniques at work, but also how Wallace was able to manipulate linguistic variables on all levels of language, a distinctive characteristic of his

---

[26] Ibid., 20.
[27] McCaffery, "An Expanded Interview with David Foster Wallace," 32.

personal voice that readers may not consciously register.[28] Letzler[29] discusses several of *Jest*'s endnotes in terms of establishing the narrator's authority and/ or reliability, such as notes 216 ("No clue") and 223 ("though what the hell 'ALGOL' is is anybody's guess") (both 1036), which establish that the narrator is not omniscient, but he does not see a similar purpose for endnote 8 (984), reproduced later, citing it specifically as prototypical "cruft"—that is, "junk text, simultaneously too excessive and too vacuous to be worth anyone's attention."[30]

> 8. I.e.: psylocibin; Happy Patches[a]; MDMA/Xstasy (bad news, though, X); various low-tech manipulations of the benzene-ring in methoxy-class psychedelics, usually home-makable; synthetic dickies like MMDA, DMA, DMMM, 2CB, para-DOT I-VI, etc.—though note this class doesn't and shouldn't include CNS-rattlers like STP, DOM, the long-infamous West-U.S.-Coast "Grievous Bodily Harm" (gamma hydroxybutyric acid), LSD-25 or -32, or DMZ/M.P. Enthusiasm for this stuff seems independent of neurologic type.
>
> [a]Homemade transdermals, usually MDMA or Muscimole, with DDMS or the over-counter-available DMSO as the transdermal carrier. (984)

Contra Letzler's strange theory that Wallace *wanted* people to skim his work (an idea I suspect would have given the author his proverbial "howling fantods"), the opening line of this note deploys multiple poetic devices to attract the reader's attention, to ensure that a reader won't simply glance, think "list," and turn back to the main text: the list begins with "psylocibin," which has an internal identity rhyme: (saɪ lə'saɪ bɪn). "Happy Patches" likewise consists of three open syllables (lacking consonantal coda) followed by a closed syllable, with the first and third syllables rhyming: [hæ pi 'pæ t͡ʃəz], also showing consonance, in this case of the salient, popping /p/ sounds. "MDMA," breaks the metrical pattern, as a natural reading of this initialism is iambic whereas the previous two items were trochaic, but this provides another yet another tetrasyllabic list item with internal rhyme and internal consonance. The repeated diphthong in *psilocybin* is the same as in the first syllable of the introductory phrase "I.e." [ˌʔaɪ 'ʔiː], creating a strong sense of assonance. (Wallace could easily have begun his list with *e.g., for instance, to wit, viz.*—or without any lead-in at all.)

---

[28] Shapiro, "The Poetic Language of David Foster Wallace."
[29] David Letzler, "Encyclopedic Novels and the 'Cruft' of Fiction: *Infinite Jest*'s Endnotes," *Studies in the Novel* 44, no. 3 (Fall 2012): 302–24.
[30] Ibid., 308.

The vowels in the first four items of the list are all non-back, non-round vowels (all the stressed vowels are front vowels, with a few unstressed central schwas), echoing the front vowels in "I.e." I do not argue that Wallace was conscious of any *particular* element of phonological patterning—it may be that he simply thought his list "sounded good," without thinking much about why. He didn't invent the names of (some of) these drugs, but he did choose which ones to use in their canonical form and which slang references to substitute. (The Urban Thesaurus[31] lists several dozen slang terms for psilocybin, for instance.) Some of the ostensible drug names further down in the list appear to be Wallace's own inventions within the novel, including "DMMM" and "DMZ/M.P." (M.P. presumably refers to Michael Pemulis, adolescent drug peddler, who claims that his supply of DMZ is "unprecedentedly potent" (212).) In addition to selecting specific terms, Wallace had to order the items within the list.

The phonological patterning draws readers in, challenging the temptation to skim, encouraging readers "to choose to be engaged."[32] Another effect is to create a strong contrast with the parenthetical comment that interrupts the list after the first few items: "(bad news, though, X)" breaks all the established patterns. The back rounded vowels of "news" (/u/) and "though" (/o/) stand out vividly from the string of front unrounded vowels, pulling readers out of the list, as does the visual cue of the parentheses, and the unexpected adjective following the string of nouns. If the purpose of the endnote were simply to list "designer class drugs," the parenthetical comment would flout Grice's maxim of quantity (being more information than required), relation, and arguably of manner as well.[33] The flouting forces a speech act re-analysis, reinforced by the subsequent use of an imperative structure ("note that"), with its underlying "you" subject, in another piece of personal commentary. The narrator provides not just information about drugs, but evidence of his own personality and lived experience, as well as a warning to the reader to stay away from these drugs.

A warning is felicitous, according to Searle,[34] if the utterance counts as an attempt to get the hearer to recognize that a future event (which the speaker believes will happen) would be detrimental to the hearer. *Jest's* narrator believes that it would be bad for readers to take these drugs. Not

---

[31] http://urbanthesaurus.org/.
[32] Hayes-Brady, *The Unspeakable Failures of David Foster Wallace*, 105.
[33] H. Paul Grice, "Logic and Conversation," in *The Philosophy of Language*, ed. A. P. Martinich (Oxford: Oxford University Press, 1985), 159–70.
[34] John R. Searle, *Speech Acts: An Essay in the Philosophy of Language* (Cambridge: Cambridge University Press, 1969), 67.

only does he tell readers that X is "bad news," he ends the note with personal commentary that would flout maxims if the speech act function of the note were misinterpreted: "Enthusiasm for this stuff seems to be independent of neurologic type." Although "this stuff" could refer to every drug mentioned, including the "mild designer class drugs," or just to the "CNS [Central Nervous System]-rattlers," this observation can be seen as obeying the maxims of quantity and relation only if the speech act is correctly interpreted as a warning: the narrator anticipates that readers may mistakenly believe that only certain "types" have enthusiasm for (and thus get addicted to) drugs (which in turn implies that readers might freely indulge without such results). Indeed, returning to the main text following the endnote, the narrator goes on to explain that the cycle of doing enough drugs "to basically short out the whole motherboard . . . and slowly recover" may "work surprisingly well" "if your basic wiring's OK to begin with," but only for a short time "before it starts to creep up on you" (52).

Repeated use of the discourse marker *though* in the endnote is more evidence that the narrator is countering readers' expected stance, attempting to persuade or convince. That he cares enough about readers to issue such a warning (but indirectly, not in an authority-figure, preachy way) is another step in the emergent relationship between reader and narrator. Wallace repeats essentially the same maneuver in the next endnote, in case readers missed it here, with the direct warning "be advised" (984), and repeatedly thereafter. Readers might not be interested in the scientific names of drugs or their classification, or which company produces them. The allusion to the "good old folks over at Sanofi-Winthrop Pharm-Labs, Inc." (984) is, as Holl[35] points out, "a colloquial antipode to those scientific expressions" which "defangs the whole paragraph." That is, the real function of endnote 12 is to remind readers that they don't *need* to be knowledgeable about all this stuff, that their friend, the narrator, is there to tell them whatever they need to know.

Wallace's infrequent use of second person in *Jest* is quite different from his more striking and metafictional use of it in "Octet," in which, as Dawson[36] points out, the pronoun refers to "a fictional version of the authorial narrator . . . yet it is also clear that the narrator is attempting to address readers through his self-directed apostrophe": "You are, unfortunately, a fiction writer. You are attempting a cycle of very short belletristic pieces" (145); "You know that this is a very bad corner to have painted yourself into, as a

---

[35] Rainer Holl, *The Narrative Game: The Reading of David Foster Wallace's Infinite Jest as Play* (Hamburg: Anchor Academic Publishing, 2013), 7.
[36] Paul Dawson, *The Return of the Omniscient Narrator: Authorship and Authority in Twenty-First Century Fiction* (Columbus: The Ohio State University Press, 2013), 75.

fiction writer" (152); "You're still going to title the cycle 'Octet.'"(152, fn 6). By making the artifice so apparent, Wallace hoped to reveal "the fibrillating self of the 'real' author." *Jest* has other metafictional devices (including the endnotes in general, and the wonderful mock "filmography" of James O. Incandenza in particular (endnote 24), which is highly intertextual both with other elements of the novel itself and other real-world texts and films), but the use of first and second pronouns in *Jest*, though relatively infrequent, straightforwardly distinguishes the "I" of the narrator and the "you" of the reader, echoing Wallace's use of pronouns in his nonfiction.

Positive Politeness

In addition to the use of first and second person, other positive politeness strategies abound in Wallace's writing, fostering solidarity with readers who might otherwise be intimidated by his scope of knowledge and imagination. In fact, Wallace exemplifies almost every positive politeness strategy discussed by Brown and Levinson (1987):[37] he expresses strong and certain opinions (viz. note 8's "doesn't and shouldn't include"), confidently (and optimistically) claims to know things he couldn't possibly know (like the contents of others' thoughts), swears freely and uses all sorts of slang (both of which, Niedzielski and Preston[38] point out are used "for solidarity or in-group marking"). Hayes-Brady[39] notes that Wallace doesn't just appeal to the reader's common sense, he flatters it. For those readers who cannot identify with his narrators and alter egos, the consciousness of difference presents a constant threat to their positive face, requiring a great deal of positive politeness to offset.

Wallace's narrator frequently claims common ground with readers, assuming shared reference to all kinds of popular culture (especially television shows such as *M*A*S*H, Bewitched, As the World Turns, Jeopardy, The Late*

---

[37] Following anthropological theory, Penelope Brown and Stephen Levinson, *Politeness: Some Universals in Language Usage* (Cambridge: Cambridge University Press, 1987) assume tension between individuals' "negative face" (the desire to be independent and autonomous, free from imposition) and "positive face" (the desire to be liked and accepted, part of the group). "Negative" and "positive" are not value judgments, just complementary opposites. Speakers use politeness strategies (also categorized according to which type of face they address) to offset the face threats they anticipate, taking into account the variables of social distance (vs. intimacy) and power, both of which are continually re-negotiated through the use (or nonuse) of politeness strategies.

[38] Niedzielski and Preston, *Folk Linguistics*, 183.

[39] Hayes-Brady, *The Unspeakable Failures of David Foster Wallace*, 165.

Show with David Letterman). On the other hand, his allusions to more intellectual fare are generally coded. Without literary scholars to point out a paraphrase of an opening sentence of one of Kafka's or Borges's fictions, that a character's name is taken from Dostoevsky, and so on, many readers simply would not know. Thus, Wallace avoids alienating the audience who doesn't recognize such allusions, while creating a sense of in-group inclusion for the audience that does. His work also has many puns and "gags," confessing a "grossly sentimental affection . . . for stuff that's nothing but funny, and which I sometimes stick in for no other reason than funniness."[40] Wallace is "widely acknowledged as one of the funniest writers of his generation. . . . He is deeply playful and often transgressive writing exhibits a sense of proximity and intimacy."[41] The puns and gags work similarly to the veiled allusions: readers who "get" the jokes feel like Wallace is winking directly at them; others are not alienated, because they do not realize that a joke has been attempted. Essentially, to borrow terminology from film and media studies, Wallace left "Easter eggs" for readers.

Wallace's frequent use of "redacted Q&A narrative format" (which Thompson[42]) traces back to influence from Manuel Puig), in which the questions are never heard or seen, may also simulate a conversation with readers, as he imagines and responds to readers' questions—much as he commonly uses ellipses within conversations to indicate fraught (meaningful) silence, forcing inferences based on the flouting of Grice's maxims of conversation. The ending of *Broom* mid-sentence ("I'm a man of my" [467]) works on several different levels, linguistically. Kelly[43] argues that "because there is no real ambiguity concerning the next word in the sentence, the reader's agency is in fact negated," which ignores the everyday reality of conversational practice, in which people often trail off without finishing their sentences, especially when the ending is predictable. Failure to end a sentence can project a sense of intimacy and trust (as in the commonly held claim of couples in sync that they finish each other's sentences), as well a lack of a desire to end the conversation. Kelly characterizes this as "a *gesture* toward an open system and readerly dialogue, rather than an achievement of it,"[44] but it is unclear how any piece of fiction would actually achieve dialogue in the realistic conversational sense. What Kelly refers to as "dialogue" is openness

---

[40] McCaffery, "An Expanded Interview with David Foster Wallace," 24.
[41] Wilson Kaiser, "Humor after Postmodernism: David Foster Wallace and Proximal Irony," *Studies in American Humor*, New Series 3, no. 28 (2013): 31–44, esp. 32.
[42] Thompson, *Global Wallace*, 65.
[43] Kelly, "Development Through Dialogue," 273.
[44] Ibid.

of interpretation, and although readers understand exactly which word is projected to end the sentence, they are in no way forced to *agree* with that sentence as a true representation of speaker Rick Vigorous's character. Nor is the speech act function of the sentence self-evident, much less the intended pragmatic interpretation of leaving the sentence dangling, a clear violation of Grice's maxims of quantity and manner. An incomplete utterance may reflect anticipation of *disagreement*, an overt signal of reluctance to initiate conflict. In a different context, trailing off might indicate that the speaker is unsure of how to phrase a thought, which could be interpreted either as a request for help from the interlocutor in choosing a word. As Wallace put it, "FYI, there happens to be a whole subdiscipline of linguistics called Pragmatics that essentially studies the way statements' meanings are created by various contexts" (*CTL* 93). It may sound naïve to critics (especially now so many years later), but I know one reader at least who did literally speak back to the book at this point, saying, "Are you kidding me? You can't just end a book mid-sentence!"

Thompson[45] briefly discusses Wallace's "vocal reproductions," including "use of 'like' as vocalized pause," "frequent use of colloquialisms," and "reliance on contractions," none of which are particularly unique to Wallace's writing. More interesting and distinctive is Wallace's penchant for starting sentences with multiple conjunctions ("and but," "and but so," even "and but so then"), which Thompson[46] says "gives the prose an idiomatic, spoken quality . . . a frenetic, breathless tone" and Hayes-Brady[47] says gives "the sense that the reader is simply reading the continuation of an earlier train of thought." Wallace himself put this at the top of a list of his own stylistic quirks that he did not wish the copyeditor of *Infinite Jest* to attempt to edit away (HRC Wallace Papers, container 20.5):

—Multiple conjunctions at the start of independent clauses.
—Commas before prepositions at the end of sentences.
—Hyphens to form compound nouns.
—Sentence-fragments following exceptionally long sentences.

Wallace was obviously well aware that *and* and *but* have distinct uses in conversation. Not only did he highlight the distinction between these

---

[45] Thompson, *Global Wallace*, 225.
[46] Ibid., 223.
[47] Hayes-Brady, *The Unspeakable Failures of David Foster Wallace*, 143.

conjunctions in his copy of Kolln's[48] *Rhetorical Grammar* (89), but he also included a discussion of this in a handout for his English composition students (dated September 25, 2002, and titled "YOUR LIBERAL-ARTS $ AT WORK" [all-caps in the original]):

> 2. *And* is a conjunction; so is *so*. Except in dialogue between particular kinds of characters, you never need both conjunctions. "He needed to eat, *and so* he bought food" is incorrect. In 95% of cases like this, what you want to do is cut the *and*." (HRC Wallace Papers, Teaching Materials, container 32.9)

Although a speaker may have a false start and abruptly change conjunctions mid-utterance without anyone particularly noticing it, the deliberate stringing together of conjunctions in writing is initially defamiliarizing. Eventually, however, this serves a connective purpose, creating cohesion across Wallace's works. Far from just a verbal tic, the combinations convey a sense of breathless excitement (as Thompson noted), but also an indication that what follows will be complicated, not just what Wallace thinks goes along with what has previously been communicated (as Hayes-Brady noted), but also what contradicts previous assumptions, what follows logically, what causes and what is caused. In some sense, this provides justification for (and warning of) Wallace's long-windedness, but there is also a sweetness that works against any interpretation of aggression or showing off. The narrator is not just excited by the story, he is eager and happy to tell it to readers; the expression of emotion and the assumption that readers will be equally excited by what he has to tell are further classic positive politeness strategies.

Wallace also incorporated conversational markers of vocal hesitation ("there seems to be some, umm, personal stuff getting dredged up and worked out here" [CTL 104]) and a variety of conversational discourse markers (as discussed by Schiffrin[49]) such as *well*, *like*, and *you know*, even though he certainly knew that these are frequently "regarded as meaningless, or, worse, 'dumb' and 'bad habits.'"[50] The palpable sense of playfulness underlying these uses, evident also in his extraordinary lexical creativity, undoubtedly helps to mitigate this "offense." Wallace delighted in idiosyncratic nonce-formations, which are on display not just once but three times in the example of *Jest's* endnote 8 quoted earlier in this chapter: *home-makable*, *CNS-rattlers*, and

---

[48] Martha Kolln, *Rhetorical Grammar: Grammatical Choices, Rhetorical Effects*, 3rd ed. (Boston: Allyn & Bacon, 1989).
[49] Deborah Schiffrin, *Discourse Markers* (Cambridge: Cambridge University Press, 1987).
[50] Niedzielski and Preston, *Folk Linguistics*, 268.

over-counter-available (984). Unlike other qualities that an author might project onto a character in his or her fiction, such lexical creativity on the part of a character or narrator would not be possible were it not shared by the author himself. Morrissey and Thompson praise his "inventive constructions,"[51] although Cioffi[52] deems this "more showing off, more hostility toward the reader." Wallace's lexical innovations also often function as deliberate attempts to break expectations for a more formal register (as seen in that same example of endnote 8), an attempt to lessen the negative face threat involved in overly formal uses of language that would imply social distance.

Burn[53] describes Wallace's "parallel projects bleeding into each other," and Thompson[54] points out, for example, the similarity of "Pop Quiz 4" in "Octet" to the Barry Loach story in *Infinite Jest*. Wallace acknowledged that he was "not subtle at all about repeating things in certain works." This, too, is reminiscent not just of conversation in general, but of long-term relationships: friends and partners hear some of the same stories told over and over again.

Wallace would likely have taken positive politeness strategies even further in TPK, just as he went further in claiming identity with the narrator. The opening chapter of the novel as published is only two paragraphs long; each paragraph contains both second-person pronouns ("like a mother's soft hand on your cheek" [1], and "your shoes' brand incised in the dew" [2]) and imperative structures ("Look around you" [1], and "Read these" [2]). The use of "doubly-deictic you" in fiction, simultaneously includes intradiegetic perspectivizer and extradiegetic reader to facilitate blends of projected storyworld possible selves.[55] The first paragraph ends with an explicit first-person-plural thesis statement: "We are all of us brothers." There could not be a more direct appeal to solidarity with the reader.

That many Wallace readers have been passionate about this author, feeling that they have truly connected with the mind that produced these works, is not surprising, given the intentional blurring of the author/narrator distinction, and given the intensely personal revelations made by the narrator and some alter ego characters. Cioffi[56] argues that *Jest* is a

---

[51] Morrissey and Thompson, "The Rare White at the Window," 8.
[52] Cioffi, "An Anguish Become Thing," 167.
[53] Stephen J. Burn, "'A Paradigm for the Life of Consciousness': Closing Time in *The Pale King*." *Studies in the Novel* 44, no. 4 (2012): 371–88, esp. 373.
[54] Thompson, *Global Wallace*, 104.
[55] Martínez, *Storyworld Possible Selves*.
[56] Frank Louis Cioffi, "'An Anguish Become Thing': Narrative as Performance in David Foster Wallace's *Infinite Jest*," *Narrative* 8, no. 2 (2000): 161–81, esp. 170.

"disturbing" text, because it forces the reader into the role of a performer; that the reader "must come to a self-conscious realization that his [sic] behavior resembles that of the drug addicts Wallace's novel focuses on" (170). He speaks of the inability he felt, as a reader, to skip over distressing, brutal scenes; powerless as an addict to forego his fix. I can't argue with his personal, subjective response, but I felt no more loss of control, no loss of dignity or perspective than I would listening to a close friend who needs to vent, to process, to share. It is readers' awareness of the ongoing conversation with the narrator/author that prevents them from overinvesting in the lives of the characters, despite the empathy evoked. Readers willingly cede control to a master conversationalist, flattered that he has taken such time and effort to entertain and instruct them.

Wallace shared detailed and intimate knowledge of many subjects, not just the pharmacology of drugs or the biological reactions to them, but less disturbing topics as well, for instance the game of tennis (which the author played at a competitive level in his youth), and he did not confine himself to areas of knowledge that paralleled his lived experience. He researched major plots and themes (e.g., in preparation for TPK, he took accounting courses[57]), but rather minor points as well—for instance, the first short paragraph of TPK lists twenty-one different types of plants and grasses, many of which I had never heard of before. Wallace's 1990 review of Martone admits that "the question of how much erudition a fiction writer gets to require of his reader is, of course, eternally vexed." The reverse is equally vexed: How much erudition does a reader demand or desire the writer to demonstrate? Although Wallace's many extended displays of knowledge potentially threaten readers' negative face (as they may feel "put down" by the implicit assertion of the author's own authority and their relative lack thereof), the research these displays obviously required is also somehow flattering—that not content with his own (already impressive) breadth of knowledge, Wallace spent many hours studying these minor details on behalf of his readers, and wanted to share that research with us. (The effect of this upon a contemporary audience accustomed to continuous and effortless access to information may be somewhat dampened; *Jest* was published before Google existed.)

Wallace is famous for his syntactic complexity, seemingly endless sentences with multiple levels of subordination,[58] strings of prepositional

---

[57] Cockfield, "David Foster Wallace on Tax Policy, How to Be an Adult, and Other Mysteries of the Universe," 93.
[58] de Bourcier, "They All Sound Like David Foster Wallace."

phrases,[59] strings of adjectives unbroken by commas (forcing readers to consider potential interactions between the descriptors rather than simply an additive, list interpretation).[60] As with Wallace's use of rare and specialized vocabulary, this display of syntactic authority potentially threatens readers' negative face, but is simultaneously flattering to the audience, optimistically assuming that the reader will devote some effort to make sense of it and appreciate it. (The self-selecting audience returns the compliment, knowing that however smart they are to "get it," Wallace had to be much smarter to write it.) Part of the appeal comes in recognizing that Wallace was not merely asserting his own authority, but risking his own positive face. Americans often judge speakers harshly for being "*too* correct . . . because the forms are 'too snooty' and the speakers 'too high-falutin.'"[61] Niedzielski and Preston[62] document in particular "folk prejudice against long sentences."

Another potential threat to readers' negative face is Wallace's tendency to go on and on and on. Wallace poked fun at his own narrative style (and critics' response to it), by creating surrogates in TPK and allowing them to criticize one another's storytelling and conversation, such as "Irrelevant Chris" Fogle, who tells extremely long stories "full of useless, apparently irrelevant detail. . . . This charge could also be levelled at the entire novel, even in its unpublished state."[63] When, in the middle of a conversation about attraction and loneliness, Shane Drinion goes off on a long tangent about radio expense protocols, his IRS co-worker Meredith Rand responds,

> Can I say that one of the reasons you come off as a little boring is that you don't seem like you have any sense of what the real topic of a conversation is? . . . What do you imagine is going through the other person's mind when you're ranting like that? Do you just automatically assume they're interested? Who cares about radio accounting if you're not tasked to it? (464)

Rand herself then proceeds to tell a seemingly endless story, prompting Drinion to observe that "certain parts you tend to repeat, or say over again only in a slightly different way. These parts add no new information, so

---

[59] Heather Houser, "Infinite Jest's Environmental Case for Disgust," in *The Legacy of David Foster Wallace*, ed. Samuel Cohen and Lee Konstantinou (Iowa City: University of Iowa Press, 2012), 118–42.
[60] Shapiro, "The Poetic Language of David Foster Wallace."
[61] Walt Wolfram and Ralph Fasold, *The Study of Social Dialects in American English* (Englewood Cliffs, NJ: Prentice Hall, 1974), 19.
[62] Niedzielski and Preston, *Folk Linguistics*, 265.
[63] Boswell, "Author Here," 35.

these parts require more work to pay attention to" (501). There is never any suggestion, however, that one should *not* pay such close attention, despite the effort involved. On the contrary, Drinion is able to achieve such a pure state of attention, when engaged in his work and when listening to Rand, that he is unaware that he is literally, physically (albeit just slightly) levitating off his seat. Wallace's "notes and asides" (some handwritten and marginal) were published with the unfinished main text, including the relevant observation that

> Drinion is *happy*. Ability to pay attention. It turns out that bliss—a second-by-second joy + gratitude at the gift of being alive, conscious—lies on the other side of crushing, crushing boredom. Pay close attention to the most tedious thing you can find (tax returns, televised golf), and in waves, a boredom like you've never known will wash over you and just about kill you. Ride these out, and it's like stepping from black and white into color. Like water after days in the desert. Constant bliss in every atom. (546)

Negative Politeness

Wallace's evident mastery of language as well as many different fields of knowledge in which readers could not claim equal expertise, together with his monopoly of the "conversation," pose inherent threats to readers' negative face, but it would be risky for Wallace to directly flatter readers' negative face to offset these threats, as overt deference could appear to be mocking readers. A safer strategy was to threaten his own negative face, using hedges and disclaimers occasionally, but often showcasing aggressive and dysphemistic self-deprecation. (That is, in order to avoid the appearance of sucking up to readers, he instead repeatedly put himself down.) In a letter to Ann Fadiman's creative writing class at Yale, Wallace wrote about "Narrator Persona challenges, more specifically the Asshole Problem":

> I'm sure you guys have seen it—it's death if the biggest sense the reader gets from a critical essay is that the narrator's a very critical person, or from a comic essay that the narrator's cruel or snooty. Hence the importance of being just as critical about oneself as one is about the stuff/people one's being critical of.[64]

---

[64] Fadiman, "Afterword," 761.

In his scathing review of John Updike's[65] *Towards the End of Time*, Wallace purports not to understand protagonist's Ben Turnbull's attitude, because "it never once occurs to him that the reason he's so unhappy is that he's an asshole" (n.p.). Wallace couldn't fathom such a lack of self-awareness; he interrogated himself at every turn, and frequently found himself wanting: "I can be kind of a snob and an asshole" (*ASFTINDA* 228), for instance. Joffe[66] interprets Wallace as claiming here *not* to be an asshole, unlike Ben, but given Wallace's frequent admission to the contrary, this seems unlikely, although I agree that it is a rhetorical bid for sympathy: readers are presumed to prefer a self-aware and apologetic asshole over an un-self-aware, unapologetic one. Surely, being an asshole is not a simple binary categorization, but a question of degree.

Thompson[67] points out that "Wallace's commitment to identifying his own shortcomings on many issues is done unsparingly." Cunningham[68] argues that *Jest* illustrates both the benefits and risks of "perpetual confrontation with oneself," as this kind of unflinching self-examination is the only way to acknowledge and overcome one's weaknesses, but getting hypnotized by what Wallace called "the constant monologue inside your head" (*Water* 50) can also lead to the trap of solipsism.

Hypermasculinity

Brown and Levinson's politeness theory is theoretically gender neutral, but life is not—and Wallace's voice is not just masculine, but hypermasculine. This may explain why "the majority . . . of Wallace's readership appears to be male, contrary to his own persistent (and perhaps affected) invocation of the she-reader."[69] Holland[70] and Hayes-Brady[71] have excellent discussions

---

[65] "John Updike, Champion Literary Phallocrat, Drops One: Is This Finally the End for Magnificent Narcissists?" *The New York Observer* (October 13, 1997). https://observer.com/1997/10/john-updike-champion-literary-phallocrat-drops-one-is-this-finally-the-end-for-magnificent-narcissists/
[66] Joffe, "In the Shadows," 39.
[67] Thompson, "Wallace and Race," 207.
[68] Josh Cunningham, "'The Hazards of Being Free': Thinking About Not Thinking in *Infinite Jest*." 2019. MA Thesis, *CUNY Academic Works*, 3. https://academicworks.cuny.edu/cc_etds_theses/739.
[69] Hayes-Brady, "Personally I'm Neutral on the Menstruation Point," 63.
[70] Mary K. Holland, "'By Hirsute Author': Gender and Communication in the Work and Study of David Foster Wallace," *Critique: Studies in Contemporary Fiction* 58, no. 1 (2016), 64–77. DOI: 10.1080/00111619.2016.1149798.
[71] Hayes-Brady, "'. . .': Language, Gender, and Modes of Power in the Work of David Foster Wallace" "Personally I'm Neutral on the Menstruation Point"; *The Unspeakable Failures of David Foster Wallace*.

of Wallace's awareness and apparent appreciation of feminist theory. Joffe[72] traces Wallace's "crisis in white Midwestern male identity" (117) throughout his work, to which I will add just a few linguistic observations.

The consistent narrative persona employed across Wallace's works embodies without exception all the gendered stereotypes first detailed in Robin Lakoff's *Language and Woman's Place* (1975),[73,74] some of which have already been considered in terms of politeness strategies: He has strong and certain opinions which he seldom hedges nor over-exaggerates (he does not fear that he will not be attended to, causing him to "speak in italics" (56–7)); he confidently claims to know things he can't possibly know (like the contents of others' thoughts); he jokes, swears, does not euphemize, doesn't use ritual frozen phrases of politeness (despite using a lot of conversational strategies and discourse markers, Wallace's narrator seldom uses *please, thank you, I'm sorry, excuse me*, at least not ironically), doesn't use words relating to traditional "woman's work" (needlecrafts, housework, more specific color terms) or "empty" adjectives (*nice, cute*); he never uses "intensive" *so* (although he uses the conjunction very frequently); he feels free to break whatever rules he feels like. Whether these stereotypes reflect current or past reality (and to what extent they may reflect socially constructed gender identities beyond a binary categorization) is not the point here; readers recognize these as gendered stereotypes and consciously or unconsciously code the voice accordingly. Especially in works in which the narrator is mostly hiding (such as *Jest*, in which the narrator is most evident in the endnotes), where his words are the only information we have about him, such impressions probably achieve even greater prominence than they would in a face-to-face conversation. Even the amount of detail given and the resulting length of Wallace's novels and essays codes as masculine, as men are given more latitude to engage in lengthy monologues, to hold the floor without seeking input from others.

Hayes-Brady and Holland suggest that Wallace never successfully empathized with women, always viewing them as unfathomably other. I have tried to argue that Wallace did empathize with Clenette, Yolanda, Amber, and others, but it may also be true that he overempathized with males, falling into logical fallacies as a result, as Bloom[75] warns. Wallace's narrators and

---

[72] Joffe, "*In the Shadows.*"
[73] Lakoff, *Language and Woman's Place*.
[74] It would be more precise to say that Wallace's narrator *avoids* all aspects of "women's language," as Lakoff has been justly criticized for providing only a list of characteristics of how women supposedly deviate from an implied masculine norm.
[75] Paul Bloom, *Against Empathy: The Case for Rational Compassion* (New York: Ecco, 2016).

protagonists certainly display frequent "himpathy," in which "a privileged man's side of the story" comes both first and last, resulting in empathy for male perpetrators of violence rather than for their usually female victims,[76] as illustrated most prominently throughout BIHM. Holland[77] finds "little, if any, development in Wallace's thinking about the threat posed to the (female) other by the (male) self's desire," while acknowledging "his anxiety about the ways in which he might be complicit" in the continued subjugation of women.

A recent *Atlantic Monthly* article[78] centered around the pernicious association of "genius" and "maleness," pointedly observing that Mary Karr didn't just remind the world of Wallace's abusive stalking and violence toward her (which he had admitted, and was included in his biography), she "reminds the world, indeed, that it needed the reminding in the first place. The horror stories had simply been subsumed into the broader story (the 'greater good') of Wallace's personal genius." Wallace, the man, was no doubt a much less admirable creature than "Wallace," the fictional persona, despite his deliberate attempts to blur the distinction. (This isn't a malicious jab at the dead author, whom I obviously nevertheless admire—who among us can live up to the image we'd rather project to the world? The greater one's ability to control the projected image, the greater the gap that may emerge between the reality and the fictionalized image.)

What keeps "Wallace" from being *toxically* masculine (in pop psychological terms, which have expanded the definition of the term rather dramatically from its original use) is precisely the odd nature of the conversation he offers to readers. He may be guilty of "mansplaining," feeling entitled "to hold forth . . . without asking,"[79] but he is presumably explaining to male and female readers alike and does not typically condescend to readers by explaining things they ought to already know. More importantly, he cannot invade readers' personal space to demand attention. Any reader who so wishes may simply put down the book, ending the "conversation" without being forced into an uncomfortable act of rudeness. Those who choose to keep reading *invite* Wallace to continue.

As with nationality, ethnicity, and regionality, Wallace's choice to voice a category of identity disproportionately does not celebrate that identity. White males are undoubtedly overrepresented and privileged in Wallace's work, yet

---

[76] Manne, *Down Girl*, 34.
[77] Holland, "By Hirsute Author," 65.
[78] Garber, "David Foster Wallace and the Dangerous Romance of Male Genius."
[79] Kate Manne, *Down Girl: The Logic of Misogyny* (Oxford: Oxford University Press, 2017), 304.

the harsh spotlight shone upon them is not flattering. Aubry's[80] description of *Jest* describes most of Wallace's work: "Case after case of highly educated, middle-class, typically male characters who are incapable of expressing, accessing, or sustaining modes of affect, including love, sorrow, and joy." This fails to note one important exception, however; the narrator expresses all of these and more, and often does succeed in sharing them with readers.

One of the "exotic new facts" that "you will acquire" if you spend "a little time around a Substance-recovery halfway facility" (*Jest* 200) is that "*pace*[81] macho bullshit, public male weeping is not only plenty masculine but can actually feel *good*" (201). Although well over a hundred of these "facts" are presented, this is the only one that the narrator specifically distances himself from, with the one-word parenthetical comment: "(reportedly)." Even when explicitly calling out "macho bullshit" and apparently giving men permission to cry in public, the narrator cannot bring himself to admit that he has done so. This is the perfect encapsulation of Wallace's performative masculinity: the awareness that it is harmful and isolating, the apparently inability to change (despite such awareness), and the subsequent impulse to turn it into a joke, clearly hoping that if readers share the humor, they will excuse the macho bullshit. (This is, fittingly, the same strategy used to address "the Asshole problem.")

Wallace is undoubtedly *easiest* to read for heterosexual white males who can identify directly with his hypermasculine narrator, but there are many "storyworld possible selves" with which other readers may identify, including not just the "'socially isolated' individual possible self, which is probably a feared or undesired representation,"[82] but the more flattering role that Wallace's narrators explicitly project for readers: the educated and intelligent self who gets the jokes and references, who appreciates being spoken to in this manner. One can only speculate what Wallace's response would have been to the world being reminded of his abuses in the #MeToo movement— my guess is that after some predictable defensiveness and characteristic soul-searching, he would have produced the world's most gut-wrenching, self-excoriating, beautifully poetic apology. I do not know whether he would have actually learned from the experience, or whether those he abused would have accepted any apology from him—but that he would have *written* in response seems incontrovertibly obvious.

---

[80] Aubry, "*Infinite Jest* and the Recovery of Feeling," 100.
[81] Wallace surely intended *contra*, here. The Latin *pace* is typically used not just for disagreement, but to indicate good will toward a person being contradicted, as in "This usage is unusual, *pace* Wallace."
[82] Martínez, *Storyworld Possible Selves*, 69.

Whether in fiction or creative nonfiction, with or without a first-person narrator (let alone one with his same name), Wallace's style is so distinctive that anyone who had read one of his pieces could pick up another and recognize him in it. As Boswell[83] argues, "Reading a David Foster Wallace novel, short story, or essay is tantamount to learning the 'rules' of his game." I agree with Boswell that it is a game worth learning, yielding "a special, surprisingly intimate zone of communication, of subjective interaction, that is unlike anything else in contemporary literature."

Wallace's recursive ventriloquation (to borrow a term from Bakhtin) creates an almost overwhelming echo chamber: Wallace's voice speaks through a narrator (always somewhat fictionalized, even when not a distinct, named character), the narrator in turn often speaks through sound-alike characters, via free indirect discourse that includes his own ventriloquizing of yet other characters' speech. The homogenous quality of most of these voices makes this multiplicity more manageable for readers, but also fosters an actual sense of relationship with the author, the sense that whatever name is attached, it is always Wallace speaking. Whether one sees this as the author's strength or weakness is largely determined by one's reaction to that distinctive voice. This would seem to emphasize the loneliness of "Dave Wallace," continually creating new imaginary friends to share his point of view. Franzen[84] shares that both he and Wallace saw fiction as "neutral middle ground on which to make a deep connection with another human being," and that the formulation they "agreed to agree on" is that fiction is "a way out of loneliness." On the other hand, because of Wallace's ventriloquation, readers who can identify feel like they have not just made a connection with a single mind but have stepped into a whole likeminded community. In this sense, Wallace's narrative persona simultaneously embodies polar opposites of the masculine "ideal": the independent loner (who needs nobody but himself) and the perfect team member (speaking with one voice, all working toward the same goal).

---

[83] Boswell, "Author Here: The Legal Fiction of David Foster Wallace's The Pale King," 19.
[84] Jonathan Franzen, "Recollections," [Remarks from a Memorial Service for David Foster Wallace Held October 23, 2008] *Sonora Review* 55 (2009): 41–4.

10

Language and Humanity

In Wallace's work, the depiction of dialects represents rather than enacts "realism": it is representational not only in the sense that various voices do exist and always have co-existed in the United States, that they do have unequal prominence and prestige, but also as a signal that the *character* is "keeping it real," not trying to pose or front or pass. In some cases, this may be active resistance to the pressure to assimilate or to aspire to upper-class norms; in others, it is less an act of resistance than a lack of access. It is not necessary that the dialect depictions themselves be entirely realistic to achieve those ends; Wallace was neither linguist nor ethnographer; he was a *creative* writer, even when ostensibly writing nonfiction. His allegiance was to his writing and to the relationship he was attempting to cultivate with readers, not to "reality." In a 1993 interview, he distanced himself explicitly from a view of fiction as "travelogue": "It *used to be* a way to take people to foreign lands and exotic cultures, or to important people, and give readers access to worlds they didn't have before."[1] It even seems fitting that Wallace got at least some details wrong, whether this was intentional or accidental, as the worlds presented in his writing are always skewed and off-kilter. It seems that Wallace placed too much trust in his ability to mimic and too little effort into researching actual dialect features (and didn't think it really mattered, didn't worry about offending), and that readers were often too awed by Wallace's linguistic skills, so evident in other ways, to question the accuracy of his dialect portrayals.

Linguistic Relativism

Dawson[2] argues that Wallace's writing highlights "characterological cognitive self-awareness"—that is, that his representation of consciousness is not just

---

[1] Hugh Kennedy and Geoffrey Polk, "Looking for a Garde of Which to Be Avant: An Interview with David Foster Wallace," in *Conversations with David Foster Wallace*, ed. Stephen J. Burn (Jackson: University of Mississippi Press, 2012), 11–20, esp. 19, emphasis added.
[2] Dawson, *The Return of the Omniscient Narrator*, 189.

mimetic, but "a means for interrogating the relation of language and thought." Others have already explored how Wallace's earliest work plays with the linguistic determinism of Wittgenstein's *Tractatus*, the view that language shapes the perception of reality. Linguist Edward Sapir's[3] magnum opus, *Language*, published in the same year as *Tractatus*, argues for a weaker connection between language and thought, what is often now referred to as linguistic relativism, or the "Sapir-Whorf hypothesis" (based also on the research of Sapir's student, Benjamin Lee Whorf), according to which, because each language reflects reality differently, its speakers tend to unconsciously and uncritically accept certain default categorizations. Presumably, different dialects within a language also encode and encourage subtly different worldviews. Wallace's non-native dialects (particularly Marathe and Schtitt) represent different philosophies, although there is little reason to believe that it is the native languages of those speakers that shaped those philosophies. Wallace's portrayals of ethnic and regional US dialects argue against stronger views of linguistic relativism: speakers of different dialects share fairly similar worldviews, and speakers ostensibly from the same dialect community are nonetheless carefully distinguished, showing the power of individuals to forge their own identities.

In *Jest*, Michael Pemulis makes a forceful distinction between *map* and *territory*: "It's snowing on the goddam *map*, not the *territory*, you *dick*" (333, emphasis original), reiterated even more forcefully a few pages later ("the *map*, not the clusterfucking *territory*" [338]). It is possible that Wallace learned of Korzybski's famous dictum that "the map is not the territory," a warning that symbols for reality should not be confused with reality itself, in one of his college philosophy courses. Korzybski was an engineer and independent scholar who developed a field called "general semantics," which he viewed as including, but going beyond the linguistic subfield known as semantics. Linguists have largely dismissed his work as unsupported by evidence, although the above slogan is unobjectionable. Wallace would not have had much truck with Korzybski's proscriptions of particular usages such as avoidance of "to be" as grammatical copula (the "*is* of identity"), which he thought caused "many human semantic difficulties."[4] (That is, a statement such as "Gately is a criminal" could create a false equation in people's minds, causing them to think that Gately is *foremost* or *only* a criminal, that he *is* what we call him. Training ourselves to avoid such usages, to say instead "Gately committed crimes," would supposedly lead to clearer thinking.)

---

[3] Edward Sapir, *Language* (New York: Harcourt, Brace, & World, 1921).
[4] Alfred Korzybski, *Science and Sanity: An Introduction to Non-Aristotelian Systems and General Semantics* (Lakeville, CT: International Non-Aristotelian Library Publishing Co., 1933), 339.

Wallace argued against this type of extreme prescriptivism, which judges some uses of language as *objectively* superior to others, as some *languages* superior to others, in A&AU.

No matter how many times Pemulis verbalizes the distinction ("You can only launch against the *territory*. Not against the *map*" [338]), the Eschaton map *does* become the territory. An abstract argument about symbols and their relationship to reality, about a game that symbolizes warfare and world domination—"Real-world snow isn't a factor if it's falling on the fucking *map*!" [334])—becomes a real-world struggle for control of the game. Instead of symbolically fighting, aiming tennis balls for "the gear that *maps* what's real," the players begin aiming at each other, then eventually forego the symbol of the launched tennis balls as well, fighting hand-to-hand, resulting in actual injuries. Words matter, but words do not control reality.

Language as Shibboleth

As noted in Chapter 1, language has always been used to distinguish "us" and "them," often with very high stakes attached. In the Hebrew Bible (Judg. xii: 4-6), Gileadites forced people to pronounce the word *shibboleth*, because the Ephramites supposedly pronounced the initial *shin* differently); the penalty for the wrong pronunciation was death. Then, as now, language was seen as indexing one's "real" identity. The conversation in French between Poutrincourt and Steeply undercover as a woman reporter in *Jest* contains Wallace's clearest use of language as shibboleth: it is "the vulgate Québecois *transperçant*, whose idiomatic connotation of doom Poutrincourt shouldn't have had any reason to think the Parisian-speaking Steeply would know" (1052) that tells Steeply his cover has been blown.

Wallace himself appears to have failed the shibboleth test himself, as many readers view his misrepresentations of AAE (particularly in the "Clenette" section of *Jest*) as proof that Wallace could not empathize across ethnic difference. He might have argued that point with them, but he would likely have approved of the underlying assumptions that language use matters, and that it reflects who people actually are.

Language as Problem and Solution

Wallace's ongoing attempt to capture regional and ethnic dialects challenged readers to "Identify, don't Compare," as the Alcoholics Anonymous mantra embedded throughout *Jest* advocates. I imagine that this was also a challenge he continued to issue to himself, to counteract his own "SNOOT-y" tendencies. He believed "that our linguistic choices can often have nonlinguistic consequences of pretty obvious practical or ethical significance"[5]—that is, that they trigger social judgments and discrimination—but not that the linguistic choices have ethical or moral significance in and of themselves.

Turnbull[6] explores the deep morality expressed in Wallace's theory of attention, as articulated in *Water*, which advocates "a richer conception of [other, unknown] people as having, like us, genuine inner lives."[7] This theory of attention urges us away from automatic, unconscious reactions toward a fuller awareness and appreciation of all things, including language use. We're all "stuck in here, in language, but we're all in here together," Wallace told McCaffery;[8] "It's not that language *is* us, but we're still *in* it, inescapably" (45).

When Hal Incandenza says, "I am not what you see and hear" (*Jest* 13), he speaks for everyone; communication is always imperfect, and language cannot fully bridge the distance between minds. Ironically, though, this is *especially* true for speakers of stigmatized dialects, whose way of speaking is so heavily judged that what they say is often ignored. I agree with Kelly[9] and Hayes-Brady[10] on "the conceptual centrality of sincere communication to Wallace's writing, both within and without the text," but this doesn't mean that he never employed irony to further the cause of a sincere message.[11] Readers are more willing to accept such an observation from a speaker of the most privileged dialect in the United States than they are from speakers of stigmatized dialects. I do not read this as Wallace claiming victimization (as Joffe[12] might), but rather as an expression of the limitations of verbal communication that affect everybody, albeit not equally.

Cunningham[13] argues that what distinguishes Wallace from the postmodernists (what makes him *post*-postmodern) is that he was not content to expose "the arbitrariness and constructedness of the stories and ideologies

---

[5] Alexis Burgess, "How We Ought to Do Things with Words," in *Gesturing Toward Reality: David Foster Wallace and Philosophy*, ed. Robert K. Bolger and Scott Korb (New York: Bloomsbury, 2014), 5–18, esp. 16.
[6] Daniel Turnbull, "*This Is Water* and the Ethics of Attention: Wallace, Murdoch, and Nussbaum," in *Consider David Foster Wallace: Critical Essays*, ed. David Hering (Los Angeles and Austin: Sideshow Media Group Press, 2010), 209–17.
[7] Ibid., 210.
[8] McCaffery, "An Expanded Interview with David Foster Wallace," 44.
[9] Kelly, "David Foster Wallace and the New Sincerity in American Fiction."
[10] Hayes-Brady, *The Unspeakable Failures of David Foster Wallace*, 19.
[11] Cf. Kaiser, "Humor after Postmodernism."
[12] Joffe, "In the Shadows."
[13] Cunningham, "The Hazards of Being Free," 5.

people believe to make sense of modern life," but sought to "also offer a meaningful, if not *hopeful*, way forward out of the rubble of disillusionment." Language is part of the problem: it allows people to conceal and mislead, it keeps groups divided, it never perfectly communicates meanings—but it is also part of the solution. Wallace believed that "language and linguistic intercourse is, in and of itself, redeeming, remedy-ing."[14] We can choose to avoid automatic, reflexive, negative judgments of people's language, to pay attention to the meanings they wish to express, which would allow us to "Identify" rather than "Compare." We can find or form communities that support individuals, finding commonality and universality of experience across acknowledged differences, rather than communities that require erasure of individual differences in order to fit in.

Wallace deemed the term "discourse community" "a rare piece of academic jargon that's actually a valuable addition to SWE because it captures something at once very complex and very specific that no other English term quite can" (*CTL* 98). Alcoholics Anonymous is presented in *Jest* as a healthy discourse community because everyone learns not just to signal their in-group identity by echoing the rather-simplistic-yet-deeply-profound slogans, not only to learn to speak in their own authentic voices but also "to listen . . . with an empathy ('identification') that manages to quiet a certain habitual cynicism and negativity."[15] Wallace explicitly specified that this crosses cultural, racial, and ethnic divides—"no matter what the color or fellowship" (*Jest* 345)—perhaps that it also crosses linguistic divides is too self-evident to warrant mention. McGurl[16] notes that Wallace's conception of a "therapeutic community" revolves around "individual ethical choices" rather than political questions or challenges to the political system," and Williams[17] agrees that "the rehabilitation of the individual is Wallace's chief concern, and he hopes that improvement of the community will follow." Individual readers might disagree with this as a philosophical matter, seeing it as a cop-out, preferring writers to take more explicitly political stances—but that would be a very different writer, not Wallace.

Wallace's alter ego characters typically do not live up to the goal of empathetic, nonjudgmental identifying, but his narrators often do. Readers are challenged to bear witness to all kinds of horrors and indignities; the

---

[14] McCaffery, "An Expanded Interview with David Foster Wallace," 33.
[15] Paul Jenner, "Don't Compare, Identify: David Foster Wallace on John McCain," in *Consider David Foster Wallace*, ed. David Hering (Los Angeles and Austin: Sideshow Media Group Press, 2010), 199–208, esp. 203.
[16] McGurl, "The Institution of Nothing," 36.
[17] Williams, "*Something Real American*," 170.

pain of this is made bearable by identifying with the always deeply ethical perspective of the narrator. Wallace presented his own endless anxieties both as human and specifically as author,[18] not because they were greater than other people's, but because they were his; the implication that readers will respond with understanding and care is flattering to their positive face, as was the implication of reciprocity—that if readers could articulate their own anxieties and traumas (in their own dialects), "Dave Wallace" would identify and care.

In *Water*, Wallace concludes that "there is no such thing as not worshipping. Everybody worships. The only choice we get is *what* to worship" (99–101; italics in original). Wallace's choice was language and the power of narrative. Those who share that choice cannot help but respond to the masterful way Wallace wielded language, somehow creating "words that are not and never can be words" (487) (as Lucien Antitoi was not able to do). He could not sound "a bell-clear and nearly maternal call-to-arms in all the world's well-known tongues" (489) (as the release of Lucien's soul from his body did); for Wallace's fans, the muddied call-to-arms in English will have to suffice.

---

[18] Cf. Holland, "By Hirsute Author," 60–70.

Acknowledgments

This book would not have been written without the support and encouragement of Stephen Burn, whose comments were very helpful and to whom I am deeply grateful.

The Harry Ransom Center in Austin, Texas, is an academic heaven; I wish I could have spent longer there. I hadn't applied for a fellowship, so many thanks to my dear friends Lauren Buxbaum and Harold Wilensky for putting me up and putting up with me.

Enormous thanks are due to all of my colleagues and students in the Department of English & Linguistics at Truman State University, especially students in my Fall 2017 "Linguistics and Literary Criticism" class, who spent more than a few days chewing over the opening of *Infinite Jest*, and who made me realize that not nearly enough linguistic criticism had been done on Wallace, and inspired me to step up for it. Extra special thanks to the twenty students who took the *Infinite Jest* class with me in Fall 2018 and helped me see it through fresh eyes.

Infinite thanks are due to Alan, Clara, and Fred Garvey, and Iris Shapiro for all sorts of things, every day. I do not thank my errant brother Paul, although he is much missed since he moved away.

Bibliography

Alexander, Matthew. "David Foster Wallace and Repressive Taboos: Clenette Henderson, Yrstruly and the Identity Politics of Representation." *FORUM: University of Edinburgh Postgraduate Journal of Culture & the Arts*, no. 24 (2017): 1–10.

Alim, H. Samy. "Introducing Raciolinguistics: Racing Language and Languaging Race in Hyperracial Times." In *Raciolinguistics: How Language Shapes Our Ideas about Race*, ed. Alim, H. Samy, John R. Rickford, and Arnetha F. Ball. Oxford: Oxford University Press, 2016, 1–30.

Alim, H. Samy. *You Know My Steez: An Ethnographic and Sociolinguistic Study of Styleshifting in a Black American Speech Community*. Durham, NC: Duke University Press/The American Dialect Society, 2004.

Allbritten, Rachael Meghan. *Sounding Southern: Phonetic Features and Dialect Perceptions*. PhD Dissertation, Georgetown University, 2011.

Araya, Jorge. 2015. "Why the Whiteness?: Race in *The Pale King*." In *Critical Insights: David Foster Wallace*, ed. Philip Coleman. New York: Grey House Publishing/Salem Press, 2015, 238–51.

Ash, Sharon. "Social Class." In *The Handbook of Language Variation and Change*, ed. J. K. Chambers, Peter Trudgill, and Natalie Schilling-Estes. Malden, MA: Blackwell, 2004, 402–22.

Atwood, E. Bagby. *The Regional Vocabulary of Texas*. Austin: The University of Texas Press, 1962.

Aubry, Timothy "*Infinite Jest* and the Recovery of Feeling." Chapter 3 of *Reading as Therapy: What Contemporary Fiction Does for Middle-Class Americans*. Iowa City: University of Iowa Press, 2011, 97–126.

Babb, Valerie. *Whiteness Visible: The Meaning of Whiteness in American Literature and Culture*. New York: New York University Press, 1998.

Babcock, Rebecca Day. "Folk-Linguistic Attitudes in Eastern Massachusetts." *Open Journal of Modern Linguistics* 4, no. 03 (2014): 415.

Bailey, Guy, and Jan Tillery. "The Lone Star State of Speech (Texas)." In *American Voices: How Dialects Differ from Coast to Coast*, ed. Walt Wolfram and Ben Ward. Malden, MA: Blackwell, 2006a, 36–4.

Bailey, Guy, and Jan Tillery. "Sounds of the South." In *American Voices: How Dialects Differ from Coast to Coast*, ed. Walt Wolfram and Ben Ward. Malden, MA: Blackwell, 2006b, 11–16.

Bakhtin, Mikhail. *The Dialogic Imagination*. Austin: University of Texas Press, 1981.

Baugh, Albert Croll, and Cable, Thomas. *A History of the English Language*, 3rd ed. Englewood Cliffs, NJ: Prentice Hall, 1978.

Baugh, John. *Black Street Speech*. Austin: The University of Texas Press, 1983.

Baugh, John. "Linguistic Profiling and Discrimination." In *The Oxford Handbook of Language and Society*, ed. Ofelia García, Nelson Flores, and Massimiliano Spotti. Oxford: Oxford University Press, 2017, 349–68.

Baugh, John. "Steady: Progressive Aspect in Black Vernacular English." *American Speech* 59, no. 1 (1984): 3–12.

Benzon, Kiki. "'Yet Another Example of the Porousness of Certain Borders': Chaos and Realism in *Infinite Jest*." In *Consider David Foster Wallace: Critical Essays*, ed. David Hering. Los Angeles and Austin: Sideshow Media Group Press, 2010, 101–12.

Bernstein, Cynthia. "More Than Just Yada Yada Yada (Jewish English)." In *American Voices: How Dialects Differ from Coast to Coast*, ed. Walt Wolfram and Ben Ward. Malden, MA: Blackwell, 2006, 252–7.

Birkerts, Sven. "The Alchemist's Retort." Review of *Infinite Jest*, by David Foster Wallace. *The Atlantic Monthly* (February 1996). https://www.theatlantic.com/magazine/archive/1996/02/the-alchemists-retort/376533/

Bissell, Tom. "Foreword" to 20th anniversary edition of *Infinite Jest*. Boston: Little, Brown, & Co., 2016, xi–xv.

Bloom, Paul. *Against Empathy: The Case for Rational Compassion*. New York: Ecco, 2016.

Boswell, Marshall. "Author Here: The Legal Fiction of David Foster Wallace's The Pale King." *English Studies* 95, no. 1 (2014): 25–39.

Boswell, Marshall. *Understanding David Foster Wallace*. Columbia: University of South Carolina Press, 2003.

Bourdieu, Pierre. *Language and Symbolic Power*. Translated by Gino Raymond and Matthew Adamson. Cambridge: Harvard University Press, 1991.

Brown, Penelope, and Stephen Levinson. *Politeness: Some Universals in Language Usage*. Cambridge: Cambridge University Press, 1987.

Bucher, Matt, Nick Maniatis and Kathleen Fitzpatrick. "How to Read *Infinite Jest*." Infinite Summer website. June 17, 2009. http://infinitesummer.org/archives/215

Bucholtz, Mary. *White Kids: Language, Race, and Styles of Youth Identity*. New York: Cambridge University Press, 2011.

Burgess, Alexis. "How We Ought to Do Things with Words." In *Gesturing Toward Reality: David Foster Wallace and Philosophy*, ed. Robert K. Bolger and Scott Korb. New York: Bloomsbury, 2014, 5–18.

Burn, Stephen J. "'A Paradigm for the Life of Consciousness': Closing Time in *The Pale King*." *Studies in the Novel* 44, no. 4 (2012): 371–88.

Burn, Stephen J. "Toward a General Theory of Vision in Wallace's Fiction." *English Studies* 95, no. 1 (2014): 85–93. Doi: 10.1080/0013838X.2013.857858

Cameron, Deborah. *Verbal Hygiene*. London and New York: Routledge, 2003.

Campbell-Kibler, Kathryn. "Accent, (ING), and the Social Logic of Listener Perceptions." *American Speech* 82, no. 1 (2007): 32–64.

Carkeet, David. "The Dialects in Huckleberry Finn." *American Literature* 51, no. 3 (1979): 315-32.

Carver, Craig. *American Regional Dialects*. Ann Arbor: University of Michigan Press, 1987.

Cayton, Andrew R. L., and Susan E. Gray, eds. *The American Midwest: Essays on Regional History*. Bloomington and Indianapolis: Indiana University Press, 2001.

Chambers, Jack K., and Peter Trudgill. *Dialectology*. Cambridge University Press, 1998.

Charity Hudley, Anne H., Christine Mallinson, Mary Bucholtz, Nelson Flores, Nicole Holliday, Elaine Chun, and Arthur Spears. (2018). "Linguistics and Race: An Interdisciplinary Approach Towards an LSA Statement on Race." *Proceedings of the Linguistic Society of America* 3 (2018): 8:1-14. https://journals.linguisticsociety.org/proceedings/index.php/PLSA/article/view/4303. Doi: 10.3765/plsa.v3i1.4303.

Cheshire, Jenny. "Sex and Gender in Variationist Research." In *The Handbook of Language Variation and Change*, ed. J. K. Chambers, Peter Trudgill, and Natalie Schilling-Estes. Malden, MA: Blackwell, 2004, 423-43.

Christian, Donna, Walt Wolfram, and Nanjo Dube. "Variation and Change in Geographically Isolated Communities: Appalachian English and Ozark English." National Science Foundation Report. 1984. https://files.eric.ed.gov/fulltext/ED246682.pdf

Cioffi, Frank Louis. "'An Anguish Become Thing': Narrative as Performance in David Foster Wallace's *Infinite Jest*." *Narrative* 8, no. 2 (2000): 161-81.

Clare, Ralph. "The Politics of Boredom and the Boredom of Politics in David Foster Wallace's *The Pale King*." *Studies in the Novel* 44, no. 4 (2012): 428-46.

Cockfield, Arthur. "David Foster Wallace on Tax Policy, How to Be an Adult, and Other Mysteries of the Universe." *Pittsburgh Tax Review* 12 (2015): 89-109.

Cohen, Samuel. "The Whiteness of David Foster Wallace." In *Postmodern Literature and Race*, ed. Len Platt and Sara Upstone. Cambridge: Cambridge University Press, 2015, 228-43.

Cohen, Samuel. "To Wish to Try to Sing to the Next Generation: *Infinite Jest*'s History." In *The Legacy of David Foster Wallace*, ed. Samuel Cohen and Lee Konstantinou. Iowa City: The University of Iowa Press, 2012, 59-79.

Cole, Roger W. "Literary Representation of Dialect: A Theoretical Approach to the Artistic Problem." *The USF Language Quarterly* 14, nos. 3-4 (1986): 3-8.

Collins, Katherine A., and Richard Clément. "Language and Prejudice: Direct and Moderated Effects." *Journal of Language and Social Psychology* 31, no. 4 (2012): 376-96.

Coughlan, David. "'Sappy or No, It's True': Affect and Expression in *Brief Interviews with Hideous Men*." In *Critical Insights: David Foster Wallace*, ed. Philip Coleman. New York: Grey House Publishing/ Salem Press, 2015, 160-75.

Crystal, David. *The Language of Stories*. Woodstock, NY: The Overlook Press, 2004.
Cunningham, Josh, "'The Hazards of Being Free': Thinking About Not Thinking in *Infinite Jest*." (2019). MA Thesis, CUNY Academic Works. https://academicworks.cuny.edu/cc_etds_theses/739
Daalder, Jurrit. "Wallace's Geographical Metafiction." In *The Cambridge Companion to David Foster Wallace*, ed. Ralph Clare. Cambridge: Cambridge University Press, 2018, 220–34.
Davies, Catherine Evans. "'We Digress': Kathryn Tucker Windham and Southern Storytelling Style." *Storytelling, Self, Society* 4, no. 3 (2008): 167–84.
Davies, Mark. *The Corpus of Contemporary American English (COCA): 560 Million Words, 1990-Present*. (2008–) https://corpus.byu.edu/coca/.
Davies, Mark. *The Corpus of Historical American English (COHA):1810s–2000s*. (2008–). https://corpus.byu.edu/coha/.
Dawson, Paul. *The Return of the Omniscient Narrator: Authorship and Authority in Twenty-First Century Fiction*. Columbus: The Ohio State University Press, 2013.
de Bourcier, Simon. "'They All Sound Like David Foster Wallace': Syntax and Narrative in *Infinite Jest*, *Brief Interviews with Hideous Men*, *Oblivion* and *The Pale King*." *Orbit: A Journal of American Literature* 5, no. 1 (2017): 1–30. Doi: 10.16995/orbit.207
Derdeyn, LeeAnn. "Love the Jackalope: Historicity, Relational Identity, and Naming in David Foster Wallace's 'Lyndon.'" *College Literature* 45, no. 4 (Fall 2018): 747–72.
Dettmar, Kevin J. H. "Afterword." In *The David Foster Wallace Reader*, ed. Bonnie Nadell, et al. New York: Back Bay Books/Little, Brown and Company, 2015, 20–1.
Donahue, Anne Marie. "David Foster Wallace Winces at the Suggestion That His Book Is Sloppy in Any Sense." In *Conversations with David Foster Wallace*, ed. Stephen J. Burn. Jackson: University of Mississippi Press, 2012, 70–72.
Drummond, Rob. *Researching Urban Youth Language and Identity*. London: Palgrave Macmillan, 2018.
Dudar, Helen. "A Whiz Kid and His Wacky First Novel." In *Conversations with David Foster Wallace*, ed. Stephen J. Burn. Jackson: University of Mississippi Press, 2012, 8–10.
Eckert, Penelope. *Linguistic Variation as Social Practice: The Linguistic Construction of Identity in Belton High*. Malden, MA: Blackwell, 2000.
Ellerhoff, Steve Gronert. "Proteus Bound: Pinning *Girl with Curious Hair* under Short Story Theory." In *Critical Insights: David Foster Wallace*, ed. Philip Coleman. New York: Grey House Publishing/Salem Press, 2015, 112–27.
Engles, Tim. 2015. "White Male Nostalgia in Don DeLillo's *Underworld*." In *Postmodern Literature and Race*, ed. Len Platt and Sara Upstone. Cambridge: Cambridge University Press, 2015, 195–210.

Esau, Helmut, Norma Bagnall, and Cheryl Ware. "Faulkner, Literary Criticism, and Linguistics." *Language and Literature* 7, nos. 1–3 (1982): 7–62.

Fadiman, Anne. "Afterword." In *The David Foster Wallace Reader*, ed. Bonnie Nadell, et al. New York: Back Bay Books/Little, Brown and Company, 2015, 759–62.

Fanning, Charles. *The Irish Voice in America: 250 Years of Irish-American Fiction*. 2nd ed. Lexington: University Press of Kentucky, 2000.

Farr, Marcia, ed. *Ethnolinguistic Chicago*. Mahwah, NJ: Lawrence Erlbaum Associates, 2004.

Fennelly, Katherine. "Prejudice Toward Immigrants in the Midwest." In *New Faces in New Places: The Changing Geography of American Immigration*, ed. Douglas S. Massey. New York: Russell Sage Foundation, 2008, 151–78.

Ferrence, Matthew J. *All-American Redneck: Variations on an Icon, from James Fenimore Cooper to the Dixie Chicks*. Knoxville: The University of Tennessee Press, 2014.

Fitzpatrick, Jim. "Beantown Babble (Boston, MA)." In *American Voices: How Dialects Differ from Coast to Coast*, ed. Walt Wolfram and Ben Ward. Malden, MA: Blackwell, 2006, 63–9.

Foer, Jonathan Safran. *Everything Is Illuminated*. Boston: Houghton Mifflin, 2002.

Folb, Edith A. *Runnin' Down Some Lines: The Language and Culture of Black Teenagers*. Cambridge: Harvard University Press, 1980.

Foster, Graham. "A Blasted Region: David Foster Wallace's Man-Made Landscapes." In *Consider David Foster Wallace: Critical Essays*, ed. David Hering. Los Angeles and Austin: Sideshow Media Group Press, 2010, 37–48.

Fought, Carmen. "California Students' Perceptions of, You Know, Regions and Dialects?" In *Handbook of Perceptual Dialectology*, vol. 2, ed. Dennis Preston and Daniel Long. Amsterdam: John Benjamins, 2002, 113–34.

Fox, Aaron A. *Real Country: Music and Language in Working-Class Culture*. Durham, NC and London: Duke University Press, 2004.

Frantzen, Mikkel Krause. "Finding the Unlovable Object Lovable: Empathy and Depression in David Foster Wallace." *Studies in American Fiction* 45, no. 2 (2018): 259–79.

Franzen, Jonathan. "Recollections." [Remarks from a Memorial Service for David Foster Wallace Held October 23, 2008]. *Sonora Review* 55 (2009): 41–4.

Frazer, Timothy C. "An Introduction to Midwest English." In *American Voices: How Dialects Differ from Coast to Coast*, ed. Walt Wolfram and Ben Ward. Malden, MA: Blackwell, 2006, 101–5.

Freudenthal, Elizabeth. "Anti-interiority: Compulsiveness, Objectification, and Identity in *Infinite Jest*." *New Literary History* 41, no. 1 (Winter 2010): 191–211.

Friedman, Claire. "How to Read *Infinite Jest*." *The New Yorker Magazine*. Print edition November 5, 2018; Online October 29, 2018. https://www.newyorker.com/magazine/2018/11/05/how-to-read-infinite-jest

Garber, Megan. "David Foster Wallace and the Dangerous Romance of Male Genius." *The Atlantic Monthly* (May 9, 2018). https://www.theatlantic.com/entertainment/archive/2018/05/the-world-still-spins-around-male-genius/559925/

Garner, Bryan A. *A Dictionary of Modern American Usage*. New York: Oxford University Press, 1998.

Gass, William. *Omensetter's Luck*. New York: Penguin, 1966.

Giaimo, Genie. "Talking Back Through 'Talking Black': African American English and Agency in Walter Mosley's Devil in a Blue Dress." *Language and Literature* 19, no. 3 (2010): 235–47.

Giles, Howard, ed. *Communication Accommodation Theory: Negotiating Personal Relationships and Social Identities Across Contexts*. Cambridge: Cambridge University Press, 2016.

Gold, David L. "The Speech and Writing of Jews." In *Language in the USA*, eds. Charles A. Ferguson and Shirley Brice Heath. Cambridge and New York: Cambridge University Press, 1989, 273–92.

Gordon, Matthew J. "Straight Talking from the Heartland (Midwest)." In *American Voices: How Dialects Differ from Coast to Coast*, ed. Walt Wolfram and Ben Ward. Malden, MA: Blackwell, 2006, 106–11.

Green, Lisa J. *African American English: A Linguistic Introduction*. Cambridge and New York: Cambridge University Press, 2002.

Grice, H. Paul. "Logic and Conversation." In *The Philosophy of Language*, ed. A. P. Martinich. Oxford: Oxford University Press, 1985, 159–70.

Gross, Terry. "*Fresh Air* Interview with David Foster Wallace." National Public Radio. March 5, 1997.

Habick, Timothy. "Farmer City, Illinois: Sound Systems Shifting South." In "*Heartland English*": *Variation and Transition in the American Midwest*, ed. Timothy C. Frazier. Tuscaloosa: University of Alabama Press, 1993, 97–124.

Hall-Lew, Lauren, and Nola Stephens. "Country Talk." *Journal of English Linguistics* 40, no. 3 (2012): 256–80.

Hartley, Laura. "The Consequences of Conflicting Stereotypes: Bostonian Perceptions of U.S. Dialects." *American Speech* 80, no. 4 (2005): 388–405. https://digitalcommons.georgefox.edu/lang_fac/16.

Haugen, Einar. "Dialect, Language, Nation." *American Anthropologist* 68, no. 4 (1966): 922–35.

Hayes-Brady, Clare. "'…': Language, Gender, and Modes of Power in the Work of David Foster Wallace." In *A Companion to David Foster Wallace Studies*, ed. Marshall Boswell and Stephen J. Burn. New York: Palgrave Macmillan, 2013, 131–50.

Hayes-Brady, Clare. "'Personally I'm Neutral on the Menstruation Point': David Foster Wallace and Gender." In *Critical Insights: David Foster Wallace*, ed. Philip Coleman. New York: Grey House Publishing/Salem Press, 2015, 63–77.

Hayes-Brady, Clare. *The Unspeakable Failures of David Foster Wallace: Language, Identity, and Resistance*. New York: Bloomsbury Academic, 2017.

Hering, David. *David Foster Wallace: Fiction and Form*. New York: Bloomsbury Publishing USA, 2017.

Hering, David. "Infinite Jest: Triangles, Cycles, Choices, & Chases." In *Consider David Foster Wallace*, ed. David Hering. Los Angeles and Austin: Sideshow Media Group Press, 2010, 89–100.

Hickey, Raymond. *Irish English : History and Present-Day Forms*. Cambridge: Cambridge University Press, 2007.

Hoberek, Andrew. "The Novel after David Foster Wallace." *A Companion to David Foster Wallace Studies*, ed. Marshall Boswell and Stephen J. Burn. New York: Palgrave Macmillan, 2013, 211–38.

Hodson, Jane. *Dialect in Film and Literature*. New York: Palgrave Macmillan, 2014.

Holland, Mary K. "'By Hirsute Author': Gender and Communication in the Work and Study of David Foster Wallace." *Critique: Studies in Contemporary Fiction* 58, no. 1 (2016): 64–77. Doi: 10.1080/00111619.2016.1149798

Holl, Rainer. *The Narrative Game: The Reading of David Foster Wallace's Infinite Jest as Play*. Hamburg: Anchor Academic Publishing, 2013.

Houser, Heather. "Infinite Jest's Environmental Case for Disgust." In *The Legacy of David Foster Wallace*, ed. Samuel Cohen and Lee Konstantinou. Iowa City: University of Iowa Press, 2012, 118–42.

Howard, Gerald. "Afterword." In *The David Foster Wallace Reader*, ed. Bonnie Nadell, et al. New York: Back Bay Books/Little, Brown and Company, 2015, 63–4.

Hudson, Cory M. "David Foster Wallace Is Not Your Friend: The Fraudulence of Empathy in David Foster Wallace Studies and 'Good Old Neon.'" *Critique: Studies in Contemporary Fiction* 59, no. 3 (2018): 295–306.

Hurt, R. Douglas. "Midwestern Distinctiveness." In *The American Midwest: Essays on Regional History*, ed. Andrew R. L. Cayton and Susan E. Gray. Bloomington and Indianapolis: Indiana University Press, 2001, 160–79.

Irvine, Judith T. "'Style' as Distinctiveness: The Culture and Ideology of Linguistic Differentiation." In *Style and Sociolinguistic Variation*, ed. Penelope Eckert and John R. Rickford. Cambridge: Cambridge University Press, 2001, 21–43.

Irvine, Judith T. and Susan Gal. "Language Ideology and Linguistic Differentiation." In *Regimes of Language Ideologies, Politics, and Identities*, ed. Paul V. Kroskrity. Santa Fe, NM: School of American Research Press, 2000, 35–84.

Ives, Sumner. "A Theory of Literary Dialect." *Tulane Studies in English* 2 (1950): 137–82.

Jackson, Edward and Joel Nicholson-Roberts. "White Guys: Questioning *Infinite Jest*'s New Sincerity." *Orbit: A Journal of American Literature* 5, no.1 (2017): 1–28. Doi: 10.16995/orbit.182

Jansen, Brian Douglas. "'On the Porousness of Certain Borders': Attending to Objects in David Foster Wallace's *Infinite Jest*." *ESC: English Studies in Canada* 40, no. 4 (2014): 55–77.
Jenner, Paul. "Don't Compare, Identify: David Foster Wallace on John McCain." In *Consider David Foster Wallace*, ed. David Hering. Los Angeles and Austin: Sideshow Media Group Press, 2010, 199–208.
Joffe, Daniela Franca. *'In the Shadows': David Foster Wallace and Multicultural America*. Ph.D. Dissertation, University of Cape Town, 2017. http://open.uct.ac.za/handle/11427/26899
Joffe, Daniela Franca. "No Man's Land: David Foster Wallace and Feminist America." *The Journal of David Foster Wallace Studies* 1, no. 1 (forthcoming): 1–. https://s3.amazonaws.com/academia.edu.documents/56681900/Joffe_JDFWS_copyedited.pdf
Johnstone, Barbara. "Features and Uses of Southern Style." In *English in the Southern United States*, ed. Stephen J. Nagle and Sara L. Sanders. Cambridge: Cambridge University Press, 2006, 189–207.
Jones, Gavin. *Strange Talk: The Politics of Dialect Literature in Gilded Age America*. Berkeley: University of California Press, 1999.
Kaiser, Wilson. "Humor after Postmodernism: David Foster Wallace and Proximal Irony." *Studies in American Humor*, New Series 3, no. 28 (2013): 31–44. http://www.jstor.org/stable/23823875
Kelly, Adam. "David Foster Wallace and the New Sincerity in American Fiction." In *Consider David Foster Wallace*, ed. David Hering. Los Angeles and Austin: Sideshow Media Group Press, 2010, 131–46.
Kelly, Adam. "Development Through Dialogue: David Foster Wallace and the Novel of Ideas." *Studies in the Novel* 44, no. 3 (2012): 267–83.
Kennedy, Hugh, and Geoffrey Polk. "Looking for a Garde of Which to Be Avant: An Interview with David Foster Wallace." In *Conversations with David Foster Wallace*, ed. Stephen J. Burn. Jackson: University of Mississippi Press, 2012, 11–20.
Kiesling, Scott F. *Language, Gender, and Sexuality: An Introduction*. Abingdon and New York: Routledge, 2019.
Kinzler, Katherine D. and Jasmine M. DeJesus. "Northern = Smart and Southern = Nice: The Development of Accent Attitudes in the U.S." *Quarterly Journal of Experimental Psychology* 66, no. 6 (2013): 1146–58. Doi: 10.1080/17470218.2012.731695
Kirkham, Sam. "Intersectionality and the Social Meanings of Variation: Class, Ethnicity, and Social Practice." *Language in Society* 44, no. 5 (2015): 629–52. Doi: 10.1017/S0047404515000585
Klayman, Joshua. "Varieties of Confirmation Bias." In *Decision Making from a Cognitive Perspective. The Psychology of Learning and Motivation*, Vol. 32, ed. Jerome Busemeyer, Reid Hartie and Douglas L. Medin. New York: Academic Press, 1995, 385–418.
Kolln, Martha. *Rhetorical Grammar: Grammatical Choices, Rhetorical Effects*, 3rd ed. Boston: Allyn & Bacon, 1989.

Konstantinou, Lee. "Unfinished Form." *Los Angeles Review of Books* (July 6, 2011). https://lareviewofbooks.org/article/unfinished-form/#
Konstantinou, Lee. "The World of David Foster Wallace." *Boundary 2*, 40, no. 3 (September 2013): 59–86.
Korzybski, Alfred. *Science and Sanity: An Introduction to Non-Aristotelian Systems and General Semantics*. Lakeville, CT: International Non-Aristotelian Library Publishing Co., 1933.
Labov, William. *Language in the Inner City: Studies in the Black English Vernacular*. Vol. 3. Philadelphia: University of Pennsylvania Press, 1972a.
Labov, William. *Principles of Linguistic Change: Internal Factors*. Oxford: Blackwell, 1994.
Labov, William. *Sociolinguistic Patterns*. Philadelphia: University of Pennsylvania Press, 1972b.
Labov, William, Sharon Ash and Charles Boberg. "A National Map of the Regional Dialects of American English." 1997. https://www.ling.upenn.edu/phono_atlas/NationalMap/NationalMap.html
Laferriere, Martha. "Ethnicity in Phonological Variation and Change." *Language* 55, no. 3 (1979): 603–17.
Lakoff, Robin. *Language and Woman's Place*. New York: Harper & Row/Colophon, 1975.
Lambert, Wallace E., Richard C. Hodgson, Robert C. Gardner, and Samuel Fillenbaum. "Evaluational Reactions to Spoken Languages." *The Journal of Abnormal and Social Psychology* 60, no. 1 (1960): 44.
LeClair, Tom. "The Prodigious Fiction of Richard Powers, William Vollman, and David Foster Wallace." *Critique* 38, no. 1 (Fall 1996): 12–37.
Le Page, Robert and Andrée Tabouret-Keller. *'Acts of Identity': Creole-Based Approaches to Language and Ethnicity*. Cambridge: Cambridge University Press, 1985.
Letzler, David. "Encyclopedic Novels and the 'Cruft' of Fiction: *Infinite Jest*'s Endnotes." *Studies in the Novel* 44, no. 3 (Fall 2012): 302–24.
Levis, John. "Learners' Views of Social Issues in Pronunciation Learning." *Journal of Academic Language & Learning* 9, no. 1 (2015): 42–55.
Levy, Joshua. "The Social Stratification of (r) in Boston." *Toronto Working Papers in Linguistics* 33, no. 1 (2010): 1–12.
Lippi-Green, Rosina. *English with an Accent*. London and New York: Routledge, 1997.
Lipsky, David. *Although of Course You End Up Becoming Yourself: A Road Trip with David Foster Wallace*. New York: Broadway Books, 2010.
Lipsky, David. "The Lost Years and Last Days of David Foster Wallace." In *Conversations with David Foster Wallace*, ed. Stephen J. Burn. Jackson: University of Mississippi Press, 2012, 161–83.
Macauley, Ronald K. S. "'Coz It Izny Spelt When They Say It': Displaying Dialect in Writing." *American Speech* 66, no. 3 (1991): 280–91.
Mair, Christian. "Literary Sociolinguistics: A Methodological Framework for Research on the Use of Nonstandard Language in Fiction." *Arbeiten aus*

Anglistik und Amerikanistik 17, no. 1 (1992): 103–23. https://www.jstor.org/stable/43023593

Manne, Kate. *Down Girl: The Logic of Misogyny*. Oxford: Oxford University Press, 2017.

Martínez, María-Ángeles. *Storyworld Possible Selves. Applications of Cognitive Linguistics*, Vol. 37. Berlin: De Gruyter Mouton, 2018.

Martone, Michael. *The Blue Guide to Indiana*. Tuscaloosa: University of Alabama Press, 2001.

Martone, Michael. "Footnotes & Endnotes." *Sonora Review* 55 (2009): 51–8.

Martone, Michael. *Fort Wayne Is Seventh on Hitler's List: Indiana Stories*. Bloomington: Indiana University Press, 1990.

Martone, Michael, ed. *A Place of Sense: Essays in Search of the Midwest*. Iowa City: Iowa Humanities Board, 1988.

Max, D. T. *Every Love Story Is a Ghost Story: A Life of David Foster Wallace*. New York: Viking, 2012.

McCaffery, Larry. "An Expanded Interview with David Foster Wallace." In *Conversations with David Foster Wallace*, ed. Stephen J. Burn. Jackson: University Press of Mississippi, 2012, 21–52.

McGurl, Mark. "The Institution of Nothing: David Foster Wallace in the Program." *Boundary 2* 41, no. 3 (2014): 27–54. Doi 10.1215/01903659-2812061

McHugh, Patrick. "Cultural Politics, Postmodernism, and White Guys: Affect in *Gravity's Rainbow*." *College Literature* 28, no. 2 (Spring 2001): 1–28.

McIlwaine, Shields. *The Southern Poor-White from Lubberland to Tobacco Road*. Norman: University of Oklahoma Press, 1939.

McWhiney, Grady. *Cracker Culture: Celtic Ways in the Old South*. Tuscaloosa: University of Alabama Press, 1988.

Mendoza-Denton, Norma. *Homegirls: Language and Cultural Practice Among Latina Youth Gangs*. Malden, MA: Blackwell, 2008.

Miley, Mike. "… And Starring David Foster Wallace as Himself: Performance and Persona in *The Pale King*." *Critique: Studies in Contemporary Fiction*, 57, no. 2 (2016): 191–207. Doi: 10.1080/00111619.2015.1028611

Miller, Laura. "The Salon Interview: David Foster Wallace." In *Conversations with David Foster Wallace*, ed. Stephen J. Burn. Jackson: University of Mississippi Press, 2012, 58–65.

Milroy, James, and Lesley Milroy. "Linguistic Change, Social Network and Speaker Innovation." *Journal of Linguistics* 21, no. 2 (1985): 339–84.

Minnick, Lisa Cohen. *Dialect and Dichotomy: Literary Representations of African American Speech*. Tuscaloosa: University of Alabama Press, 2007.

Moore, Stephen. "In Memoriam David Foster Wallace." *Modernism/Maturity* 16, no. 1 (2009): 1–24.

Morgan, Marcyliena. "'Nuthin' But a G Thang': Grammar and Language Ideology in Hip Hop Identity." In *Sociocultural and Historical Contexts of African American English*, ed. Sonja L. Lanehart. Amsterdam and Philadelphia: John Benjamins Publishing, 2001, 187–210.

Morrison, Toni. *Playing in the Dark: Whiteness and the Literary Imagination*. Cambridge: Harvard University Press, 1992.

Morrissey, Tara, and Lucas Thompson. "'The Rare White at the Window': A Reappraisal of Mark Costello and David Foster Wallace's *Signifying Rappers*." *Journal of American Studies*, 49, no. 1 (2015): 77–97.

Moyer, Alene. "Exceptional Outcomes in L2 Phonology: The Critical Factors of Learner Engagement and Self-Regulation." *Applied Linguistics* 35, no. 4 (2014): 418–40.

Mura, David. "White Writing Teachers (or David Foster Wallace vs. James Baldwin)." *Journal of Creative Writing Studies* 1, no. 1 (2016): 1–7. http://scholarworks.rit.edu/jcws/vol1/iss1/7

Murray, Thomas E. "Positive *anymore* in the Midwest." In *"Heartland English": Variation and Transition in the American Midwest*, ed. Timothy C. Frazier. Tuscaloosa: University of Alabama Press, 1993, 173–86.

Nagy, Naomi, and Patricia Irwin. "Boston (r): Neighbo(r)s Nea(r) and Fa(r)." *Language Variation and Change* 22, no. 2 (2010): 241–78.

Natalini, Roberto. "David Foster Wallace and the Mathematics of Infinity." In *A Companion to David Foster Wallace Studies*, ed. Marshall Boswell and Stephen J. Burn. New York: Palgrave Macmillan, 2013, 43–57.

Negra, Diane. "The Irish in Us: Irishness, Performativity, and Popular Culture." In *The Irish in US*, ed. Diane Negra. Durham, NC: Duke University Press, 2006, 1–19.

Nichols, Catherine. "Dialogizing Postmodern Carnival: David Foster Wallace's *Infinite Jest*." *Critique: Studies in Contemporary Fiction* 43, no. 1 (2001): 3–16.

Niedzielski, Nancy A., and Dennis R. Preston. *Folk Linguistics*. Berlin: De Gruyter Mouton, 2000.

Nugent, Benjamin. *American Nerd: The Story of My People*. New York: Scribner, 2008.

Oliva, Leo E. "Kansas: A Hard Land in the Heartland." In *Heart Land: Comparative Histories of the Midwestern States*, ed. James H. Madison. Bloomington: Indiana University Press, 1988, 248–75.

Olsen, Lance. "Termite Art, or Wallace's Wittgenstein." *The Review of Contemporary Fiction* 13, no. 2 (1993): 199.

Oster, Judith. *Crossing Cultures: Creating Identity in Chinese and Jewish American Literature*. Columbia: University of Missouri Press, 2003.

Padilla Cruz, Manuel. "Interlocutor-Related and Hearer-Specific Causes of Misunderstanding: Processing Strategy, Confirmation Bias and Weak Vigilance." *Research in Language* 15, no. 1 (2017): 11–36.

Paulson, Steve. "Wallace in the #MeToo Era: A Conversation with Clare Hayes-Brady." *Los Angeles Review of Books* (September 10, 2018). https://lareviewofbooks.org/article/david-foster-wallace-in-the-metoo-era-a-conversation-with-clare-hayes-brady/

Pederson, Lee. "Dialects." In *The Cambridge History of the English Language*, vol. 6: *English in North America*, ed. John Algeo. Cambridge: Cambridge University Press, 2001, 253–90.

Pichler, Pia, and Nathanael Williams. "Hipsters in the Hood: Authenticating Indexicalities in Young Men's Hip-Hop Talk." *Language in Society* 45, no. 4 (2016): 557–81.

Platt, Len and Sara Upstone. *Postmodern Literature and Race*. New York: Cambridge University Press, 2015.

Potts, Sam. n.d. http://sampottsinc.com/ij/IJ_Diagram.pdf.

Preston, Dennis R. "Language with an Attitude." In *The Handbook of Language Variation and Change*, ed. J. K. Chambers, Peter Trudgill, and Natalie Schilling-Estes. Malden, MA: Blackwell, 2004, 40–66.

Preston, Dennis R. "The Li'l Abner Syndrome: Written Representations of Speech." *American Speech* 60, no. 4, (1985): 328–36.

Pynchon, Thomas. *Gravity's Rainbow*. New York: Viking, 1973.

Quinn, Paul. "'Location's Location': Placing David Foster Wallace." In *A Companion to David Foster Wallace Studies*, ed. Marshall Boswell and Stephen J. Burn. New York: Palgrave Macmillan, 2013, 87–106.

"Race and Hispanic Origin." 1990 *Massachusetts Census*, Table 6: 24. https://www2.census.gov/library/publications/decennial/1990/cp-1/cp-1-23.pdf

Ramal, Randy. "Beyond Philosophy: David Foster Wallace on Philosophy, Wittgenstein, and the Dangers of Theorizing." In *Gesturing Toward Reality: David Foster Wallace and Philosophy*, ed. Robert K. Bolger and Scott Korb. New York: Bloomsbury, 2014, 177–98.

Rhode, Jason. "Why Insufferable People Love *Infinite Jest*." *Paste Magazine.com* (June 29, 2018). https://www.pastemagazine.com/articles/2018/06/why-insufferable-people-love-infinite-jest.html

Ribbat, Christoph. "Seething Static: Notes on Wallace and Journalism." In *Consider David Foster Wallace: Critical Essays*, ed. David Hering. Los Angeles and Austin: Sideshow Group Press, 2010, 187–98.

Rickford, John R., and Russell John Rickford. *Spoken Soul: The Story of Black English*. New York: Wiley, 2000.

"Ricky tick." *Urban Dictionary*. http://www.urbandictionary.com

Riney, Timothy J. "Linguistic Controversies, VBE Structures, and Midwest Attitudes." In *"Heartland English": Variation and Transition in the American Midwest*, ed. Timothy C. Frazier. Tuscaloosa: University of Alabama Press, 1993, 81–93.

Rios, Diane. "Chicana: A Negative Connotation?" *La Prensa San Diego* (October 13, 2000). http://www.laprensa-sandiego.org/archieve/october13/chicana.htm

Roache John. "'The Realer, More Enduring and Sentimental Part of Him': David Foster Wallace's Personal Library and Marginalia." *Orbit: A Journal of American Literature* 5, no. 1, (2017). Doi: 10.16995/orbit.142

Ronkin, Maggi, and Helen E. Karn. "Mock Ebonics: Linguistic Racism in Parodies of Ebonics on the Internet." *Journal of Sociolinguistics* 3, no. 3 (1999): 360–80.

Rosa, Jonathan. *Looking Like a Language, Sounding Like a Race: Raciolinguistic Ideologies and the Learning of Latinidad*. New York: Oxford University Press, 2019.

Rubin, Louis D., Jr. *A Gallery of Southerners*. Baton Rouge: Louisiana State University Press, 1982.

Russell, Emily. "Some Assembly Required: The Embodied Politics of *Infinite Jest*." *Arizona Quarterly: A Journal of American Literature, Culture, and Theory* 66, no. 3 (2010): 147–69.

Ryan, Ellen Bouchard, and Howard Giles, eds. *Attitudes Towards Language Variation: Social and Applied Contexts*. London: Edward Arnold, 1982.

Sapir, Edward. *Language*. New York: Harcourt, Brace, & World, 1921.

Sartre, Jean-Paul. "Why Write?" In *Critical Theory Since Plato*, ed. Adams Hazard, Rev. ed. Fort Worth: Harcourt Brace Jovanovich, C1992 [1948], 984–92.

Saussure, Ferdinand de. *Course in General Linguistics*. New York: McGraw-Hill, 1966.

Schechner, Mark. "Behind the Watchful Eyes of Author David Foster Wallace." In *Conversations with David Foster Wallace*, ed. Stephen J. Burn. Jackson: University Press of Mississippi, 2012, 104–9.

Schegloff, Emanuel, Gail Jefferson, and Harvey Sacks. "A Simplest Systematics for the Organization of Turn-Taking for Conversation." *Language* 50, no. 4 (1974): 696–735.

Schiffrin, Deborah. *Discourse Markers*. Cambridge: Cambridge University Press, 1987.

Schiffrin, Deborah. "Jewish Argument as Sociability." *Language in Society* 13, no. 3 (1984): 311–35.

Schildkraut, Deborah J. "American Identity and Attitudes Toward Official English Policies." *Political Psychology* 24, no. 3 (2003): 469–99.

Schneider, Edgar. "Shakespeare in the Coves and Hollows? Toward a History of Southern English." In *English in the Southern United States*, ed. Stephen J. Nagle and Sara L. Sanders. Cambridge: Cambridge University Press, 2006, 17–35.

Schwartzburg, Molly. "Observations on the Archive at the Harry Ransom Center." In *The Legacy of David Foster Wallace*, ed. Sam Cohen and Lee Konstantinou. Iowa City: Iowa University Press, 2012, 241–59.

Shapiro, Mary. "The Poetic Language of David Foster Wallace." *Critique: Studies in Contemporary Fiction* 60, no. 1 (2019): 24–33. Doi: 10.1080/00111619.2018.1441121.

Shapiro, Stephen. "From Capitalist to Communist Abstraction: *The Pale King*'s Cultural Fix." *Textual Practice* 28, no. 7 (2014): 1249–71.

Sheridan, Mark. "Interpret You, INTERPRET-ME? Or, Fictional Pasts and Fictional Futures: The Predecessors and Contemporaries of David Foster Wallace." In *Critical Insights: David Foster Wallace*, ed. Philip Coleman. New York: Grey House Publishing/Salem Press, 2015, 78–93.

Shorrocks, Graham. "Non-Standard Dialect Literature and Popular Culture." In *Speech Past and Present. Studies in English Dialectology in Memory of Ossi Ihalainen*, ed. Juhani Klemola, Merja Kytö and Matti Rissanen. Frankfurt: Peter Lang, 1996, 385–411.

Skaggs, Merrill Maguire. *The Folk of Southern Fiction*. Athens: University of Georgia Press, 1972.

Sloane, Peter. "The Divided Selves of David Foster Wallace." *Tropos* 1, no. 1 (2014): 67–73.

Smith, Zadie. "*Brief Interviews with Hideous Men*: The Difficult Gifts of David Foster Wallace." In *Changing My Mind: Occasional Essays*. London: Hamish Hamilton, 2009, 257–300.

Smitherman, Geneva. "Language and African Americans: Movin On Up a Lil Higher." *Journal of English Linguistics* 32, no. 3 (2004): 186–96.

Smitherman, Geneva. *Talkin and Testifyin: The Language of Black Americans*. Detroit: Wayne State University Press, 1977.

Spears, Arthur K. "The Black English Semi-Auxiliary *Come*." *Language* 58 (1982): 850–72.

Spinner, Samuel. "Reading Jewish." *Publications of the Modern Language Association* 134, no. 1 (2019): 150–6.

Staes, Toon., "Rewriting the Author: A Narrative Approach to Empathy in *Infinite Jest* and *The Pale King*." Studies in the Novel 44, no. 4 (Winter 2012): 409–27.

Szmrecsanyi, Benedikt, and Bernd Kortmann. "The Morphosyntax of Varieties of English Worldwide: A Quantitative Perspective." *Lingua* 119, no. 11 (2009): 1643–63.

Tannen, Deborah. "New York Jewish Conversational Style." *International Journal of the Sociology of Language* 30 (1981): 133–50.

Tarkington, Booth. "The Middle West." *Harper's Monthly Magazine* 106 (1902): 75–83.

Thomas, Erik R., and Guy Bailey. "Segmental Phonology of African American English." In *The Oxford Handbook of African American Language*, ed. Sonja Lanehart. Oxford, UK: Oxford University Press, 2015, 403–19.

Thompson, Lucas. "David Foster Wallace's Germany." *Comparative Literature Studies* 56, no. 1 (2019): 1–30.

Thompson, Lucas. *Global Wallace: David Foster Wallace and World Literature*. New York: Bloomsbury Publishing, 2016.

Thompson, Lucas. "Wallace and Race." In *The Cambridge Companion to David Foster Wallace*, ed. Ralph Clare. Cambridge: Cambridge University Press, 2018, 204–19.

Trillin, Calvin. "The Midwest Is What's Left Over." *The New York Times*, September 9, 1974, 35.

Trudgill, Peter. "Sex, Covert Prestige and Linguistic Change in the Urban British English of Norwich." *Language in Society* 1, no. 2 (1972): 179–95.

Turnbull, Daniel. "*This Is Water* and the Ethics of Attention: Wallace, Murdoch, and Nussbaum." In *Consider David Foster Wallace: Critical Essays*, ed. David Hering. Los Angeles and Austin: Sideshow Media Group Press, 2010, 209–17.

Ukeles, Jacob B., Ron Miller, Peter Friedman, and David Dutwin. 2010 *Metropolitan Chicago Jewish Community Study*. Berman Jewish Databank. https://www.jewishdatabank.org/databank/search-results/study/576

Wallace, Sally Foster. *Practically Painless English*. Englewood Cliffs, NJ: Prentice Hall, 1989 [1980].
Walsh, Ryan, and Jordyn Bonds. *The David Foster Wallace Audio Project*, n.d. http://www.dfwaudioproject.org/
Warren, Andrew. "Narrative Modeling and Community Organizing in *The Pale King* and *Infinite Jest*." *Studies in the Novel* 44, no. 4 (2012): 389–408.
Williams, Iain. *"Something Real American": David Foster Wallace and Authenticity*. Ph.D. Dissertation, University of Edinburgh, 2016. https://www.era.lib.ed.ac.uk/bitstream/handle/1842/31007/Williams2016.pdf
Wirth-Nesher, Hana. *Call It English: The Languages of Jewish American Literature*. Princeton: Princeton University Press, 2006.
Wisely, Karen, and Joel Zapata. "Why I Call Myself Chicana." Video clip from oral history interview with Lilia Escajeda. Amarillo, TX: Civil Rights in Black and Brown Interview Database July 6, 2016. https://crbb.tcu.edu/clips/2533/why-i-call-myself-chicana.
Wittgenstein, Ludwig. *Philosophical Investigations*. Malden, MA: Wiley-Blackwell, 2009 [1953].
Wittgenstein, Ludwig. *Tractatus Logico-Philosophicus*. New York: Routledge, 2013 [1921].
Witzling, David. 2015. "Postmodern Prose and the Discourse of the 'Cultural Jew': The Cases of Mailer and Foer." In *Postmodern Literature and Race*, ed. Len Platt and Sara Upstone. Cambridge: Cambridge University Press, 2015, 160–76.
Wolfram, Walt. "The Grammar of Urban African American Vernacular English." *Handbook of Varieties of English* 2 (2004): 111–32.
Wolfram, Walt, and Ralph Fasold. *The Study of Social Dialects in American English*. Englewood Cliffs, NJ: Prentice Hall, 1974.
Wolfram, Walt, and Natalie Schilling-Estes. *American English*. 2nd ed. Malden, MA: Blackwell, 2006.
Wollitz, Michael Gibson. "Figurant Society: Post-Postmodernity and David Foster Wallace's *Infinite Jest*." (2009). MA Thesis, Georgetown University. https://repository.library.georgetown.edu/bitstream/handle/10822/552982/WollitzMichaelGibson.pdf?sequence=1.

Index

academese 11, 42, 95
African American English
    (AAE) 19, 40, 50–79,
    141, 163, 197
Alexander, Matthew 67, 164
alter ego 1, 98, 102, 136, 145, 150,
    173, 176, 199. *See also*
    "Dave Wallace"
American Heritage Dictionary 8,
    12, 143
anti-Semitism 89, 92
Araya, Jorge 29, 52–3, 61, 67, 77,
    82–4, 105
Asian/Asian American 4, 32, 82–3,
    168
the asshole problem 189–90, 193
Aubry, Timothy 52, 175, 193

Bakhtin, Mikhail 5, 14, 194
Barth, John 98, 129, 147, 173
Benzon, Kiki 29
Birkerts, Sven 40 n.28
Bissell, Tom 8
Boston 22, 64, 83–7, 102–3, 124,
    139, 159–70, 178
Boswell, Marshall 5, 29, 55, 70, 98,
    128–30, 133, 147, 172, 174,
    177, 188, 194
Bourdieu, Pierre 20
Burn, Stephen J. 156, 186
burnout identity 140, 167–9

Cioffi, Frank 186
Clare, Ralph 6 n.19
Cockfield, Arthur 6 n.19, 187 n.57
code-switching 17, 71–2, 90, 95,
    108, 142
Cohen, Samuel 13, 54, 67, 105, 142,
    148, 164

Costello, Mark 54, 85
Coughlan, David 54, 56, 144
covert prestige 18, 109, 115, 161
cultural appropriation 20, 48,
    89–90
Cunningham, Josh 190, 198

Daalder, Jurrit 136–8
"Dave Wallace" (narrative
    persona) 4, 6, 30, 32, 77,
    112, 144–5, 171–94, 200
Dawson, Paul 181, 195–6
de Bourcier, Simon 11, 55–6, 187
DeLillo, Don 48
Derdeyn, LeeAnn 4, 153
Dettmar, Kevin J. H. 144
dialect features
    adverbs without-*ly* 122, 126–7,
        129, 143
    ain't 62, 66, 67, 69, 71, 76, 95,
        126, 130–1, 138, 141,
        149–50, 153, 165
    ax vs. *ask* 69, 76
    counterfactual *like to* 76, 106,
        120, 127
    double modals 66, 120, 127
    "drawl" 120, 123
    future tense forms 57, 62, 65,
        68, 73, 75, 76, 120
    habitual (invariant) *be* 57, 65–6,
        76
    -in vs.*-ing* 43, 63, 66, 69, 74–6,
        91, 122, 126–7, 141
    multiple negation 19, 59, 63, 66,
        68, 71, 75, 76, 95, 114, 131,
        138, 141, 147, 150, 153, 165
    narrative present tense 57, 66,
        71, 76
    negative inversion 66, 71, 76

nonstandard relative clauses 58–9, 63, 69, 71, 76, 131
null copula/auxiliary 57, 62, 65, 76
past tense forms 57, 63, 71–2, 114, 129–31, 153
perfective *done* 57, 62, 76, 120, 127, 141
reflexive infix-*own*- 66, 76
"twang" 121–3, 148
unmarked possessors 63, 66, 68, 72, 76
unmarked verbs 43, 65, 68, 73, 76
unstressed syllables 66, 71, 74, 76, 126, 168
vowel shifts 120, 145–6, 160
where [x] is at construction 131, 141, 153
y(')all 65, 76, 120, 122, 127, 132
dialogism 5, 14. *See also* heteroglossia; ventriloquation
discourse community 15, 199

Ellerhoff, Steve Gronert 93, 128 n.36
empathy 24, 27, 41, 56, 70–1, 78, 85, 107, 133, 153–4, 166, 175, 177–8, 187, 191–2, 197, 199
ethnicity 4, 19, 22–5, 27–31, 47–100, 102–4, 107–8, 111–15, 125, 132, 137, 160, 163, 166–8, 197, 199. *See also* African American; European American; Irish American; Italian American; Jewish American; Latinx; white European/European American 4, 32, 33, 81–5, 107, 137, 168. *See also* white identity
eye dialect 37, 69, 74, 165

Fadiman, Ann 8, 148–9, 189
Foer, Jonathan Safran 89
folk linguistics 3, 6, 19–20, 24, 31, 75, 103–5, 108, 118, 137, 185, 188
Foster, Graham 101
Frantzen, Mikkel Krause 56, 70 n.87
Franzen, Jonathan 1, 145, 194
Freudenthal, Elizabeth 7 n.21, 162

Garner, Bryan 8, 10, 105, 114
Gass, William 18–19, 128–9
gender 15, 23, 28–9, 108–10, 113, 164, 170, 190–4
German 31, 32, 34–6, 43, 92, 99–100, 131
Grice, H. Paul/gricean implicature 180–1, 183–4

Hayes-Brady, Clare 2, 4–5, 28, 38, 45, 51, 54, 64, 88, 96, 109–10, 123, 133, 146, 152, 175, 180, 182, 184, 190–1, 198
Hering, David 3, 14, 34, 139, 142, 145, 150–1, 154
heteroglossia 14, 29, 33, 111
Hoberek, Andrew 162
Holl, Rainer 181
Holland, Mary K. 190–2, 200
Howard, Gerald 8, 12
Hudson, Cory M. 7

Infinite Summer (website) 67, 70
Irish/Irish American 22, 36–7, 84, 85–7, 103, 160
Italian/Italian American 54, 82, 90, 103, 160

Jackson, Edward 61
Jansen, Brian Douglas 6 n.19, 29
Jewish American 23, 53, 64, 81, 85, 87–100, 160

Index 219

jock identity 4, 79, 107–9, 122, 167–9, 172
Joffe, Daniela Franca 2, 25, 52, 61, 68, 136, 140, 175, 190, 191, 198

Kaiser, Wilson 183 n.41, 198 n.11
Karr, Mary 1, 125, 159, 192
Kelly, Adam 5, 13, 14–15, 45, 183, 198
Konstantinou, Lee 155, 173–4
Korzybski, Alfred 196

Labov, William 6 n.20, 57, 93, 103, 105, 120 n.21, 161
Lakoff, Robin 112, 191
Latin (language) 36, 131, 147, 152, 193 n.81
Latinx 3, 49–50, 84, 168
LeClair, Tom 13
Lelchuk, Alan 88, 93
Letzler, David 165, 179
linguistic insecurity 105, 108, 115, 123–4, 151, 161
Lipsky, David 11, 13, 16, 52, 92, 143
literalization 45, 133

McCaffery, Larry 6 n.17, 7 n.25, 8 n.33, 12, 17 n.65, 21 n.89, 23 n.96, 118 n.4, 174 n.10, 175 n.13, 178 n.27, 183 n.40, 198, 199 n.14
McGurl, Mark 1, 34, 54, 60, 85, 96, 155–6, 168, 199
marginalia 10, 14, 56, 118, 122, 138, 149, 173, 189
Martone, Michael 138–9, 187
Max, D.T. 1, 13, 18, 93, 159, 177, 192
melting pot 3, 23, 28, 78, 84, 100, 112, 115. *See also* white identity
Midwestern 102, 106, 108, 115, 122, 131, 135–58

Midwesternisms 155–8
Miley, Mike 172, 174
mimesis 5, 29–30, 127, 172, 196
misogyny 25. *See also* sexism
Moore, Stephen 13
Morrissey, Tara 55, 186
Morrison, Toni 52, 59, 60, 73, 78
Mura, David 59, 77, 83

Nadell, Bonnie 88
names (of Wallace characters) 13, 30, 34, 35, 38–42, 43, 64, 82, 92, 93, 98–9, 122, 125, 132–3, 146, 151, 153–5
narcissism 68, 112
Natalini, Roberto 175
Native American 129, 132
nerd identity 4, 9, 79, 107–9, 122, 167–9, 172
Nichols, Catherine 5, 14
Nicholson-Roberts, Joel 61
non-native speakers 27–45, 89, 196

O'Connor, Flannery 118, 130
Olsen, Lance 5
Ozick, Cynthia 52, 87–8

performativity 6, 47, 88, 113, 115, 117, 124, 128, 142, 148, 152, 193
politeness 93, 119, 127, 173, 182–90, 191
postmodernism 47–8, 88, 174, 198–9
Potts, Sam 164
prejudice 1, 6, 16, 21, 24–5, 27, 31, 88, 92, 111, 115, 118–19, 138, 152, 188, *See also* anti-Semitism; misogyny; racism; sexism
prescriptivism 9–10, 42, 143, 197. *See also* SNOOT; "Standard Written English" (SWE)
Pynchon, Thomas 43, 48

Quinn, Paul   101, 141, 150

racism   24, 27, 30–1, 33, 34, 37, 49–54, 67, 70, 71, 77, 83, 86, 112, 114, 173
Ramal, Randy   146
realism   2, 14, 17, 23–4, 30, 75, 88, 102, 112, 120, 178, 183, 195
Ribbat, Christoph   148, 150
r-lessness   19, 66, 120, 160–4, 167
Roache, John   10
Roth, Philip   88, 93
rural speech   104, 106, 109, 115, 121–2, 126, 133, 135–7, 140–1, 147
Russell, Emily   7 n.23

the Sapir-Whorf hypothesis   196
Schwartzburg, Molly   14 n.53
sexism   24, 127, 173. *See also* misogyny
Shapiro, Stephen   7 n.22
Sheridan, Mark   173
shibboleth   23, 197
Sloane, Peter   7 n.24
Smith, Zadie   23
SNOOT   9, 51, 94, 130, 141, 176, 198
solipsism   28, 52, 68, 112, 190
Southern   19, 22, 102, 106, 108, 112, 115, 117–33, 136–7, 140–1, 147–8
Spanish (language)   34, 147
speech acts   172, 176, 180–1, 184
Staes, Toon   69, 165, 174, 177
"standard written English" (SWE)   10, 57–8, 63, 72–5, 77, 141, 199

Thompson, Lucas   14, 28, 32–3, 34–5, 38, 50–1, 53, 55, 64, 66, 75, 85, 88, 107, 118, 128, 183–6, 190
Trillin, Calvin   143
Turnbull, Daniel   198

ventriloquation   176, 194

Wallace, David Foster (works)
"Another Pioneer"   139
"Authority and American Usage" (A&AU)   1, 5, 9–11, 22, 48, 50–1, 55–7, 75, 93, 114, 122, 141–2, 197
Brief Interviews with Hideous Men (BIHM)   23, 29, 55–6, 70, 82, 177, 192
The Broom of the System (*Broom*)   5, 9, 13, 15, 52–3, 61–3, 110, 113, 125–8, 173, 174, 183–4
"Consider the Lobster"   111
"Democracy and Commerce at the U.S. Open"   54, 111
"Derivative Sport in Tornado Alley"   136, 139, 144, 169
"Everything is Green"   114
Fate, Time, and Language   9
"Getting Away from..."   136, 142, 144, 148–50
"Here and There"   145
"Host"   135
"Incarnations of Burned Children"   121
Infinite Jest (*Jest*)   1–3, 8–9, 11, 13–14, 17, 20, 24, 30–6, 39–45, 50, 60–1, 64–79, 82–7, 98, 99–100, 102, 107–8, 110, 114, 120, 139, 159–69, 174–82, 184–7, 190–1, 193, 196–200
Avril Incandenza   9, 42
Clenette Henderson   60, 66–72, 75, 77–9, 166, 191
Don Gately   30–3, 36–7, 40, 50, 60–1, 67–8, 99, 123–4, 161–4, 175, 178
Gerhardt Schtitt   32, 34–6, 110
Hal Incandenza   9, 31–2, 40, 50, 68, 78, 82, 99, 110, 112, 162, 167–9, 174, 176–8, 198

Index

Hugh Steeply   15–16, 40–5, 100, 110, 177, 197
Joelle van Dyne   9, 60–1, 70, 117, 122–4, 161
Kate Gompert   44, 50, 70, 161–2, 175
Michael Pemulis   86–7, 99, 166–9, 196–7
Ortho Stice   121–2
Rémy Marathe   15–16, 40–45, 98, 177
Roy Tony   58, 72–3, 74–5, 77
Yolanda Willis   68, 71–2, 75, 77, 79, 99, 191
yrstruly   164–6
"John Billy"   117, 128–33, 152, 153
"Lyndon"   37–8, 64–5, 110, 113, 125, 153
"My Appearance"   13, 110
"Octet"   181–2, 186
The Pale King (TPK)   6, 15, 29, 42, 52–3, 77, 82–5, 105–7, 136, 138, 139, 144, 155–6, 171, 173, 186–9
"The Planet Trillaphon…"   144
"Say Never"   33–4, 88, 90, 92, 93–8, 99, 111

Signifying Rappers   54
"Solomon Silverfish"   60, 64–6, 88–94, 97–8, 110
"The Suffering Channel"   115, 144, 150–5
"A Supposedly Fun Thing I'll Never Do Again"   32–3, 48, 111
This is Water (*Water*)   45, 53–4, 190, 198, 200
"Twenty-Four Word Notes"   11–12
"The View from Mrs. Thompson's"   136, 138, 140, 144, 147
"Westward the Course of Empire Takes Its Way"   98–9, 144, 147–8, 174
Warren, Andrew   162–3
white identity   3–5, 53, 55, 77, 81–9, 97–9, 102–3, 108–9, 111–12. *See also* European American; melting pot
Williams, Iain   106, 199
Wittgenstein, Ludwig   5, 146, 153, 196
Wollitz, Michael Gibson   164

Yiddish   64, 89–91, 94, 98–100, 131–2

www.ingramcontent.com/pod-product-compliance
Lightning Source LLC
Chambersburg PA
CBHW072232290426
44111CB00012B/2065